First World War
and Army of Occupation
War Diary
France, Belgium and Germany

7 DIVISION
20 Infantry Brigade
Border Regiment
2nd Battalion
5 October 1914 - 30 November 1917

WO95/1655/1

The Naval & Military Press Ltd
www.nmarchive.com
Published in association with The National Archives

Published by

The Naval & Military Press Ltd

Unit 10 Ridgewood Industrial Park,
Uckfield, East Sussex,
TN22 5QE England
Tel: +44 (0) 1825 749494

www.naval-military-press.com

www.nmarchive.com

This diary has been reprinted in facsimile from the original. Any imperfections are inevitably reproduced and the quality may fall short of modern type and cartographic standards.

© Crown Copyright
Images reproduced by permission of The National Archives, London, England, 2015.

Contents

Document type	Place/Title	Date From	Date To
Heading	WO95/1655/1		
Heading	20th Brigade. 7th Division. 2nd Battalion The Border Regiment October 1914		
War Diary	Southampton	05/10/1914	05/10/1914
War Diary	Zebrugge Belgium	06/10/1914	07/10/1914
War Diary	St. Andre Belgium	08/10/1914	08/10/1914
War Diary	Leffingham	09/10/1914	09/10/1914
War Diary	Destelberghen	10/10/1914	11/10/1914
War Diary	Somergem	12/10/1914	12/10/1914
War Diary	Thielt.	13/10/1914	13/10/1914
War Diary	Den Aap	14/10/1914	14/10/1914
War Diary	Ypres	15/10/1914	15/10/1914
War Diary	On the march	15/10/1914	15/10/1914
War Diary	Zillebeke	16/10/1914	16/10/1914
War Diary	Zanvoorde	17/10/1914	18/10/1914
War Diary	Kruiseik	19/10/1914	19/10/1914
War Diary	Kruiseik Hill	20/10/1914	26/10/1914
War Diary	Zanvoorde	27/10/1914	27/10/1914
War Diary	Zonnebeke	28/10/1914	31/10/1914
War Diary	Zanvoorde	01/11/1914	01/11/1914
Heading	20th Brigade. 7th Division. 2nd Battalion The Border Regiment November 1914		
War Diary	Zanvoorde	01/11/1914	01/11/1914
War Diary	Veldhoek	02/11/1914	05/11/1914
War Diary	Locre	06/11/1914	06/11/1914
War Diary	Meteren	06/11/1914	17/11/1914
War Diary	Sailly	18/11/1914	01/12/1914
Miscellaneous	A Form. Messages And Signals.		
Miscellaneous	2nd Battalion Border Regiment		
Miscellaneous	20th Infantry Brigade.		
Heading	20th Brigade. 7th Division. 2nd Battalion The Border Regiment December 1914		
War Diary	Sailly	01/12/1914	30/12/1914
Miscellaneous	7th Division CR-611. 20th Infantry Brigade.	12/12/1914	12/12/1914
Heading	20th Infantry Brigade. 7th Division. 2nd Battn. The Border Regiment. January 1915		
War Diary	Sailly	04/01/1915	28/01/1915
Heading	20th Infantry Brigade. 7th Division. 2nd Batt. The Border Regiment. February 1915 Attached: Reconnaissance Reports. Honours & Awards.		
War Diary	Near Fleurbaix	01/02/1915	08/02/1915
War Diary	Fleurbaix	09/02/1915	09/02/1915
War Diary	Sailly	10/02/1915	13/02/1915
War Diary	Near Fleurbaix	14/02/1915	26/02/1915
War Diary	Sailly	27/02/1915	28/02/1915
Heading	Reconnaissance Reports.		
Miscellaneous	Reconnaissance Report on part of the German trenches immediately S.E. of La Cordonnerie Farm.	08/02/1915	08/02/1915
Miscellaneous	Reconnaissance Report on enemy Line in Front of No. 6.7.8 Pivot Posts.	08/02/1915	08/02/1915

Map	Sketch to illustrate reconnaissance report on German Trenches		
Miscellaneous	To O.C. 2nd Border Regt. (Reconnaissance Report)	08/02/1915	08/02/1915
Miscellaneous	Reconnaissance report on Enemy's Lines	08/02/1915	08/02/1915
Heading	Honours And Awards.		
Miscellaneous	2nd Battn Border Regiment Honours & Rewards for Services granted to the Battalion during February.		
Heading	20th Infantry Brigade. 7th Division. 2nd Battn. The Border Regiment. March 1915. Attached: Account of the Operations 10th/14th March. Appendices.		
Heading	Account of the Operations 10th /14th March.		
War Diary	Sailly	01/03/1915	04/03/1915
War Diary	Rostraete	04/03/1915	08/03/1915
War Diary	Estaires	09/03/1915	10/03/1915
War Diary	N. of Neuve Chapelle	11/03/1915	14/03/1915
War Diary	Laventie	15/03/1915	16/03/1915
War Diary	Estaires	17/03/1915	25/03/1915
War Diary	La Gorgue	26/03/1915	31/03/1915
Miscellaneous	2nd Battalion Border Regt. Roll of Officers (Combatant)	16/03/1915	16/03/1915
Heading	Appendices.		
Miscellaneous	2nd Border Regiment.	27/03/1915	27/03/1915
Miscellaneous	Special Order by Brigadier-General F.S.Heyworth CB. D.S.O. Commanding 20th Infantry Brigade.	15/03/1915	15/03/1915
Miscellaneous	IVth Corps Orders.	14/03/1915	14/03/1915
Miscellaneous	R.A.M.C.	27/03/1915	27/03/1915
Miscellaneous	Account of the Operation 10th to 14th March, 1915	14/03/1915	14/03/1915
Miscellaneous	Account of the Operations 10th to 14th March, 1915	21/03/1915	21/03/1915
Miscellaneous	2nd Bn Border Regiment		
Miscellaneous	Head Q. XXth Bde.		
Heading	War Diary		
Heading	20th Infantry Brigade. 7th Division. 2nd Battn. The Border Regiment. April 1915 Attached: Appendix.		
War Diary	Laventie	01/04/1915	04/04/1915
War Diary	Fauquissart.	05/04/1915	07/04/1915
War Diary	Laventie	08/04/1915	25/04/1915
War Diary	Fauquissart	26/04/1915	27/04/1915
War Diary	Laventie	28/04/1915	30/04/1915
Miscellaneous	Appendix.		
Miscellaneous	Field Marshall Sir S.D.P. French. G.C.B, OM. G.C.V.O. K.C.M.G.		
Heading	20th Infantry Brigade. 7th Division. 2nd Battn. The Border Regiment. May 1915		
War Diary	N. of Neuve Chapelle	01/05/1915	05/05/1915
War Diary	Laventie	06/05/1915	09/05/1915
War Diary	Rouges Bancs.	10/05/1915	10/05/1915
War Diary	Bethune	11/05/1915	12/05/1915
War Diary	Hinges	13/05/1915	15/05/1915
War Diary	Festubert.	16/05/1915	17/05/1915
War Diary	Rue L'Epinette	18/05/1915	18/05/1915
War Diary	Hinges	19/05/1915	19/05/1915
War Diary	Busnes	20/05/1915	31/05/1915
Heading	20th Infantry Brigade. 7th Division. 2nd Battn. The Border Regiment. June 1915.		
War Diary	Gorre	01/06/1915	04/06/1915
War Diary	Givenchy	05/06/1915	05/06/1915
War Diary	Les Harisoirs	06/06/1915	12/06/1915

Type	Location	Start	End
War Diary	Marias	13/06/1915	13/06/1915
War Diary	Givenchy	14/06/1915	14/06/1915
War Diary	Gorre	15/06/1915	18/06/1915
War Diary	Givenchy	19/06/1915	23/06/1915
War Diary	Locon	24/06/1915	25/06/1915
War Diary	Beuvry	26/06/1915	27/06/1915
War Diary	Cuinchy	27/06/1915	30/06/1915
War Diary	20th Infantry Brigade. 7th Division. 2nd Battn. The Border Regiment. July 1915		
War Diary	Busnes	01/07/1915	13/07/1915
War Diary	Lestrem	14/07/1915	17/07/1915
War Diary	Lacouture	18/07/1915	26/07/1915
War Diary	Lestrem	27/07/1915	31/07/1915
Heading	20th Infantry Brigade. 7th Division. 2nd Battn. The Border Regiment. August 1915		
War Diary	Robecq	01/08/1915	17/08/1915
War Diary	Locon	18/08/1915	26/08/1915
War Diary	Near Marias.	27/08/1915	30/08/1915
War Diary	Near Locon	31/08/1915	31/08/1915
Heading	20th Inf. Bde. 7th Div. 2nd Battn. The Border Regiment. September 1915. Attached: Battalion Operation Orders. Brigade Narrative of Events on Recent Operations.		
War Diary	Novelles	01/09/1915	02/09/1915
War Diary	Nr. Vermelles	03/09/1915	04/09/1915
War Diary	Labourse	05/09/1915	05/09/1915
War Diary	Mi Bernonchon	06/09/1915	12/09/1915
War Diary	Labourse	13/09/1915	13/09/1915
War Diary	Nr Vermelles	14/09/1915	17/09/1915
War Diary	Labourse	18/09/1915	23/09/1915
War Diary	Noyelles	24/09/1915	31/09/1915
Heading	Battalion Operation Orders.		
Miscellaneous	Operation Orders By Lieut Col E. Ide S Thorpe	24/09/1915	24/09/1915
Heading	Brigade Narrative of events on the Recent Operations.		
Miscellaneous	Narrative of Events on the recent operations. September 24th	10/10/1915	10/10/1915
Heading	20th Inf. Bde. 7th Div. 2nd Battn. The Border Regiment. October 1915		
War Diary	Cambrin	01/10/1915	10/10/1915
War Diary	Beuvry	10/10/1915	16/10/1915
Miscellaneous	Bethune	17/10/1915	17/10/1915
War Diary	L'Ecleme	18/10/1915	19/10/1915
War Diary	Near Hinges	20/10/1915	24/10/1915
War Diary	Bethune	25/10/1915	31/10/1915
War Diary	Bethune	28/10/1915	28/10/1915
Heading	20th Infantry Brigade. 7th Division. 2nd Battn. The Border Regiment. November 1915		
War Diary	Bethune	01/11/1915	01/11/1915
War Diary	E of Givenchy	03/11/1915	03/11/1915
War Diary	Hingette	04/11/1915	08/11/1915
War Diary	Le Quesnoy	09/11/1915	10/11/1915
War Diary	E of Givenchy	11/11/1915	12/11/1915
War Diary	Le Quesnoy	13/11/1915	14/11/1915
War Diary	E of Givenchy	16/11/1915	16/11/1915
War Diary	Le Quesnoy	17/11/1915	17/11/1915
War Diary	Hingette	18/11/1915	30/11/1915

Heading	20th Infantry Brigade. 7th Division. 2nd Battn. The Border Regiment. December 1915		
War Diary	E of Festubert.	01/12/1915	01/12/1915
War Diary	Le Hamel	02/12/1915	02/12/1915
War Diary	Gonneham	03/12/1915	07/12/1915
War Diary	Saleux	08/12/1915	08/12/1915
War Diary	Breilly (10 K.m. West of Amiens)	09/12/1915	31/12/1915
Heading	20th Brigade. 7th Division. 2nd Battalion Border Regiment. January 1916.		
War Diary	Breilly	01/01/1916	04/01/1916
War Diary	Buigny-L'Abbe	05/01/1916	28/01/1916
War Diary	Breilly	29/01/1916	31/01/1916
Heading	20th Brigade. 7th Division. 2nd Battalion Border Regiment February 1916		
War Diary	Breilly	01/02/1916	01/02/1916
War Diary	Poulainville	02/02/1916	02/02/1916
War Diary	La Houssoye	03/02/1916	03/02/1916
War Diary	Buire sur L'Ancre	04/02/1916	11/02/1916
War Diary	Meaulte	12/02/1916	19/02/1916
War Diary	Trenches	22/02/1916	29/02/1916
Miscellaneous	OC ACD Company	21/02/1916	21/02/1916
Miscellaneous	Dear Colonel	21/02/1916	21/02/1916
Miscellaneous	The Brigade Major 20th Inf. Brigade.	21/02/1916	21/02/1916
Miscellaneous	To Adjutant 2nd Border Regt.	23/02/1916	23/02/1916
Miscellaneous	To Adjutant 2nd Border Regt.	25/02/1916	25/02/1916
Miscellaneous	I Further beg to submit the following names of men whose conduct was noteworthy	23/02/1916	23/02/1916
Miscellaneous	The Brigade Major 20th Infantry Brigade.	24/02/1916	24/02/1916
Miscellaneous	Report on attack on night of 22nd inst	23/02/1916	23/02/1916
Heading	20th Brigade. 7th Division. 2nd Battalion Border Regiment March 1916		
War Diary	Meaulte	01/03/1916	04/03/1916
War Diary	Trenches	10/03/1916	10/03/1916
War Diary	Meaulte	11/03/1916	31/03/1916
Heading	20th Brigade. 7th Division. 2nd Battalion Border Regiment April 1916		
War Diary	Trenches X 26c to E3c	01/04/1916	03/04/1916
War Diary	Meaulte-and-Becordel	03/04/1916	06/04/1916
War Diary	Bray	08/04/1916	13/04/1916
War Diary	Trenches F.11.c	14/04/1916	20/04/1916
War Diary	Trenches	21/04/1916	21/04/1916
War Diary	Bray	22/04/1916	22/04/1916
War Diary	Corbie	23/04/1916	27/04/1916
War Diary	Vaux	28/04/1916	30/04/1916
Map	B2 Subsector Scale 1/5000.		
Heading	20th Brigade. 7th Division. 2nd Battalion Border Regiment May 1916		
War Diary	Vaux-sur-Somme	01/05/1916	06/05/1916
War Diary	Bois Des Tailles	07/05/1916	17/05/1916
War Diary	Grovetown	18/05/1916	22/05/1916
War Diary	Grantown	23/05/1916	23/05/1916
War Diary	Bois Des Tailles	24/05/1916	31/05/1916
Heading	20th Brigade. 7th Division. 2nd Battalion Border Regiment June.1916		
War Diary	?	01/06/1916	10/06/1916
War Diary	?	11/06/1916	21/06/1916

War Diary	Grantown	22/06/1916	24/06/1916
War Diary	Mericourt	25/06/1916	25/06/1916
War Diary	Morlancourt	25/06/1916	30/06/1916
Miscellaneous	Operation Order by Lieut Col E Thorpe Commanding 2Bn Border Regt.	26/06/1916	26/06/1916
Heading	20th Inf. Bde. 7th Div. 2nd Battn. The Border Regiment. July 1916.		
Heading	War Diary 2nd Battn. Border Regiment. 1st-31st July 1916. Vol 18		
War Diary		01/07/1916	22/07/1916
War Diary	Breilly	23/07/1916	31/07/1916
Miscellaneous	7th Division No. G.1/444. 20/BM/647.	03/08/1916	03/08/1916
Miscellaneous	7th Division. Narrative of Operations From 1st to 5th July, 1916.	01/07/1916	01/07/1916
Miscellaneous	7th Division. Narrative of Operations From 11th to 20th July, 1916.	11/07/1916	11/07/1916
Miscellaneous			
Miscellaneous	Report on part taken by the 2nd Border Regt. in the engagement by Mametz on the 1st July 1916	07/07/1916	07/07/1916
Miscellaneous	To The adjutants 2nd Border Regt.	05/07/1916	05/07/1916
Miscellaneous	Report of Part taken in recent Fighting by B-Coy 2nd Bn The Border Rgt.		
Miscellaneous	The Adjutant 2 Border Rgt.	06/07/1916	06/07/1916
Miscellaneous	Report on the Part Taken by "C" Company in the recent Operations	06/07/1916	06/07/1916
Miscellaneous	The adjutant 2nd Border Rgt.	06/07/1916	06/07/1916
Heading	20th Brigade. 7th Division. 2nd Battalion Border Regiment August 1916.		
Heading	War Diary 2nd Battalion Border Regiment From 1/8/1916 to 31/8/1916		
War Diary	Breilly	01/08/1916	12/08/1916
War Diary	Buire	13/08/1916	25/08/1916
Heading	20th Brigade. 7th Division. 2nd Battalion Border Regiment September 1916		
Heading	War Diary 2nd Battn Border Regiment From 1st September 1916 To 30th September 1916. Vol 20		
War Diary	Buire	01/09/1916	09/09/1916
War Diary	Airaines	10/09/1916	17/09/1916
War Diary	Bailleul	18/09/1916	30/09/1916
Miscellaneous	Headquarters 20th Inf. Bde.	11/09/1916	11/09/1916
Miscellaneous	Report on movements of the 2nd Bn Border Regt. from the 3rd to 8th Sept-1916	10/09/1916	10/09/1916
Miscellaneous	Narrative of Events in the recent Operations September 24th	24/09/1916	24/09/1916
Miscellaneous	Operations Orders by Lieut Col & I des thorpe Comdg 2nd Bn Border Rgt.	24/09/1916	24/09/1916
Heading	20th Brigade. 7th Division. 2nd Battalion Border Regiment October 1916		
Heading	War Diary 2nd Battalion Border Regiment. Period:- From 1st October 1916 to 31st October 1916.		
War Diary	Le Bizet.	01/10/1916	07/10/1916
War Diary	Pont De Nieppe	10/10/1916	19/10/1916
War Diary	Le Bizet	20/10/1916	31/10/1916
Heading	20th Brigade. 7th Division. 2nd Battalion Border Regiment November 1916.		

Type	Description	From	To
Heading	War Diary 2nd Battn. Border Regiment From 1st November 1916 to 30th November 1916.		
War Diary		01/11/1916	30/11/1916
Heading	20th Brigade. 7th Division. 2nd Battalion Border Regiment December 1916		
Heading	War Diary 2nd Battalion Border Regiment. Period From 1-12-1916 to 31-12-1916		
War Diary	Trenches (K 35a 3.0 to K 35d 56)	01/12/1916	01/12/1916
War Diary	Mailly-Maillet	02/12/1916	05/12/1916
War Diary	Bertrancourt	06/12/1916	31/12/1916
Heading	7th Division. 20th Inf. Bde. 2nd Border Regiment. January 1917.		
Miscellaneous	War Diary 2nd Battalion Border Regiment From 1st January 1917. to 31st January 1917.		
War Diary	Mailly-Maillet	01/01/1917	23/01/1917
War Diary	Beauval	24/01/1917	31/01/1917
Heading	7th Division 20th Inf. Bde. 2nd Border Regiment. February 1917.		
Miscellaneous	War Diary. 2nd. Battalion Border Regiment. From 1st February 1917 to 28th February 1917.		
War Diary	Pernois	01/02/1917	16/02/1917
War Diary	Beauval	17/02/1917	18/02/1917
War Diary	Bus.	19/02/1917	19/02/1917
War Diary	Bertrancourt	20/02/1917	22/02/1917
War Diary	Mailly-Maillet	23/02/1917	28/02/1917
Heading	7th Division 20th Inf. Bde. 2nd Border Regiment March 1917.		
Heading	War Diary 2nd Battalion Border Regiment Period From 1st March 1917 to 31st March 1917		
War Diary	Mailly Maillet	01/03/1917	05/03/1917
War Diary	Bertrancourt	06/03/1917	24/03/1917
War Diary	Courcelles	25/03/1917	31/03/1917
Miscellaneous	Administrative Order for For forthcoming Operations by Major G.E Beaty Pownall Commdg 2nd Border Regt.	25/03/1917	25/03/1917
Miscellaneous	Operation Order by Major G.E Beaty. Pownall Commdg 2nd Border Regt.	25/03/1917	25/03/1917
Miscellaneous	Officer Commanding, 9th Devon Regt. 2nd Border Regt. 2nd Gordon Highlanders.	29/03/1917	29/03/1917
Miscellaneous	Report on advance by "A" company, 8th Devon Regiment on 28th March, 1917.	28/03/1917	28/03/1917
War Diary	Ervillers	04/04/1917	05/04/1917
War Diary	Blainzeville	06/04/1917	11/04/1917
War Diary	Courcelles	12/04/1917	12/04/1917
War Diary	Ablainzeville	13/04/1917	30/04/1917
Miscellaneous	Operations Order by G.E. Beaty. Pownall Commdg 2nd Border Regt.	01/04/1917	01/04/1917
Miscellaneous	Operation Order by Major G.E. Beaty. Pownall Commdg 2nd Border Regt.	04/04/1917	04/04/1917
Miscellaneous	Operation Order by Major G.E. Beaty. Pownall Commdg 2nd Border Regt.	05/04/1917	05/04/1917
Miscellaneous	Operation Orders by Lieut Col E. I de B Thorpe D.S.O. Commdg 2nd Bn Border Regt	11/04/1917	11/04/1917
Miscellaneous	Operation Orders by Lieut Col E. I de B Thorpe D.S.O. Commdg 2nd Bn Boder Regt.	12/04/1917	12/04/1917
Miscellaneous	Operation Order by Lieut E. I de B Thorpe D.S.O. Commdg 2nd Border Regt.	20/04/1917	20/04/1917

Miscellaneous	Operation Order by Lieut E. I de B Thorpe D.S.O. Commdg 2nd Border Regt.	26/04/1917	26/04/1917
Miscellaneous	Operation Orders By Lieut E. I de B Thorpe D.S.O. Comdg, 2nd Bn. Border Regt.	28/04/1917	28/04/1917
Miscellaneous	Lieut Col E. I de B Thorpe D.S.O. Comdg, 2nd Border Regt.	28/04/1917	28/04/1917
Miscellaneous	2nd Bn Border Regiment List of officer and Wants Officer- April 1917	00/04/1917	00/04/1917
Miscellaneous	Warrant Officers.		
Heading	7th Division. 20th Inf. Bde. 2nd Border Regiment. May.1917.		
War Diary	Ablainzeville	01/05/1917	03/05/1917
War Diary	Gomiecourt Mory	04/05/1917	16/05/1917
War Diary	Ablainzevelle	17/05/1917	31/05/1917
Heading	7th Division. 20th Inf. Bde. 2nd Border Regiment. June 1917.		
War Diary	Ablainzevelle	01/06/1917	25/06/1917
War Diary	Mory	26/06/1917	30/06/1917
Heading	7th Division. 20th Inf. Bde. 2nd Border Regiment. July 1917.		
War Diary	Mory	01/07/1917	31/07/1917
Heading	7th Division. 20th Inf. Bde. 2nd Border Regiment. August 1917.		
War Diary		01/08/1917	31/08/1917
Heading	7th Division. 20th Inf. Bde. 2nd Border Regiment. September 1917.		
War Diary	Linde Goed Farm	01/09/1917	30/09/1917
Heading	7th Division. 20th Inf. Bde. 2nd Border Regiment. October 1917.		
War Diary		01/10/1917	31/10/1917
Heading	7th Division. 20th Inf. Bde. 2nd Border Regiment. November 1917.		
War Diary		01/11/1917	30/11/1917

WO 95/16551

20th Brigade.

7th Division.

2nd BATTALION

THE BORDER REGIMENT

OCTOBER 1 9 1 4

2/Border Rgt"
20th Bde

Army Form C. 2118.

WAR DIARY
or
INTELLIGENCE SUMMARY.
(Erase heading not required.)

Instructions regarding War Diaries and Intelligence Summaries are contained in F.S. Regs, Part II. and the Staff Manual respectively. Title pages will be prepared in manuscript.

Hour, Date, Place	Summary of Events and Information	Remarks and references to Appendices
5/10/14 Southampton	The Battalion embarked. A & B Companies sailed on SS "Minneapolis" and H.Q. Companies on SS "Turcoman"	
7am 6/10/14 Zeebrugge, Belgium	G & D Companies disembarked, entrained for BRUGES - thence by march route to ST. ANDRE and billeted	
9am 7/10/14 "	A & B Companies disembarked, entrained for BRUGES - thence by march route to ST. ANDRE and joined remainder of Battalion in billets	
11am 8/10/14 ST. ANDRE	Battalion proceeded by march route to LEFFINGHAM and arrived about 6pm and billeted	
6am 9/10/14 LEFFINGHAM	Battalion marched to OSTEND and entrained for GHENT. Arrived at GHENT at 11am. Left GHENT about 4pm and entrenched at DESTELBERGHEN at night.	
10/10/14 DESTELBERGHEN	Battalion completed trenches during the day.	
4am 11/10/14 "	Battalion was relieved in trenches by French Marines. At 8am the Battalion proceeded by forced march to SOMERGEM. The French Marines joining in the retirement of GHENT. The Town was occupied by the enemy later.	
11am 12/10/14 SOMERGEM	Battalion arrived and billeted. At 2hrs the Battalion marched to THIELT - arvd about 9pm and billeted	
13/10/14 THIELT.	At about 9am the Brigade opened fire on a hostile aeroplane flying over the town and succeeded in bringing it down.	5 S.A

(9 29 6) W 4141-463 100,000 9/14 HWV Forms/C.2118/10

Army Form C. 2118.

WAR DIARY
or
INTELLIGENCE SUMMARY.
(Erase heading not required.)

Instructions regarding War Diaries and Intelligence Summaries are contained in F.S. Regs., Part II. and the Staff Manual respectively. Title pages will be prepared in manuscript.

Hour, Date, Place	Summary of Events and Information	Remarks and references to Appendices
13/10/14 THIELT.	At 12 noon the Battalion marched to ROULERS - arrived at 4pm but entrenched at DEN AAP 2 miles outside the town as outpost to the Brigade.	
Noon 14/10/14 DEN AAP	Battalion marched to YPRES. Arrived at 11pm and billeted	
10am 15/10/14 YPRES	Battalion marched to ZILLEBEKE. The Regimental Scout Lieut Plaunt encountered a Uhlan Patrol whilst searching a wood. Shots were exchanged at close quarters - 8 of the enemy were killed and 1 was taken prisoner. 1 man (wounded) were taken prisoner. Our casualties were:- NIL. The German officer afterwards succumbed to his wounds. The Battalion entrenched at night.	
1pm " On the march		
2am 16/10/14 ZILLEBEKE	Lieut. S/ Edgerton was severely wounded, accidentally by men of his Platoon in trenches. In the Battn expected an attack he had warned his men to fire at anyone on their front. It appears that he himself, for reasons unknown walked along the front covered by his Platoon and fire was opened. The Battalion vacated the trenches in the afternoon, marched to ZANVOORDE and billeted.	
11/10/14 ZANVOORDE	Heir shell fire was expected the Battalion entrenched but billeted at night.	
2pm 18/10/14 ZANVOORDE	The Battalion marched to KRUISEIK and arrived 5pm. The outpost to the Brigade - and Gordon Highlanders came under shrapnel fire at about 6pm. The remainder of the day was quiet	

Army Form C. 2118.

WAR DIARY
or
INTELLIGENCE SUMMARY.
(Erase heading not required.)

Instructions regarding War Diaries and Intelligence Summaries are contained in F. S. Regs., Part II. and the Staff Manual respectively. Title pages will be prepared in manuscript.

Hour, Date, Place	Summary of Events and Information	Remarks and references to Appendices
9am 19/10/14 KRUISEIK.	The Brigade advanced in Artillery formation on MENIN which was occupied by the enemy. On arrival at a village AMERICA the Brigade was subjected to heavy shrapnel fire from enemy's guns firing from direction of MENIN. 2 men of the Battalion were wounded. At 3 pm the Battalion fell back and entrenched on KRUISEIK HILL leaving D Company at AMERICA as outpost. D Company returned and the Battalion completed trenches. Owing to the large amount of frontage which the Battalion had to cover (roughly 2¼ miles) and the nature of the country, two lines of Machine & Lewis in some cases were not connected up by trenches. Men complete the Battn. was entrenched thus:- B Coy (extreme left), A Coy, C Coy, 2 Platoons D Company (extreme right.) 2 Platoons D Company in reserve - 500 yards in rear. The other Battalions of the Brigade were sent out to reconnaissance but had to return owing to heavy shell fire. By night the Brigade was entrenched on KRUISEIK HILL thus:- (L to R) Grenadier Guards, Scots Guards, Border Regt., Gordon Highlanders. The line resembled a half circle.	
20/10/14 KRUISEIK HILL	Our casualties on this day were 2 killed and 2 wounded.	

Army Form C. 2118.

WAR DIARY
or
INTELLIGENCE SUMMARY.
(Erase heading not required.)

Instructions regarding War Diaries and Intelligence Summaries are contained in F.S. Regs., Part II. and the Staff Manual respectively. Title pages will be prepared in manuscript.

Hour, Date, Place	Summary of Events and Information	Remarks and references to Appendices
21/10/14 KRUISEIK HILL	Artillery bombarded all day, and rifle fire at long range. The nature of the country pushed enemy snipers to advance to within 300 yards of our trenches at certain points completely concealed. It was thought that farm houses in the vicinity of the firing line were also used for snipping parties were sent out at night to fire them. Our casualties were slight.	
22/10/14 KRUISEIK HILL	Bombardment of trenches by enemy's artillery. The Battn. was engaged at intervals day and night. 2 Lieut. T. Clauncey was killed in a farm house near his trench by a shell. The house caught fire & his body could not be recovered. Our casualties were slight.	
23/10/14 KRUISEIK HILL	Heavy bombardment of trenches by enemy's artillery. The Battalion was engaged at intervals at night. Captain R.W. Gordon was killed on this day. Our casualties were slight.	
24/10/14 KRUISEIK HILL	Several small attacks were launched by the enemy but were repulsed. The bombardment by enemy's artillery was incessant - some of the trenches being blown in by heavy artillery	

WAR DIARY
or
INTELLIGENCE SUMMARY.
(Erase heading not required.)

Army Form C. 2118.

Instructions regarding War Diaries and Intelligence Summaries are contained in F.S. Regs., Part II. and the Staff Manual respectively. Title pages will be prepared in manuscript.

Hour, Date, Place	Summary of Events and Information	Remarks and references to Appendices
25/10/14 KRUISEIK HILL	Small attacks were again made at different points but no General attack was launched by the enemy. No Artillery appeared to have been mentioned by heavy pieces and a terrific fire was directed at our trenches during the day. The enemy on B Company's front put up a white flag in the morning and Major W Allen S.O. left his trench to go over to them. He was almost instantly killed by rifle fire over to them. 2 Companies S. Staffords Regiment ✱ took up a reserve position near Brigade Headquarters 100 yards in rear. Lieut E Oblein was wounded by a shell explosion. Our casualties were 3 killed, 25 wounded.	✱ 2 Companies only. 2 Coys S. Staffs took up reserve trenches previously occupied by 2 Platoons D Coy.
26/10/14 KRUISEIK HILL	During the night of 25th - 26th the enemy had advanced considerably & had concentrated in large numbers in woods on our front. They launched an attack at about 9am and succeeded in taking the front line trenches occupied by A and B Companies — the four survivors (about 70 in all) retiring to the flanks and joining up in rear with the Scouts and Battalion Head Qr's. The enemy continued to advance in mass but were eventually held in check by the Scouts under

(9 29 6) W4141—463 100,000 9/14 H W V Forms/C. 2118/10

WAR DIARY or INTELLIGENCE SUMMARY.

Army Form C. 2118.

Hour, Date, Place	Summary of Events and Information	Remarks and references to Appendices
30/10/14 KRUISEIK HILL	Lieut Lamb Machine Gun under Lieut Watson, and Battalion Head Qrs under Lt.Col. Ovagd. "C" Company under Capt P.B.K. Marquence Seel advanced up the hill to KRUISEIK in line of Platoons to support "A" & "B" if necessary. "A" & "B" took trenches but orders were received from Brigade Head Qrs for them to return to ZANVOORDE. At about 5pm His Qrs Scouts & Machine Guns fell back on Brigade Head Quarters the 1st and 2nd Divisions having come up on our left, the attack was commenced. The Battalion marched from Brigade Head Quarters at about 8pm & rested in a field near ZANVOORDE for the night. In the afternoon 6 Company Indian Ludung ZANVOORDE in ruins on arrival marched through to YPRES and billeted.	Casualties on the day were Heavy:- Officers Killed:- Captains L & 9?? Andrews, E.K. Cholmondeley, E.K. Hes, Lieut Q.B.B. Warren. Officers wounded:- Major Y.?. Bousquet, 2nd Lieut W. Revis. Officers wounded missing:- Lieut H.O. Neigh, 2nd Lieut. Curtees, Lieut B. Hogan? Other Ranks:- Killed:- 25 Wounded:- 65 Missing:- 174
21/10/14 ZANVOORDE	The Battalion (less "C" Coy) marched to ZONNEBEKE at about 5am and rested in the grounds of a Chateau. "C" Company under Capt P.W. Seel rejoined the Battalion at 3pm. A muster roll showed 12 Officers and 538 Other ranks in the Battalion. The day was considered a day of rest & the men were re-equipped & Companies reformed.	Casualties:- Nil

Army Form C. 2118.

WAR DIARY
or
INTELLIGENCE SUMMARY.
(Erase heading not required.)

Instructions regarding War Diaries and Intelligence Summaries are contained in F.S. Regs., Part II. and the Staff Manual respectively. Title pages will be prepared in manuscript.

Hour, Date, Place	Summary of Events and Information	Remarks and references to Appendices
ZONNEBEKE 28/10/14	The Battalion remained at ZONNEBEKE but were ordered to take up a reserve position. The Battalion marched from Chateau grounds at 8pm & occupied trenches in reserve. Casualties:- Nil.	
29/10/14 Near ZONNEBEKE	At 9am orders were received to reinforce the Gordon Highlanders who were being heavily pressed. The Battalion deployed to its right using the YPRES - MENIN Road as the left and advanced on KRUISEIK HILL. On reaching the first ridge the Battalion came under terrific direct shell - machine gun and rifle fire. After an hours wait the Battn advanced under Lieut. Col. A.S. Wood who was almost immediately hit. Captain L.A. Molyneux-Seel was also hit twice from a Machine Gun in a house which became our object of attack. Captain A.S. Robeson then assumed command as Captain D.E. Warren had been slightly wounded - he continued the advance and was able to direct operations from a large shell hole. Eventually the Queens Regt. came up and relieved us. At 11pm orders were received for the Battn to return to reserve dug-outs. Our casualties were about 25 killed, 30 wounded. Lieut A.B. Johnson Lt. Geo. H. Hodgson were wounded. This day is known in the Battalion as "WINDMILL DAY".	

Army Form C. 2118.

WAR DIARY
or
INTELLIGENCE SUMMARY.
(Erase heading not required.)

Instructions regarding War Diaries and Intelligence Summaries are contained in F. S. Regs., Part II. and the Staff Manual respectively. Title pages will be prepared in manuscript.

Hour, Date, Place	Summary of Events and Information	Remarks and references to Appendices
30/10/14	The Battalion under Capt Lyl Marrow who had returned from Field Hospital received orders to move to the East of Morge to support a Cavalry Advance. The Battn proceeded & halted for the day in woods 1½ miles NW of Chateau near ZONNEBEKE. This was practically a day of rest only an occasional shell coming into wood. At 11pm orders were received to return to cross-roads HOOGE and YPRES-MENIN Roads and entrench on W. side of road facing West. Continuous line of trenches with communications was dug before daybreak. Casualties :- 1 man wounded	
31/10/14	All day the Battn was very heavily shelled. At 4pm orders to move were received - but were cancelled shortly afterwards. Eventually at 8pm the Battn marched back along the YPRES road. At 11pm the Battn moved off on a S.W. direction and came under ZANVOORDE - orders were given for the men to dig themselves in, lining the hedges, and to be concealed by daylight.	
1/11/14 ZANVOORDE	The Machine Gun with Lieut Watson & Lieut Laws were entrenched on the left of the Battalion. At about 9am Lieut Laws noticed a Battalion of enemy Infantry crossing the open from wood to wood - evidently not knowing we were in our position. He	

(9 29 6) W 4141—463 100,000 9/14 H W V Forms/C. 2118/10

20th Brigade.

7th Division.

2nd BATTALION

THE BORDER REGIMENT

NOVIMBER 1 9 1 4

2nd Border Regt.

W A R   D I A R Y

1/11/14.

ZANVOORDE

The Machine Gun with Lieut.W.Watson & Lieut C.Lamb were entrenched on the left of the Battalion.   At about 10 a.m. Lieut.Lamb noticed a Battalion of enemy Infantry crossing the open from wood to wood - evidently not knowing we were in our position.   He   (continued on next page.)

WAR DIARY
or
INTELLIGENCE SUMMARY.
(Erase heading not required.)

Army Form C. 2118.

Hour, Date, Place	Summary of Events and Information	Remarks and references to Appendices
1/11/14 ZANVOORDE	opened fire at 800 yards and did great execution - but this drew rifle and shell fire from them. By 11am they had blown the Machine Gun up and killed 4 men. They then commenced searching the wood and road with a variety of shells. The Machine Gun had to be left & the men crawled away - but at night they went back & recovered it. Casualties on this day were 6 killed, 12 wounded	
2/11/14 VELDHOEK ~~HILLEBEKE~~	Early in the morning movements of the enemy on the right front of our position were noticed and the left of I Company was brought back so as to form a continuous line and connect up with "C" Company. The Battalion formed the right of 20th Brigade. At about 10am a terrific shelling commenced and was continued until about 3hrs - very little damage was done Shortly after 3hrs bugles were heard to sound and the enemy charged (it is noteworthy to record that the noise made by them charging so alarmed the Reserve body of troops that they were fell in and prepared to assist us) - but the Battalion withheld its fire until the enemy were almost on top of us - then the signal was given and a terrific fire was poured in. The number killed is almost impossible to state but a rough estimate, about 200 to 300 killed on our front alone. The enemy retired under cover of woods - Again the bugles	

WAR DIARY or INTELLIGENCE SUMMARY.

(Erase heading not required.)

Army Form C. 2118.

Hour, Date, Place	Summary of Events and Information	Remarks and references to Appendices
	occupied and again the same scene enacted - but with the difference that the troops on our right gave way. The Battalion was in danger of being surrounded and Sgt Booth, noticing this left his trench and gallantly led up two sections which were in reserve, reoccupied the trenches which had been vacated and so kept the line intact until reinforcements came up 3 hours later. The enemy were compelled to desist. The Battalion was relieved at night and retired to woods near YPRES road as Reserve.	See congratulatory message of G.O.C. in C. 7th Division attached
3/11/14	Casualties on this day were Lieut A.W.Gerrard Killed, *2/Lt Geo.N.Hodgson Severely wounded, 14 Killed & 35 Wounded. The Battalion remained in Reserve position. The first reinforcement Captain N.J.Jackson and 98 other Ranks joined the Battalion at night.	*Died of wounds 6/11/15
4/11/14	Casualties: Nil Battalion still remained in Reserve. Very little shelling	
5/11/14	Battalion still in Reserve. At 11pm orders were received and the Battalion left the trenches and marched to LOCRE. Arrived about 3am & rested in a field for the night.	
2pm 6/11/14 LOCRE	The Battalion under Captain G.E.Warren marched to METEREN and billeted.	
6/11/14 to 13/11/14 METEREN	The Battalion remained in billets and reorganized - the men being re-equipped, clothed &c.	

Army Form C. 2118.

WAR DIARY
or
INTELLIGENCE SUMMARY.
(Erase heading not required.)

Hour, Date, Place	Summary of Events and Information	Remarks and references to Appendices
11am 14/11/14 METEREN	The Battalion proceeded by march route to BAC ST. MUIR and arrived at 3pm. (Strength 9 Offrs. 1 RSM. MCOs & men) At 5pm the Battalion proceeded to trenches at "LA BOUTILLERIE" relieving the Middlesex Regiment.	
18/11/14 to 19/11/14	The Battalion was relieved on night of 19th November and proceeded to Billets at Sailly. Casualties slight.	
19/11/14 to 21/11/14 SAILLY	In Billets. The Battalion proceeded to the trenches on night of 21st November. A draft of 97 NCOs & men joined the Battn. on 19/11/14.	
21/11/14 to 24/11/14	In trenches at ROUGE BANCS near LA CORDONNIERE FARM. The Battn. was relieved on night of 24th November and proceeded to Billets at SAILLY. Casualties - Slight.	
25/11/14 SAILLY 5pm 26/11/14 SAILLY	In Billets. 2nd Lieuts. M.Ovey & Horsley joined the Battalion. The Battalion and Gordon Highlanders under Captain MacKensie proceeded to the Trenches.	
27/11/14 and 28/11/14	In Trenches. The Battn. was relieved on night of 28th November and proceeded to Billets at SAILLY.	
29/11/14 to 1/12/14 SAILLY	In Billets. H.M. The King inspected the 7th Division on 1st December at SAILLY. Captain b Faut was awarded the D.S.O. personally by H.M. The King for gallantry at KRUISEIK in October. The Battalion under Captain N.R.S. Kerr proceeded to trenches at night.	

Forms/C. 2118/10

"A" Form.   Army Form C. 2121.

MESSAGES AND SIGNALS.   No. of Message_____

Prefix ___ Code ___ m.	Words	Charge	This message is on a/c of:	Recd. at ___ m.
Office of Origin and Service Instructions.	Sent			Date ZT
Coly	At 8-20 a.m.		___Service.	From 3/11/1914
	To *Roe*		(Signature of "Franking Officer.")	By
	By *6/duly*			

TO — Commanding Borders

Sender's Number	Day of Month	In reply to Number	A A A
* BM 92	3RD		

Following from 7TH DIV begins "Stout action of Border Regt in maintaining its trenches throughout the day although unsupported on its right is much commented AAA Congratulate Border Regt from me and tell them I am making a special report on their conduct through Corps Hd Qrs" ends.

Please inform all ranks.

From   Twentieth Bde
Place
Time   8-15 a.m.

The above may be forwarded as now corrected. (Z)

Censor.   Sd/ AC Palmer Lt for Maj

Signature of Addressor or person authorised to telegraph in his name

Bde Maj

*This line should be erased if not required.

3662 M. & Co. Ltd. Wt. W919/549—100,000. 6/14. Forms C2121/10.

2nd Battalion Border Regiment

This Battalion held a portion of the KRUSEIK position in front of YPRES during which it was exposed to particular heavy shell fire for 3 days and nights. Many of the trenches were blown in but no trench was given up by any portion of the Battalion.

On 2nd November this Battalion formed the right of the Brigade at VELDHOEK. Owing to troops on the right giving way the enemy was able to occupy some woods and so surround the right of the Border Regiment. Nevertheless the Battalion held its line for some hours until the enemy could be driven from these woods by relieving troops.

During the fighting this Battalion lost very heavily.

The devoted and firm conduct of this Battalion repeatedly called forth the admiration of the Brigadier and of the Officers in other Battalions in the same Brigade; and I myself can testify to its fortitude and determination to maintain its position at all costs; a spirit which saved a difficult and critical situation.

It is impossible to praise this Battalion too highly for its firmness and battle discipline.

20th Infantry Brigade

This Brigade had, eventually, the most difficult task to perform, as it had to hold the echoed position of Kruisek Hill.
It was impossible to abandon this point without prejudicing not only the rest of the line, but also the pivot of all contemplated offensive action.
In spite therefore, of its natural unfavourable situation, Kruisek Hill had to be held.
The 20th Brigade did this itself under constant violent Artillery fire by day and often by night. The defence was by no means passive but counter attacks were frequently and successfully made.
Later on in the halting this Brigade showed the same tenacity in defence and on one critical occasion (31st October) by its forward action, was mainly instrumental in restoring the fight.
The losses of this Brigade were very heavy.

20th Brigade.

7th Division.

2nd BATTALION

THE BORDER REGIMENT

DECEMBER 1 9 1 4

WAR DIARY
or
INTELLIGENCE SUMMARY.

Army Form C. 2118.

Hour, Date, Place		Summary of Events and Information	Remarks and references to Appendices
9pm 1/12/14	SAILLY	A draft of 570 NCOs & men, Lieut O.P.O. Drake-Brockman, 2nd Lieut O.R. Cochin and Captain R.J. Hawbury & Lieut G. Mumbey attached from H. Bedfords Regt. joined from England.	
2/12/14 to 4/12/14		In trenches. The draft remained in billets at SAILLY. The Battalion was relieved on night of 4th November and proceeded to billets at SAILLY. Casualties - Slight	
4/12/14 to 6/12/14	SAILLY	In billets. The draft was allotted to companies. Under instructions received from 20th Brigade 2 companies (A and C) Borders and 2 companies Gordon Highlanders proceeded to trenches on night of 6th December. B & D Companies remaining in billets at SAILLY.	Strength of Battalion 13 Offrs, 993 Other Ranks
11/12/14	SAILLY	B and D Companies proceeded to trenches the night relieving B & D Companies who returned to billets at SAILLY.	
12/12/14	SAILLY	A & C Companies who returned to billets at SAILLY.	
15/12/14	SAILLY	A draft of 26 NCOs & men and Lieut Yates-Boswell joined from England.	
		A & C Companies proceeded to trenches the night relieving B & D Companies who returned to billets at SAILLY.	
18/12/14		At about 11am Major Barrow received orders from 20th Brigade to 2 Companies 2nd Royal Scots Regt. to attack enemys trenches at 6.30pm. 2 Companies of Scots Guards attacking their row at Chm. In the trenches at about 2.30pm Captain 6 and 2/Lt was informed by Lieut Sawhen B Company that B and D Companies would attack at 6.30pm. At about 3pm Major G.E. Barrow arrived at the trenches with Captain H.A. Ockew and B and D Companies. Major Barrow gave orders that A & C Companies were to make the attack not B & D Companies - The left was to be road running S.E. of	

WAR DIARY
or
INTELLIGENCE SUMMARY.
(Erase heading not required.)

Army Form C. 2118.

Hour, Date, Place	Summary of Events and Information	Remarks and references to Appendices
18/12/14 (Continued)	LA CORDONNIERE FARM and the right to be the Scots Guards whose left was the SAILLY-FROMELLES ROAD. This necessitated the moving of the whole of C Company to the right. A Company also moving their position. B and D Companies were to get behind each man of A + C Companies and help them out of the trenches. The Companies were not in position until well after dark and consequently no one knew exactly their correct front or front of attack. At 6.15 pm the Companies advanced - strength about 200 men. Both A + C Companies reached the enemy's trenches without the seventh being fired on the whole time crossing the intervening distance between trenches - about 150 yards. Many casualties occurred in this advance, some of our men being hit by our own Artillery which opened fire at the same time. Owing to our Artillery fire the Companies withdrew about 50 yards, lay down and waited for orders. The order came after about 1 hour to advance again. The Companies did so but the attack failed and they retired to our own trenches and lay down in front of them. Major Warren then collected the remnants of A + C Companies and brought up 2 Platoons of B Coy under Captain N? Venture. Again they advanced to the enemy's trenches but halted in a ditch near the enemy's barbed wire - wire were cutters being required. Major Warren went back and obtained 3. On his return he said he would go and see the General who	

WAR DIARY or INTELLIGENCE SUMMARY.

Army Form C. 2118.

Hour, Date, Place	Summary of Events and Information	Remarks and references to Appendices
18/12/14 (continued)	was at LA CORDONNIERE FARM. He did so and was away 1½ hours. When he returned he found that Captain Jenkins had brought the Companies back to our trenches and as the General had ordered no further attack unless it could be done without heavy loss - further operations ceased and collecting of dead and wounded was carried on. Casualties: Capt Clauss 2i/c and 2nd Lt N Castle were wounded in first advance. Captain HA Askew being killed on top of enemy trenches (Captain Lamb died of wounds 11 days later). Lieut W S N Kennedy was wounded in second advance. Total Casualties Other Ranks:- 123 2/Lt Bd Brewer and Pte MacRae received the DCM for bringing back Captain Lamb under very heavy fire. No 10694 Pte C Jetson and No 10436 Pte F Smith were both awarded the V.C. for bringing in wounded men lying between the trenches by daylight on 19th December 1914 under heavy rifle and Machine Gun fire. B & C Companies remained in trenches and A & C Companies proceeded to billets at SAILLY.	
19/12/14		
22/12/14 SAILLY	A & C Companies proceeded to trenches at night relieving B & D Companies who returned to billets at SAILLY. Major de Warren proceeded sick to England.	

War Diary

Hour	date	Place	Summary of Events & information	Remarks
	24/12/14	SAILLY	Captain S.H. Morrall joined the Battalion	
	25/12/14	SAILLY	2nd Lieut R.Y.K Wood and 130 Other Ranks joined the Battalion. Captain S.H. Morrall took over command of the Battalion from Captain N.F. Jenkins who proceeded to England. In the morning the enemy in front of A and B Companies trenches signalled for an Officer. One went over to their trenches and an armistice was agreed upon until 11pm for the purpose of burying the dead lying between the trenches. On the night of 18th Dec. there was no firing on either side on this day, and the bodies were buried near the trenches.	
	26/12/14	SAILLY	B & D Companies proceeded to the trenches relieving A & B Companies who returned to Billets at SAILLY. The armistice was still recognized and there was no firing - the troops walking along the top as communicating trenches were so bad.	
	29/12/14	SAILLY	Lieut B.W. Wilson and 2nd Lieut N.R. Wight joined the Battalion	
	30/12/14	SAILLY	A & C Companies proceeded to the Trenches relieving B & D Companies who returned to billets. Casualties: Nil	

Confidential

7th Division G.S. - 611

20th Infantry Brigade

The GOC has had great pleasure in forwarding to Head Quarters, 4th Army Corps, a dispatch (of which this is a copy for your retention) testifying to the devoted conduct of the Officers and men of the Brigade under your command during the recent operations near Ypres.

He hopes you will take the occasion to bring his remarks to the notice of the Officers Commanding Battalions concerned.

12/12/1914

(S/d) H. Daly, Major
A.A. & Q.M.G. 7th Division

2

Of
Border Regiment

Passed for your information. Please copy and return the original despatch concerning your Battalion.

14/12/14

(S/d) H. Palmer, Staff Capt.
20th Infy Bde. 7th Divn.

20th Infantry Brigade.

7th Division.

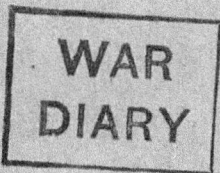

2nd BATTN. THE BORDER REGIMENT.

JANUARY

1 9 1 5

2nd Battn. The Border Regiment.

January 1915

4/1/1915	SAILLY	2nd Lieut "R.I. Newdigate and 50 Other Ranks joined the Battalion. B & D Companies proceeded to trenches relieving A & C Companies who returned to billets. Casualties:- Nil.
8/1/1915	SAILLY	A & C Companies proceeded to trenches relieving B & D Companies who returned to billets. Casualties:- 1 wounded.
9/1/1915	SAILLY	Major Colonel L. Wood resumed and took over command of the Battalion.
11/1/1915	"	2 Lieut I.S. Richardson and 110 Other Ranks joined the Battalion.
12/1/1915	"	B & D Companies proceeded to the trenches relieving A & C Companies who returned to billets. Casualties A & C :- 2 killed 2 wounded

Army Form C 2118

Hour date & Place	Summary of Events Information	Remarks
13/11/15 SAILLY	A+C Companies under Lieut-Colonel L Wood joined B+D Companies in the trenches at night	
16/11/15 SAILLY	2nd Lieuts W Wilson and AM Fraser joined the Battalion. The Battalion was relieved at night and proceeded to billets at SAILLY. Casualties 13 to 14/11/15 :- 3 Killed, 2 wounded.	
19/11/15 -"-	In billets. Captain JB Moulton and 50 Other Ranks joined the Battalion.	
20/11/15 -"-	The Battalion under Lt-Col L Wood proceeded to the trenches at night	
24/11/15 -"-	The Battalion was relieved in trenches at night and proceeded to billets at SAILLY. Casualties 20/11/15 to 24/11/15 :- 3 Killed, 2 wounded. Major RBW Moffat joined the Battalion	
26/11/15 -"-	2nd Lieut HL Cholmeley and 94 Other Ranks joined the Battalion	
28/11/15 -"-	The Battalion under Lieut-Col L Wood proceeded to the trenches at night. Casualties 28/11/15 to 31/11/15 :- 2 Killed 5 wounded.	

L Wood Lieut-Colonel
Commanding 2nd Batt Border Regiment

20th Infantry Brigade.
7th Division.

WAR DIARY

2nd BATTN. THE BORDER REGIMENT.

FEBRUARY

1 9 1 5

Attached:

Reconnaissance Reports.
Honours & Awards.

Army Form C. 2118.

WAR DIARY
or
INTELLIGENCE SUMMARY.
(Erase heading not required.)

Instructions regarding War Diaries and Intelligence Summaries are contained in F.S. Regs., Part II. and the Staff Manual respectively. Title pages will be prepared in manuscript.

Hour, Date, Place		Summary of Events and Information	Remarks and references to Appendices
1st February	Neuf Neubaux	The Battalion returned from trenches to Billets at night	
2nd "	"	In Billets - Battalion forming Brigade Reserve. Lieut M.R. Scott returned from England. 2 men of a digging party near the trenches were wounded at night.	
3rd & 4th Feby	"	In Billets - Nothing to report.	
5th Feby	"	The Battalion proceeded to the trenches at 6pm. 1 man was wounded during the night.	5.5
6th "	"	In Trenches. Casualties 1 killed, 4 wounded	
7th "	"	" " " 1 " 1 "	
8th "	"	" " " 1 " 1 "	
		Lieut N. Sutherland & 2/Lt J.W. Eubank joined the Battalion from England.	
9th "	Fleurbaix	In Trenches - Nothing to report - The Battalion proceeded to Billets at night.	
10th "	Sailly	In Billets - Battalion forming Divisional Reserve.	
11th "	"	" " - Nothing to report	
12th "	"	" " " " " " 1 man attached to RE wounded	
13th "	"	" " " " " " The Battalion proceeded to trenches at 6pm	

Army Form C. 2118.

WAR DIARY
or
INTELLIGENCE SUMMARY.
(Erase heading not required.)

Hour, Date, Place	Summary of Events and Information	Remarks and references to Appendices
14th Feby, Neuve Neuvaise	In Trenches - Casualties 4 men wounded.	
15th "	" 1 man killed. 1 man wounded.	
16th "	" A draft of 50 NCO's & men joined the Battn. from England	
17th "	In Trenches :- Casualties 2 killed, 3 wounded.	
" "	" 1 wounded. The Battn. proceeded	
18th "	to Billets at night.	
" "	In Billets - Battalion forming Brigade Reserve.	
19th "	" - Nothing to report	
20th "	" " "	
21st "	" " " The Battn. proceeded to Trenches	
22nd "	In Trenches - Casualties 2 wounded. 2nd Lieut P.W. Greetham-Strode and 60 NCO's & men joined the Battn. from England.	
23rd "	In Trenches - Casualties 3 killed, 4 wounded.	
24th "	" NIL	
25th "	Lieut R. Newdigate & 2nd Lt P.R. Cowding joined the Battn. from England. In Trenches.	
26th "	In Trenches - Casualties :- NIL. The Battalion proceeded to Billets at night	

Army Form C. 2118.

WAR DIARY
or
INTELLIGENCE SUMMARY.
(Erase heading not required.)

Instructions regarding War Diaries and Intelligence Summaries are contained in F.S. Regs., Part II. and the Staff Manual respectively. Title pages will be prepared in manuscript.

Hour, Date, Place	Summary of Events and Information	Remarks and references to Appendices
Sailly 27th Feby.	In Billets - Batln forming Divl Reserve.	for month X.9.W.25.
28th "	" " - Nothing to report.	

J.H.Marsh. Lieut. Colonel
Commanding 2nd Bn Border Regiment

RECONNAISSANCE REPORTS.

Reconnaissance Report
on part of the German
trenches immediately S.E
of La Cordonnerie Farm

For reference see attached sketch

1) ENEMY'S TRENCHES
At this point there are 3 lines of trenches. The distance between the 1st & 2nd line being from 20^x - 30^x (approx) while that between the 2nd & 3rd lines is about 100^x.

2) Communication trenches at distances of from 50^x - 60^x connected 1st & 2nd Lines all along the line. Two main ones are marked in sketch

3) Pointed Appui at night are about 50^x apart, but whether all these are occupied by day is not certain. I have not been able to locate the supports by day or night for certain but the locality marked Ⓒ is occupied by night. It seems that the supports

(Left)

(2)

might very likely be concealed behind the wood (D) as the 3rd line of trench seems to disappear behind the houses in the Rue des Turks.

4) <u>Parapet</u> about 4' – 5' high.

5) <u>Loopholes</u> spaced about 15" apart. They seem to be of 2 kinds. One which is square in section, many of these are dummy. The other kind is the steel plate pattern affording good protection, the hole for firing through seldom being in the centre but generally in one of the corners.

6) <u>Parados</u> The parados is very low a not being visible from anywhere.

7) <u>Weak points</u> There are no points which offer good opportunities

(3)

for attack neither are there any points which can be enfiladed from our trenches opposite.

8) <u>Machine Guns</u> There appear to be six or seven emplacements for M.Gs but there are only 2 or 3 guns. The positions of these weapons are constantly being changed and are hard to locate even at night for the enemy evidently have some means of concealing the flashes of the bursts of fire.

9) <u>Wire</u> The enemy has several types of wire entanglements & the depth varies, the broadest being about 15' in depth & the the narrowest about 2'. The enemy employ both trestles 30' long with wire

4

attached also the ordinary wire entanglement about +4', thick while in other places ordinary strands of wire parallel to one another about + 1'6" to 2' from the ground & staked every 10'.

10) <u>Surrounding Country</u> The country in front of the trenches is flat ab this spot but very muddy, while there is a slight dip in the ground just in front of the enemy's trenches. Country in rear very enclosed ^

^ This report was made from substance gained by observation from the trenches & from points of vantage behind them.

11) There are no saps from the enemy's lines

A. P. L. Drake Brockman Lt
2nd Border Regt
8/2/15

Reconnaissance Report on enemy's line in front of Nº 6, 7 & 8. Pivot Posts.

The enemy's parapet is about 80 yds away from Nº 8 post, 100 yards from Nº 7, & 100 yards from Nº 6. The height of the parapet is about 4 feet 6 inches.

They have a machine gun about half way between 7 & 8 posts, and another further to our right, which enfilades our trench between 8 & 9 posts.

Their loopholes are made of iron plates, & they have several of them.

I am unable to locate any retrenchments or communicating trenches, owing to the height of their parapet.

Their wire entanglements are close to their trenches, and are made in some parts of the aeroplane type.

Their line cannot be enfiladed from

2

any of my posts.

The country in front is open & between the trenches there are no ditches, but the ground is very heavy.

Owing to the enemy's trenches being so close I am unable to reconnoitre so as to ascertain the weakest points of the enemy's line.

8/2/15

A. B. Clayton Capt.
Commdg. A. Company.
2nd Border Regt.

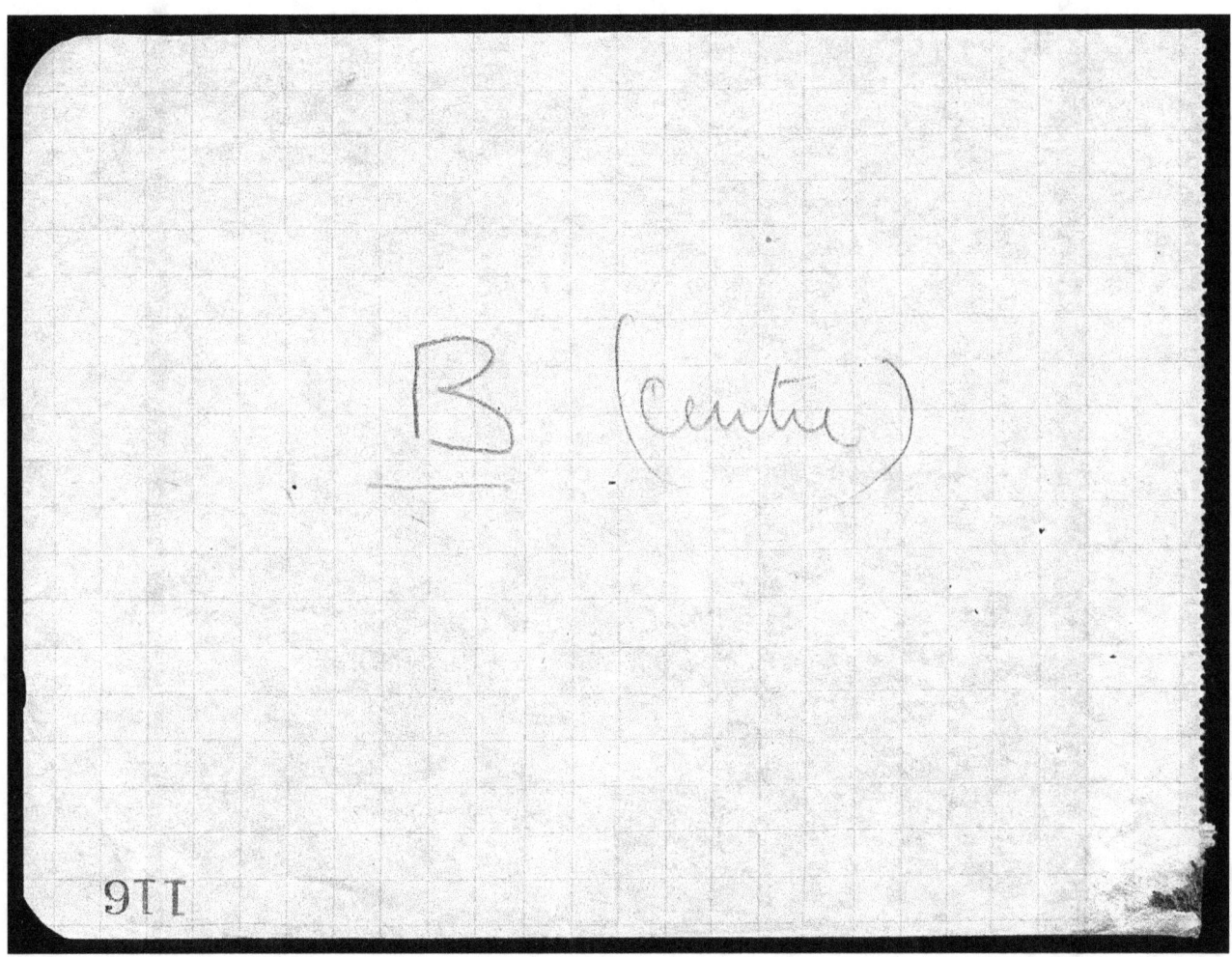

The Enemy's barbed wire in front of Post N:8 to N:6 post is formly staked in. Large stakes driven in at various angles & more than 6 strands, placed at all angles & as high as 6 feet in many places.

Immediately behind 1st Trench there is apparently one strand of barbed wire. In front of the Trenches ie between Trench & barbed wire - there are thousands of tins - apparently all refuse gone over the front of trench - in the way of tins - Immediately in front of N:8 post there is about 30ft of trench - all

sandbagged & have carefully
revetted - the balks & planks extend
well out to back & win. It has the
appearance of a wall rather
than a trench.

The 2nd line of Trenches have large
"piles" intersected with sandbags with
innumerable loopholes & appears to be
about 40ˣ behind 1st Trench.
There is a Machine Gun Exactly in line
with Left corner of F over centre of 6 post
No.
& a tree in the Trench.

Sergt. Maya Davenport

(B)
Centre

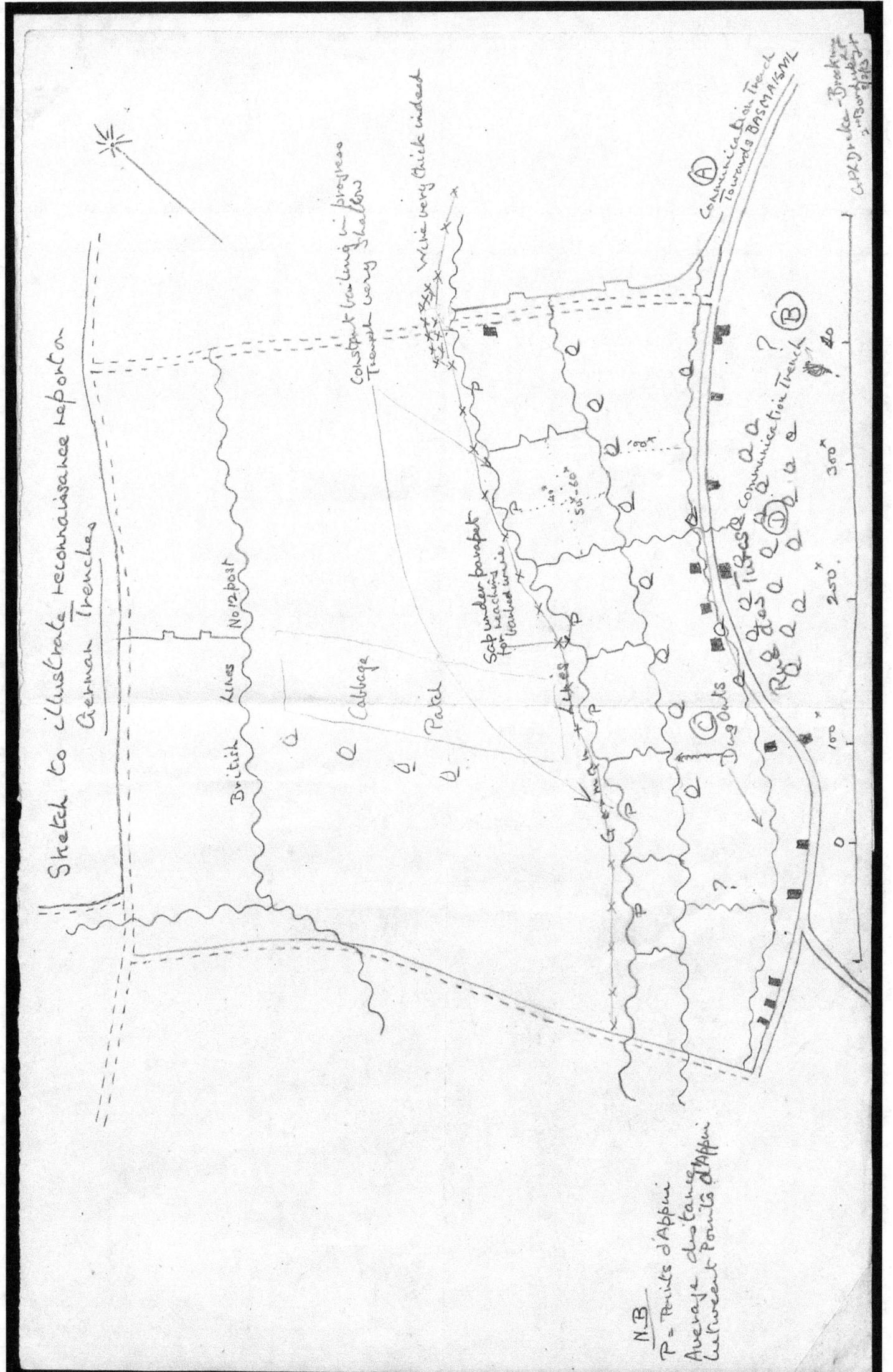

To
O.C.
2nd Border Regt

(Reconnaissance Report)

20 men with tools at the Rue [illegible] 7. q.a.m.
Slings:

8.2.15

1. **Reconnaissance report on enemy's lines** —

Parapet — appears to be in good condition, distance from "E" No. 4 & "D" posts about 100x — from No. 3 lateral 140x over FROMELLES road about 309x — from "C" lateral 200x facing road 350x — No. 2 and "A" post roughly 350x.

Height (avg) — 3 feet

Loopholes — nature of. These are fixed at the bottom of the parapet, square shape, and when not in use, appears to be blocked up by sandbags from inside the trench. These loopholes must have a great advantage as I have only seen one German firing from the top of the parapet during the time

2/ the Brigade has been in this district.

Machine Gun Positions — I have not located any gun positions in front of my post. These positions are very difficult to locate even at night when the gun is firing, the enemy appears to mask their guns in front and always set them to the flanks, by these means, no flashes can been seen.

Enfilade fire weak points — 1 Enfilade Machine Gun fire could be used from No. 2 post on trench opposite those occupied by the Guards

2

3/

Salient or Re-entrant

Observing the German line from D. post it runs parallel with ours to the Fromelles–Sailly road, beyond that it gradually falls back, causing a slight re-entrant for a distance of about 200x then appears to come forward again. At this point, I think that a machine gun anyway between 2 & 3 posts could enfilade it, if the distance be too short for such fire, I suggest that a gun placed in the vicinity of the cellar, with its shares in the above posts might be fired with advantage.

Retrenchments

None can be seen behind their lines.

Wire
height
Depth

Low wire entanglement about 10' deep, (well concealed) in front, roughly 0x4yds – behind that, a continuous wire (barbed) entanglement about 3 feet high made in sections, then wired together. The section is made up by a centre pole then 5 to 6 crosspieces, wire running from crosspiece to crosspiece. See rough sketch.

    Section   Section
 ⋈⋈⋈⋈⋈⋈⋈   ⋈⋈⋈⋈⋈⋈⋈

makes a formidable obstacle behind good trip wire.

Number of lines of trenches

During cessation of fire at Xmas time, a second line could be observed about 20 to 30x behind their first. A number of men were noticed climbing over the parapet, observing from haystack in Rue Petillon the German line could not be properly defined.

Communicating trench, location — A communicating trench between their first and second line was located during Xmas truce, near the Fromelles-Sailly road

Nature of Country. Obstacles Ditches etc. — That part of the country E. of Fromelles-Sailly road up to and beyond No. 4 post is a vegetable field chiefly mangelwurzels, a diagonal ditch runs from the right of No 4 post which joins up to the enemy's line. This ditch which is strongly wired protects the right of our post. This part of the ground would be difficult to sap on account of the natural slope of the ground towards the centre, between the two lines. That part W of the road is fallow, the abandoned trench running alongside of the road, now a ditch forms a strong obstacle. otherwise the ground would be much easier to move troops over, than that on the "E" side of the road.

Orders, framing of — Information — All information I know of is in the report with the exception that since my last tour of duty more fires than usual have been noticed in their lines this may indicate that the line has been thickened.

Weakest point — I can only suppose that the portion of the enemy's trench where

the Fromelles joins in, is
by nature the weakest point
it was also known to be
the dividing line between
the 15th & 158th Regts.

8/2/15

Brockman? M Kerr Lieut
Comdg B Company
B. Coy

A
(1st West)

HONOURS AND AWARDS.

2nd Battn Border Regiment

Honours & Rewards for Services granted to the Battalion during February

Regtl No	Rank & Name			
	Pte	Acton		Victoria Cross } (not yet notified)
	"	Smith		Victoria Cross }
51●	CSM	Davenport	VHS	⎫
9479	Sgt	Booth	R.J.	⎬
8211	Sgt	Riley	W.E.	⎬ Distinguished Conduct Medal
6615	LCpl	Brewer	R	⎬
10354	"	Wilson	JH	⎬
2873	Pte	Clark	D	⎬
9570	"	Smith	L	⎭
	Major	Bosanquet	J.T.J.	Brevet Lieut-Colonel
	Lt Col	Wood	L.J.	C.M.G.
	Major	Warren	G.E.	D.S.O.
	2/Lieut	Hutton	B	Military Cross
	Captain	Watson	W	D.S.O.

20th Infantry Brigade.

7th Division.

2nd BATTN. THE BORDER REGIMENT.

MARCH

1915

Attached:

Account of the Operations 10th/14th March.
Appendices.

ACCOUNT OF THE OPERATIONS 10TH/14TH MARCH.

WAR DIARY
or
INTELLIGENCE SUMMARY.
(Erase heading not required.)

Army Form C. 2118.

March 1915

Hour, Date, Place		Summary of Events and Information	Remarks and references to Appendices
6 a.m. 1/3/1915	SAILLY	The Battalion proceed to trenches from Divisional Reserve Billets in trenches. Casualties:- 1 Killed	
2/3/1915	SAILLY	The Battalion was relieved in the trenches at night by 16th Batn Canadian Scottish and proceeded to billets at Sailly	
3/3/1915	SAILLY		
4/3/1915	SAILLY	The Battalion proceeded by march route to ROSTRAETE near VIEUX BERQUIN, [arrived about 4pm and billeted]	
4/3/15 to 7/3/15	ROSTRAETE	The Battalion remained in billets	
2-45 pm 8/3/15	ROSTRAETE	The Battalion proceeded by march route to ESTAIRES [arrived at 5pm and billeted]	
9/3/15	ESTAIRES	in billets	
5-30 am 10/3/15	ESTAIRES	The Battalion proceeded by march route to Estaires Bridge and formed up with the 20th Brigade. It about 8am the Brigade moved off and occupied dugouts in rear of trenches occupied by 21st Infantry Brigade, acting as Reserve.	
11-15 am 11/3/15	N. of NEUVE CHAPELLE	The Battalion moved forward in support of Gordon Highlanders. The attack commenced at 11-30am, Gordon Highlanders and Grenadier Guards in front line, Border Regiment and Scots Guards in support. Whilst waiting for the Gordon Highlanders to advance the Battalion was subjected to heavy shell fire, both high explosive and shrapnel, and had many casualties. Our objective was Rue DU PIETRE. On the advance of the Gordon Highlanders being	

WAR DIARY
or
INTELLIGENCE SUMMARY.
(Erase heading not required.)

Army Form C. 2118.

Hour, Date, Place	Summary of Events and Information	Remarks and references to Appendices
12/3/15	being checked the Battalion came up in line with them and with the greater portion of our front line on their left. "A" and B Companies under Major N.O. Moffat with C and D Companies in support. A great many casualties occurred in "A" and "B" Companies from enfilade fire and in 2 Platoons of B Company when ordered to move round to the left flank. The Companies remained more or less in their positions all night but straightened the line and dug themselves in. In the early evening of the 12th C and D Companies moved forward and took up positions in trenches dug during the night in advance of A and B Companies, whilst the latter withdrew into Reserve. The Scots Guards were ordered to take up a position on our right, and the attack was to commence at 8-30am. objective Jenny Trenstoork and trenches about 600 yards to N.E. The advance at 8-30am was cancelled during to fog till 10-30am. The attack was then ordered to take place at 10-30am precisely. At 10-30am 'C' Company moved forward and immediately came under heavy Machine Gun and rifle fire with a Company of Scots Guards on their right. The attack continued for about 15 minutes but the casualties in both Regiments were so heavy	

WAR DIARY
or
INTELLIGENCE SUMMARY.

(Erase heading not required.)

Army Form C. 2118.

Hour, Date, Place	Summary of Events and Information	Remarks and references to Appendices
12/3/15	Major Lieut. Colonel L.I. Wood ordered the advance to stop until strong artillery fire to covering fire could be brought to bear. At this critical time, 20 minutes after the attack had been launched, an order arrived to say the attack would be postponed till 12.30pm. As this order did not arrive till 10.50am nothing could be done, except wait in the present position for the Artillery Bombardment. At 12 mid-day the Artillery commenced their bombardment. At about 12.20pm Lieut. Colonel Wood again gave the order to advance, although still enfiladed. The Battalion rushed on and got close up to the enemy's position and rushed it just as the guns ceased firing. The Germans came out holding up their hands and waving handkerchiefs. Some 400 prisoners were taken and large quantities of rifles, bayonets and ammunition &c. The Battalion then reorganised as quickly as possible and pushed forward in direction of red house on road - but again came under heavy enfilade fire from the right flank and having no battalion on its right had to stop and withdraw into the German trenches. Our B.Coy order to consolidate position and ground captured. the Companies were re-organised and told off to different positions of the German trenches which were greatly strengthened at night to provide against a counter-attack. The Machine Guns were brought up by hand	

WAR DIARY
or
INTELLIGENCE SUMMARY.
(Erase heading not required.)

Army Form C. 2118.

Hour, Date, Place	Summary of Events and Information	Remarks and references to Appendices
13/3/1915	under 2nd Lieut N.H.Wood, but many were hit. The two that did get up doing great execution. 2nd Lt Whichcote and 2nd Lt Fraser were killed on Thursday. The Battalion were under orders to remain in the doorway trenches and to be in reserve, ready to move forward if necessary, to support the Grenadiers and Gordon Highlanders who were to make an attack. Owing to some mistake the attack was never launched. The Battalion came under exceptionally heavy shell fire but had two casualties. The night was spent strengthening the firing line and parapets.	Total Casualties 10/3/15 to 14/3/1915. Officers Killed 2 O.Ranks 65 Wounded 13 Died of wounds 21 Wounded 186 Missing 16 Total 15 Total 288
14/3/1915	The Battalion was again heavily shelled at the morning. At 12 midnight the Battalion was relieved by the Worcester Regiment and proceeded to LAVENTIE and billeted.	
15/3/1915 LAVENTIE	In Billets.	
16/3/1915 LAVENTIE	The Battalion proceeded by march route to ESTAIRES [at 5 p.m. arrived at 9 p.m. and billeted]	
17/3/1915 ESTAIRES	In Billets.	
18/3/1915 ESTAIRES	The Battalion proceeded to trenches at 5 p.m., at RUE TILLELOY relieving the Queens Regiment.	
19/3/15 to 23/3/15	In trenches.	
24/3/1915	In trenches. Captain W.Watson D.S.O., Lieut T.W. Hackenthorpe, Lieut C.B.Love, 2nd Lieut D.N.Leck and 2/Lt O.Rauke, joined the Battalion.	
25/3/1915	The Battalion was relieved in trenches at night and proceeded to billets at LA GORGUE, arrived at 9 p.m. and billeted.	

Army Form C. 2118.

WAR DIARY
or
INTELLIGENCE SUMMARY.
(Erase heading not required.)

Instructions regarding War Diaries and Intelligence Summaries are contained in F.S. Regs., Part II. and the Staff Manual respectively. Title pages will be prepared in manuscript.

Hour, Date, Place	Summary of Events and Information	Remarks and references to Appendices
26/3/15 to 30/3/15 LA GORGUE	The Battalion remained in billets	
31/3/15 LA GORGUE	The Battalion proceeded by march route to LAVENTIE at night, arrived about 8pm and billeted	

6th April 1915

[signature] Lieut. Colonel.
Commanding 2nd Bn. The Border Regt.

72

2nd Battalion Border Regt
Roll of Officers (Combatant)

Rank	Name	Remarks
Lt. Col	Wood L.L.	
Major	Moffat F.W.	
Lieut	Lyake-Brockman G.	
2Lieut	Kerr	
"	Meetham-Steede G.	
"	Lowdang	
"	Wood N.O.H.	
"	Horsley	Joined 13/3/15
"	Johnson	" "

M Wood. Lieut. Colonel

16/3/15 Commdg 2nd Border Regt

APPENDICES.

2nd Border Regiment

The Divisional General has now received all the reports on the fighting near NEUVE CHAPELLE on the 10th - 14th March.

He desires to commend the conduct of the 2nd Border Regiment, who, owing to non-arrival of the order postponing the attack on the 12th March, attempted to attack without Artillery support. This attempt was made in a gallant manner and in spite of losses thus occasioned, the Battalion was able to successfully attack later on the same day.

The Divisional General much regrets the losses sustained by this Battalion.

March 27th 1915.

Sd/ J. Sears, Captain
A.D.C
7th Division.

Special Order by
Brigadier-General J.S. Heyworth C.B. D.S.O.
Commanding 20th Infantry Brigade.

"The Brigadier-General Commanding desires to congratulate all ranks of his Brigade on the part they have taken in the successful operations of the last five days round NEUVE CHAPELLE. The heroism and devotion to duty of the Regimental Officers, Non-Commissioned Officers and men have been beyond all praise — where all have done well it is difficult to pick out any one individual Battalion.

Although deeply deploring the loss of many gallant comrades, the Brigadier knows that all ranks must feel elated at their victory over the Germans, and he feels certain that the troops will do as well in the future as they have done in the past."

Sd/ A.B.E. Cator,
Brigade Major
15th March 1915.   20th Infantry Brigade.

IVth Corps Orders.

The following Special Order by the Lieutenant General Commanding IVth Corps is to be communicated to all ranks at once :-

"The brilliant success which the troops of the IVth Corps have achieved in the capture of NEUVE CHAPELLE is of the first importance to the Allied Cause, especially at this period of the war. The heroism and gallantry of Regimental Officers and men and the assistance afforded them by the Artillery Units is deserving of the highest praise, and the Corps Commander desires to congratulate them on the severe defeat they have inflicted on the enemy, whose losses amount to not less than 10,000 men in killed and prisoners alone. The magnificent behaviour of the Infantry Units is deserving of the highest commendation, and in deploring the loss of those gallant comrades who have given their lives for their King and Country, Sir Henry Rawlinson hopes that all Officers and men fully realise what they have accomplished in breaking through the German line is an achievement of which they should all feel justly proud.

14th March. 1915.

(Sd) A G Dallas Brig. General
General Staff. IVth Corps.

R.A.M.C.

The Divisional General has received the reports of the fighting near NEUVE CHAPELLE during the 10th - 14th March.

He desires to express his admiration and satisfaction of the devoted conduct of the Regimental Stretcher Bearers and of the Officers and men of the Bearer Detachment R.A.M.C.

These detachments worked with great devotion, skill and energy, and had cleared the ground, right up to the enemy's position, of all wounded before the Division was relieved on the night of the 14th March.

27th March 1915

Sd/- J Sears Captain
A.D.C.
7th Division.

Account of the operations 10th to 14th March. 1915

Head Quarters
20th Brigade

On the morning of 10th March we paraded close to ESTAIRES Bridge and moved off at about [?] and went into [?] ...... 21st Infantry Brigade.

[overlaid note:]
C/\
8
21.3.15.
To H.Q. XX Bde

In forwarding the attached, I would like to state, how willingly everyone did his allotted task right from the senior downwards, all having had very little sleep for several days, and the greater proportion being very young Officers — H.P.E. & men who had never been under heavy Artillery, Infantry & Machine Gun fire before.

S. Wood Lt Col
Comd 2/Border Regt

[main text continues:]
...Highlanders.
...Gordon
...front line,
...[?] in support
...Highlanders
...subjected to
...explosive
...casualties.
...E. On the
...ed we
...eater portion
...on their left. — "A" and "B" Companies under Major A.S.W. Moffat with "C" and "D" Companies in support.

A lot of casualties occurred in A and B Companies

Account of the operations 10th to 14th March, 1915

Head Quarters
20th Brigade

On the morning of 10th March we paraded close to ESTAIRES Bridge and moved off at about 8am and went into dugouts occupied by 21st Infantry Brigade. We remained there all night and paraded early next morning, 11th, at 4-15am and moved in support of Gordon Highlanders.

The attack commenced at 7-30am, Gordon Highlanders and Grenadiers in front line, Border Regiment and Scots Guards in support. Whilst waiting for the Gordon Highlanders to advance the Battalion was subjected to very heavy shell fire, both high explosive and shrapnel, and had many casualties.

Our objective was line DU PIETRE. On the advance of the Gordons being checked we came up in line and with the greater portion of our front line on their left.— "A" and "B" Companies under Major A.S.W. Moffat with "C" and "D" Companies in support.

A lot of casualties occurred in A and B Companies

(2)

from enfilade fire and in two Platoons of "B" Company when ordered to move round to the left flank.

The Companies remained more or less in their positions that night but straightened the line and dug themselves in.

In the early morning of the 12th C and D Companies moved forward and took up positions in trenches dug during the night in advance of A & B Companies, whilst the Gordons withdrew into Reserve. The Scots Guards were to take up a position on our right - we were ordered to attack at 8-30am, objective being breastwork and trenches about 600 yards to N.E. The advance at 8-30am was cancelled, owing to fog, till 10-30am. The attack was then ordered to take place at 10-30am precisely and immediately came under heavy rifle + M.G. fire. At 10-30 am "C" Company moved forward, with a Company of Scots Guards on their right. The attack continued for about 15 minutes but the casualties in both Regiments were so heavy that I ordered the advance to stop until strong artillery fire or covering fire could be brought to bear. At

(3)

At this critical time, 20 minutes after the attack had been launched, an order arrived to say the attack would be postponed till 12-30pm. As this did not arrive till 10-50am nothing could be done, except wait in their present position for the Artillery bombardment. At 12 mid-day the Artillery commenced their bombardment. At about 12-20pm I again gave the order to advance - although still enfiladed. The Battalion pushed on and got close up to the position and rushed it just as the guns ceased firing. The Germans came out holding up their hands and waving handkerchiefs - some 400 prisoners were taken and large quantities of rifles, bayonets and ammunition &c. We then reorganized as quickly as possible and pushed forward in direction of red house on road - but we again came under heavy enfilade fire from our right flank; and having no Battalion on my right I had to stop and withdraw into the German trenches, which I held - sending a

(4)

message back to that effect.

On GOC's order to consolidate position and ground captured the Companies were re-organized and told off to different positions of the German trenches which were greatly strengthened that night to provide against a counter attack. Some men of the Wilts Regt who got mixed up with my Regiment took a small portion on the left of our line. The Machine Guns were brought up by hand under 2nd Lieut. A.V.H.Wood - but had many hit - the two guns that did get up did very good work.

All the Companies did equally well and considering they were led by very young Officers, mostly all 2nd Lieuts, they shewed great gallantry.

13th. We were under orders to remain in the trenches we now occupied and to be in Reserve, ready to move forward if necessary to support the Grenadiers and Gordons should they be in need of it. Owing to some mistake the

the attack was never launched. We came under exceptionally heavy shell fire but had few casualties. The night of the 13th was spent strengthening the position and parapets.

We were again shelled all the morning of the 14th and at 12 mid-night we were relieved by the Worcester Regiment.

       I attach a separate report of Officers and Other Ranks whom I consider worthy of mention.

Total number of Casualties of Officers and other ranks during the fighting attached

21st March 1915

J. Wood
Lieut. Colonel.
Commanding 2nd Bn The Border Regt.

2nd Bn Border Regiment

Total Number of Casualties - Officers & O.Ranks during operations 10th to 14th March 1915

Officers		Other Ranks	
Killed :-	2	Killed	58
Wounded :-	13	Wounded	180
Total	15	Missing	41
		Died of wounds	7
		Total	286

C.4.

9.

Head Qrs XXTH Bde.

Re your BM 142 of 21st I beg to forward the names of Officers, NCOs and men whom I consider worthy of recommendation in connection with the recent operations 10th to 14th March.

(1) Major A.S.W. Moffat – He was continually up in the firing line both on 11th and 12th giving assistance and encouragement to the young company commanders and platoon leaders at times under heavy fire and assisted me greatly on the 12th in reorganizing the different units that had got mixed up after taking the German trenches

(2) 2nd Lieut W. Kerr, in command of "B" Company. – He did exceptionally well in

both attacks on 11th and 12th and it was in a great measure due to him for the steady way in which the men moved forward to the attack, under heavy rifle and machine gun fire.

He is a very capable leader under fire and a fine example to the men.

(3) Lieut G.P.L Drake-Brockman.- Although a very young Officer he did exceptionally well in handling his Company under heavy fire and showed good judgement.

(4) Lieut J.H. Beves (twice wounded).

He did exceptionally well on the 12th in leading and encouraging his men in the attack and he shewed a splendid example to his men

(5) No 5180 Regtl Sgt Major V.H.S Davenport.
This NCO gave me great assistance on both days of the attack, taking messages under fire to the Company Commanders - and helping to reorganise the Battalion - and units of other Corps that had got mixed up with my Battalion after taking the German trenches.

(6) No 9284 Coy Sgt Major J Groggins (wounded)
This NCO, after his Officers had been wounded handled his Company exceptionally well. - I especially noticed this NCO. - He also got his men well together against a counter attack and showed good leadership.

(7) No 9426 L.Cpl. W Hodgson – In continually taking messages for me under heavy fire.

(8) No 10340 L.Cpl. J. Robinson and No 9392 Private W Corkish – Bringing Machine Gun into action under fire and continuing to work the gun after the former had been wounded.

(9) No 6684 Sgt. T. Toner.
Company Officers statement attached.

(10) No 4565 Private H McDowell – A Coy (Killed)
Company Officers statement attached.

T Wood Lieut-Colonel
Commanding 2nd Border Regt

WAR DIARY.

20th Infantry Brigade.
7th Division.

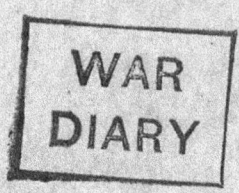

2nd BATTN. THE BORDER REGIMENT.

APRIL

1915

Attached:
    Appendix.

Army Form C. 2118.

WAR DIARY
or
INTELLIGENCE SUMMARY.
(Erase heading not required.)

April 1915

Instructions regarding War Diaries and Intelligence Summaries are contained in F.S. Regs., Part II. and the Staff Manual respectively. Title pages will be prepared in manuscript.

Hour, Date, Place		Summary of Events and Information	Remarks and references to Appendices
1st to 3rd April 1915.	LAVENTIE.	The Battalion remained in billets	
4th April 1915	LAVENTIE.	The Battalion proceeded to trenches near FAUQUISSART at 7.30 p.m.	
5th and 6th April 1915	FAUQUISSART	In trenches.	
7/4/1915	"	The Battalion was relieved in the trenches at night and proceeded to billets at LAVENTE. Casualties 4-7/4/15. 4 wounded. A draft of 100 Other Ranks joined the Battalion on this date. 2nd Lieut H Owen, who was wounded in action near NEUVE CHAPELLE in March rejoined the Battalion from hospital.	
8/4/15	LAVENTIE		
9th - 24/4/15	LAVENTIE	The Battalion remained in billets. On 19th April the Battalion with the 20th Brigade, was inspected by Field Marshal Sir J.D.P. French. After his inspection the Commander in Chief addressed the Battalion. The Battalion again proceeded to trenches near FAUQUISSART at about 9 p.m.	21/4/15. 2nd Lieut 2 McLaurin joined the Battalion. (*- Copy of address attached)
25/4/15	LAVENTIE		
26/4/15	FAUQUISSART.	The Battalion was relieved at night by 6th West Yorks Regt and proceeded to billets at LAVENTE.	
27/4/15	"		
28/4/15	LAVENTIE	A draft of 161 Other Ranks joined the Battalion. At about 9 p.m. the Battalion proceeded to trenches about 800 yards N.E. of NEUVE CHAPELLE - about to erect trenches captured by us on 12/3/15	
29th & 30/4/15		In trenches. Captain W Watson DSO was wounded on 30/4/15	

Signed, Lieut. Colonel.
Commanding 2nd Bn. The Border Regt.

APPENDIX.

Field Marshall Sir J.D.P. French. G.C.B, O.M. G.C.V.O. K.C.M.G. Commander-in-Chief. British Expeditionary Force, addressed the Battalion in the following words in a field immediately N. of ESTAIRES. on the 19th April. 1915 :-

"Officers, NCO's and men of the 2nd Battalion The Border Regiment - I have come here this afternoon as your Commander-in-Chief to thank you from the bottom of my heart for the magnificent part you took in the recent battle of NEUVE CHAPELLE. The last occasion on which I had the honour of addressing you was after the exceptionally heavy and strenuous fighting at YPRES, where you added fresh lustre to your already splendid records.

In congratulating the Battalion I then said I was sure that in the future they would acquit themselves, should the occasion offer, as creditably as they had done in the past.

At the battle of NEUVE CHAPELLE, by your gallantry. You have gained still further laurels and added still further honours to your already magnificent records. I know the part you took in this battle - You stormed a very strong redoubt of which the enemy were in possession - You came under a very heavy fire and your losses were enormous - But you took the work and 300 German prisoners. In congratulating you I thank you as your Commander-in-Chief. Not only I but your country is grateful to you for the magnificent part you have played all through the war.

I also congratulate you on the splendid front you now show in spite of your recent strenuous work and great losses. I wish you all every success in the future."

20th Infantry Brigade.
7th Division.

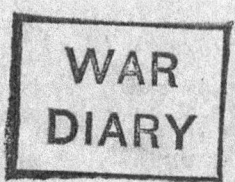

2nd BATTN. THE BORDER REGIMENT.

M A Y

1 9 1 5

Army Form C. 2118.

May 1915

WAR DIARY
or
INTELLIGENCE SUMMARY.
(Erase heading not required.)

Hour, Date, Place	Summary of Events and Information	Remarks and references to Appendices
1/5/15 to 4/5/15 NEUVE CHAPELLE	In Trenches. Casualties :- 1 Killed 9 wounded.	
5/5/15 — " —	The Battalion was relieved in trenches by West Riding Brigade and proceeded to billets at LAVENTIE	
6/5/15 to 8/5/15 LAVENTIE	In billets	
9/5/15 12.30 a.m — " —	The Battalion marched with 20th Brigade to reserve trenches near ROUGES BANCS. The Brigade being reserve to 8th Division who attacked at about 6 a.m. The attack was unsuccessful.	
10/5/15 ROUGES BANCS	The Battalion marched with the Brigade to Bethune at 9 p.m. Arrived and billeted about Daybreak.	
11/5/15 BETHUNE	In billets. 2nd Lieut R.W. Burmann joined the Battn & assumed duties of Adjutant.	
12/5/15 — " —	The Battalion marched to HINGES at 9 a.m, arrived at 12 noon and billeted.	
13/5/15 & 14/5/15 HINGES	The Battalion remained in billets.	
15/5/15 — " —	The Battalion marched to trenches at FESTUBERT at 5 p.m. The Battalion arrived in trenches at 9 p.m. Several orders had been issued as to situations on the following day. Casualties during the night by shell fire, 1 Officer in Machine Gun Section	
16/5/15 FESTUBERT.	The Brigade were allotted the task of breaking the line at two points. The London Regiment from P5 to PRINCES ROAD roughly,	

WAR DIARY or INTELLIGENCE SUMMARY

Army Form C. 2118.

May 1915 (2)

(Erase heading not required.)

Hour, Date, Place	Summary of Events and Information	Remarks and references to Appendices

150 yards and the 2nd Scots Guards from PRINCES ROAD to 150 yards to right.

At 5-15 am two Platoons of "A" Company made the assault but were startled by two of our own heavy howitzer shells which dropped after the time the bombardment should have ceased. They advanced a second time after heavy loss & gained the German trench. They were at once supported by the remaining two Platoons of "A" Company.

An attempt was made to progress further but the advance was stopped by a ditch full of water and by heavy machine gun fire which enfiladed from the left.

The guide of the B Company was then pushed over & occupied the German front line trench with orders to hold P5 of all costs. 80 Brigade Bombers were attached to the Company of this purpose. Attempts were made to bomb down the trench to the left, which was still in the hands of the Germans. About 200 yards was gained but by each occasion the ground gained had to be given up owing to the shortage of bombs. These tactics came under fire from a trench partly during each attempt and suffered very heavy losses but despite their losses P5 was held until the Battalion was relieved.

About this time the Communication trench P5, P4, which was our objective was made good.

The machine gunners with 2 guns were then sent up to a point about midway between P5 and P4 to strengthen the line. "C" and "D" Companies pushed over into the German trench & prolonged the

WAR DIARY or INTELLIGENCE SUMMARY.

(Erase heading not required.)

Army Form C. 2118

(3)

May 1915

Instructions regarding War Diaries and Intelligence Summaries are contained in F.S. Regs., Part II. and the Staff Manual respectively. Title pages will be prepared in manuscript.

Hour, Date, Place	Summary of Events and Information	Remarks and references to Appendices
	later to the night.	
	During these operations the Battalion suffered very heavily. Lieut-Col Wood D.S.O. was wounded midway between the British & German trenches and was brought in by Major Garnett & Colonel Coleman but died as soon as he reached the British trenches. Major J.S.O. McFall was in command of the two leading companies & was hit in the head in the German Communication trench P.4, P.5, & died shortly afterwards. The following Officers were also killed and wounded:—	
	Killed: 2nd Lieut H Owen, 2nd Lieut E Sinclair, Lieut E Sale, 2nd Lt W Bridgman [*], 2nd Lt G S Richardson, Lieut J Morley, 2nd Lt N A Krohn, 2nd Lt H G Byng [*]	[*] Died of Wounds.
	2nd Lieut Eric Cauce [*]	
	Wounded: 2nd Lieut S Meek, 2nd Lt H Nata, 2nd Lt S Johnson, 2nd Lt G Lindsay.	
	During the night the Battn. was relieved by the 21st Grenadier Guards on account of the serious losses it had sustained & returned to the old British line where it was re-organised by Captain O.W. Crackenthorpe who had assumed command of the Battalion.	
11/5/15 FESTUBERT	This day was spent in bringing in the wounded & burying the dead. While superintending this work Lieut J. Kerr was wounded in the leg. In the early part of the afternoon the Battalion received orders to move into reserve billets near M. about 5 P.M. The Battalion received orders to move into reserve billets near Rue L'Epinette. This was carried out as soon as it was dark. The total casualties during these operations were:—	
	Officers: Killed 110, Wounded 240, Missing 35.	
	Other Ranks: Killed 110, Wounded 240, Missing 35.	

Army Form C. 2118.

WAR DIARY
or
INTELLIGENCE SUMMARY.
(Erase heading not required.)

May 1915

Hour, Date, Place	Summary of Events and Information	Remarks and references to Appendices
18/5/15 RUE L'EPINETTE	The Battalion marched to HINGES in the afternoon and billetted.	
19/5/15 HINGES.		
20/5/15 to 30/5/15 BUSNES.	The Battalion marched to BUSNES at 2.30pm and billetted. In billets.	
	The following joined the Battalion on 20/5/1915:-	
	Lieut. Col. G.W. S. Monke, 2nd Bedford Regt, who assumed command of the Battn.	
	2nd Lieut K.W. Browne, 2/Suffolk Regt, 2/Lt. R.G. Spalding, 3/Surrey Regt.	
	2/Lt. A.P. Newton 2/Surrey Regt.	
	Draft of 146 Other Ranks joined on 20/5/15	
	Capt. P.B. Cosser + Lieut. W. Rumgates 2/York Regt joined the Battalion on 22/5/15	
	Lieut. W. Bates 3/Surrey Regt joined on 26/5/15	
	Capt. A Keaton-Oulde, 3/York Rifles, joined the Battn on 28/5/15	
	Draft of 170 Other Ranks joined on 29/5/15.	
31/5/15 BUSNES	The Battalion marched to GORRE at 2.30pm and billetted.	
	2nd Lieut K. Sheriff 3/R.W.Kent Regt joined the Battn.	

M. Eastentrop Captain
Commanding 2nd Border Regiment

20th Infantry Brigade.

7th Division.

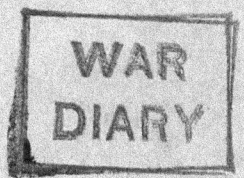

2nd BATTN. THE BORDER REGIMENT.

J U N E

1 9 1 6

20th Infantry Brigade.

7th Division.

Army Form C. 2118.

WAR DIARY
or
INTELLIGENCE SUMMARY. June 1915
(Erase heading not required.)

Hour, Date, Place		Summary of Events and Information	Remarks and references to Appendices
1/6/15	GORRE	The Battalion remained in reserve billets.	
2/6/15	GORRE	Two Platoons of A Company proceeded to the trenches in support of 6th Gordon Highlanders who attacked the German position opposite at 9.40 p.m. after the explosion of a mine. The crater was taken but was evacuated early on the morning of 10th instant May.	
3/6/15	GORRE	Two Companies proceeded to the trenches relieving 6th Bn Gordon Highlanders.	Casualties 3 - 5/6/15 2 killed 24 wounded
4/6/15	GORRE	The remainder of the Battalion proceeded to trenches in the early morning.	
5/6/15	GIVENCHY	The Battalion was relieved in the trenches by the Queens Regt. at about 6 p.m. and proceeded to billets at LES HARISOIRS.	
6/6/15 to 11/6/15	LES HARISOIRS	In billets. 2nd Lieut R.T. Baker joined the Battalion on 6/6/15. 2nd Lieut M.F. Smith, 3rd Hants Regt. " " 7/6/15.	
12/6/15	LES HARISOIRS	The Battalion proceeded to billets at MARIAS.	
13/6/15	MARIAS	2nd Lieut B.K. Ehrenborg, Lieut G. Mackie, 2nd Lieut W.N. Beaumont, Lieut A. Ratcliffe 2nd Lieut G. Aylmer 2nd Batt. Regt. joined the Battalion with a draft of 30 Other Ranks. The Battalion proceeded to the trenches at 8 p.m. relieving Royal Welch Fusiliers.	
14/6/15	GIVENCHY	The Battalion was relieved in Trenches by 2nd Gordon Highlanders and proceeded to reserve billets at GORRE. Casualties 11/6/15 :- 2 killed 7 wounded.	

WAR DIARY or **INTELLIGENCE SUMMARY.**
(Erase heading not required.)

Army Form C. 2118.

June 1915

Hour, Date, Place	Summary of Events and Information	Remarks and references to Appendices
15/6/15 to 17/6/15 GORRE	The Battalion remained in reserve billets.	
18/6/15 GORRE	A draft of 25 other ranks joined the Battalion on 17/6/15. The Battalion proceeded to the trenches relieving 2nd Gordon Highlanders	
19/6/15 GIVENCHY	in trenches. 2nd Lieut A Sheard 3rd Bn. Nth Fus. was wounded. 2nd Lieuts J.R.H. McMorran, 2nd Lt W. Dodd, V. Lyscombe, 2nd Lt D.M. Dove, 2nd Lieuts J. Ricketts, M.N. Morse, Lt P. W. Dodd, V. Lyscombe,	
20/6/15 to 23/6/15 GIVENCHY	& C.B. Kennessey, joined the Battalion. in trenches. Casualties. 2 Killed, 17 wounded. The Battalion was relieved on night of 23/6/15 by 1st. S. Staff. Regt.	
24/6/15 LOCON	and proceeded to billets at LOCON. A draft of 30 other ranks joined the Battalion and proceeded to billets. 2nd Lieuts J. Neutris, N.W. Boyne, J.W. Gates, R.G. Spalding proceeded to join the 2nd South Lancs Regt.	
25/6/15 LOCON 26/6/15 BEUVRY	The Battalion proceeded to billets at BEUVRY at 9pm.	
27/6/15 BEUVRY	The Battalion proceeded to trenches at 4.30pm relieving 1st Grenadier Guards.	
28/6/15 to 30/6/15 CUINCHY	in trenches. 2 Lieut J. Beckett was killed on 2/6/15. 2 Lieut B.F. Baker, 3rd Wilts Regt was wounded on 29/6/15. Casualties 27-30/6/15. - 8 killed, 14 wounded. The Battalion was relieved on night of 30/6/15 and proceeded to billets at BUSNES, arriving at 3am.	

D. Crankanthorpe Captain
Commanding 2nd Bn. The Border Regt.

20th Infantry Brigade.

7th Division.

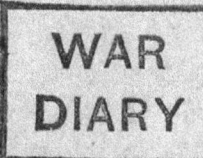

2nd BATTN. THE BORDER REGIMENT.

J U L Y

1 9 1 5

WAR DIARY
or
INTELLIGENCE SUMMARY. — July 1915
(Erase heading not required.)

Army Form C. 2118

Hour, Date, Place		Summary of Events and Information	Remarks and references to Appendices
1st to 12th July 1915	BUSNES.	The Battalion remained in billets. On 9th July 1915 the Battalion acted in conjunction with the 20th Brigade & kept the streets between BOURECQ and LILLERS on the occasion of the visit of Earl Kitchener Secretary of State for War.	2nd Lieut P.D. Mawson and 50 O.Ranks joined the Battalion on 9th July 1915.
13th July 1915	BUSNES.	The Battalion proceeded to Rescue Billets at LESTREM and arrived about 11pm.	
14th to 16th July	LESTREM.	The Battalion remained in Billets.	
17th July	LESTREM.	The Battalion proceeded to Billets at LACOUTURE and arrived about 4pm.	
18th to 20th July	LACOUTURE.	The Battalion remained in Billets.	
21st July 1915	LACOUTURE.	The Battalion proceeded to the trenches relieving 2nd Gordon Highlanders.	
22nd to 25th July 1915	In trenches	*(Casualties 6 killed, 10 wounded) — mostly "A" Coy.	* All casualties occurred owing to the parapet being blown in by enemy shell fire.
26th July 1915.		The Battalion was relieved in trenches by 2nd Warwicks Regt and proceeded to billets at LESTREM.	
27th to 30th July 1915	LESTREM.	The Battalion remained in billets.	
31st July 1915	LESTREM	The Battalion proceeded to billets at ROBECQ.	

E. Thorpe Lieut. Colonel.
Commanding 2nd Bn The Border Regt.

20th Infantry Brigade.
7th Division.

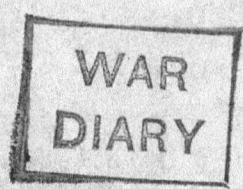

2nd BATTN. THE BORDER REGIMENT.

AUGUST

1915

Army Form C. 2118.

WAR DIARY
or
INTELLIGENCE SUMMARY. — August 1915
(Erase heading not required.)

Instructions regarding War Diaries and Intelligence Summaries are contained in F.S. Regs., Part II. and the Staff Manual respectively. Title pages will be prepared in manuscript.

Hour, Date, Place		Summary of Events and Information	Remarks and references to Appendices
1/8/15 to 16/8/15	ROBECQ	The Battalion remained at Rest Billets	August 3rd 1915. The 1st Grenadier Gds and 2nd Scots Guards were transferred to a newly formed Guards Brigade and were replaced by the 8th and 9th Bns Devon Regt
17/8/15	ROBECQ	On 6th August a draft of 40 Other Ranks joined the Battalion. The Battalion proceeded to Divisional Reserve Billets at LOCON.	
18/8/15 to 25/8/15	LOCON	Divisional Reserve Billets. On 20th August a draft of 25 Other Ranks joined the Battalion. On 21st August Captain H. Blackwood joined the Battalion from 28 Bn Royal Regt (Artists Rifles). On 22nd August 2nd Lieuts W. Day and W. Grinter joined the Battalion.	
26/8/15	LOCON	The Battalion proceeded to Reserve Trenches near MARIAS.	
27/8/15 to 30/8/15	Near MARIAS	In Reserve Trenches. Casualties :- 4 wounded	
30/8/15	" " LOCON	The Battalion proceeded to Quick Reserve Billets near LOCON.	
31/8/15	" " LOCON	The Battalion was temporarily attached to the 1st Division and proceeded to Reserve Trenches at NOYELLE being attached to 2nd Brigade	

R. Brooke Lieut-Colonel
Commanding 2nd Bn Border Regt.

20th Inf.Bde.
7th Div.

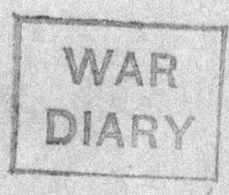

2nd BATTN. THE BORDER REGIMENT.

S E P T E M B E R

1 9 1 5

Attached:

Battalion Operation
Orders.
Brigade Narrative of
Events on Recent
Operations.

Army Form C. 2118.

WAR DIARY
or
INTELLIGENCE SUMMARY.

September 1915

(Erase heading not required.)

Instructions regarding War Diaries and Intelligence Summaries are contained in F. S. Regs., Part II. and the Staff Manual respectively. Title pages will be prepared in manuscript.

Hour, Date, Place		Summary of Events and Information	Remarks and references to Appendices
1/9/15	NOYELLES	The Battalion remained in billets in Brigade Reserve.	
2/9/15	"	The Battalion proceeded to trenches near VERMELLES	
3/9/15	Nr. VERMELLES	In trenches (Casualties 3 wounded)	
4/9/15	"	The Battalion was relieved in the trenches at night and proceeded to billets at LABOURSE. 1 draft of 31 Other Ranks joined the Battalion	
5/9/15	LABOURSE	The Battalion marched to Mt BERNONCHON at 2 p.m., arrived at 4 p.m. and billetted	
6/9/15	Mt BERNONCHON	2nd Lieut N.L. Roulgate joined the Battalion from Lord Strathcona's Horse.	
7/9/15 to 11/9/15	"	The Battalion remained in billets.	
12/9/15	"	The Battalion marched to LABOURSE at 9·30am, arrived at 11·30 am and billetted	
13/9/15	LABOURSE	The Battalion proceeded to trenches near VERMELLES at 11·30am	
14/9/15 to 16/9/15	Nr VERMELLES	In Trenches (Casualties 6 killed 2 wounded by shell fire)	
17/9/15	"	The Battalion was relieved in the trenches and proceeded to billets at LABOURSE arriving about 11 p.m.	
18/9/15	LABOURSE	In billets. 1 draft of 12 NCOs & men joined the Battalion	
19/9/15 to 22/9/15	"	In billets	
23/9/15	"	The Battalion proceeded to NOYELLE at night and billetted	

WAR DIARY
or
INTELLIGENCE SUMMARY.
(Erase heading not required.)

Army Form C. 2118.

Hour, Date, Place	Summary of Events and Information	Remarks and references to Appendices
24/9/15 NOYELLES	The 20th Inf. Bde. was ordered to form up on the night 24th-25th Sept. as a front line declaratory to an attack on 25th Sept. VERMELLES – HULLUCH ROAD – SAP 2. declaratory to an attack on 25th Sept. Information:- Enemy defences consisted of 2 well defined lines of trenches first running from FOSSE 8 Southwards to LOOS. Second 1500 yds to East running through HAISNES – CITÉ ST ELIE – HULLUCH. Our troops attacking were to swing the right eastwards, 9th Divn centre 9th Divn, swing on left. Southwards between HULLUCH and LOOS. Task:- The task of 20th Inf Bde was to clear the trenches in front enemy HULLUCH and BENEFONTAINE finishing on a line PONT-A-VENDIN Y ridge Canal Crossings. At 10 pm the Brigade began to concentrate and by 2.30 am were in position as follows:- 1st Line:- 2nd Gordon Highlders on right (in our lines) HULLUCH ROAD to SAP 1. 2 to lead off 8th Devons on the left (in our lines) SAP 1 to SAP 2. assault. 2nd Line:- 6th Gordon Highlders in support to 2nd Gordons, 2nd Border Regt. supporting 8th Devons. 3rd Line:- 9th Devons. The Battalion occupied the following trenches:- 1st Line:- OLD SUPPORT TRENCH from CHAPPEL ALLEY to FROG. LANE as follows from right to left:- 1 Machine Gun, B Company, D Company, 1 Machine Gun on left of FOSSE WAY. 2nd Line:- CURLEY CRESCENT from CHAPPEL ALLEY to 100 yds N of FOSSE WAY as follows from right to left:- 1 Machine Gun, C Coy, A Coy, 1 Machine Gun, Headquarters.	
25/9/15	At 5.50 am the attack with gas commenced. At 6.30 am the 2nd Gordons and 8th Devons left their trenches advanced at a walk up the hill to the enemy trenches. The trenches wanted were immediately occupied by 6th Gordons and the Battalion. The enemy trenches in front of 20th Inf Bde	

WAR DIARY or INTELLIGENCE SUMMARY.

Army Form C. 2118.

Hour, Date, Place	Summary of Events and Information	Remarks and references to Appendices
25/9/15	had been captured with rather heavy losses. At 11.25am the front system of enemy trenches above 20th Brigade had been captured & both 2nd Gordons & 8th Devons were steadily advancing in spite of heavy losses supported by b/y Gordons and the Battalion. During the advance an enemy trench containing 8 field guns was captured, the latter disappears. At about 11.40am the 22nd Inf. Bde (on left) were held up at POPE'S NOSE REDOUBT and 2 sections of the Battalion bombers were ordered up to try and knock down this obstruction. The bombers were unable to make any headway and the Battalion at about 1am the 8th Devons reached PITS 13, still supported by the Battalion, commenced to dig themselves in. The resistance of the enemy at POPE'S NOSE still continued at 1.30am and part of D Company under Captain A.W. Sutcliffe were ordered to attack this point. Major N. Sutcliffe led his men out with great dash & assisted by Captain H.K. Carey-Castle with half of "A" Company broke down the resistance & took the enemy in this place. However to the number of about 70. This set the example to the pres which who came on & carried the advance forward to join the remainder of the Brigade. The attack had now come to a standstill for the want of further backing and the position was that a forward line east of HULLUCH - GREEN ROADS was held connected up on the right with 10 Division but with the left in the air - behind this GUN TRENCH was held with 8 enemy guns in it which was being heavily shelled by the enemy. At 10.50am 2 Battalions of 2nd Inf. Bde were ordered to reinforce 20th Inf. Bde.	

WAR DIARY
or
INTELLIGENCE SUMMARY.
(Erase heading not required.)

Army Form C. 2118.

Hour, Date, Place	Summary of Events and Information	Remarks and references to Appendices
	but we received meanwhile from GUN TRENCH were brought up. Meanwhile messages had been received that 4th Corps were to attack HULLOCH and 21st Brigade were ordered to recede. Nothing came of this attack & the enemy continued to hold HULLOCH and CITE-ST-ELIE & were getting some troops into both places – The fronts of both villages were strongly held with Machine Guns. Besides a trench with strong wire in front. The Battalion was now in GUN TRENCH. At 4.30 say Queram sent orders to consolidate positions gained. Positions to unite 17 20th Bde Brigade at 6.30 Aug were as follows: 2nd & 10th Gordons about H.Q. H4 with a junction of 8th & 10th Devons. These were ordered to dig in & make the cross roads a strong point with the aid of two ½ cpls French mortars. 2nd Borda Reg. same 8th and 9th Devons & details. Not Bde in GUN TRENCH, in touch on the right to Lucron Y on left with 2nd Bde while were ordered to dig themselves in and RE ordered to put out wire in front. Shortly before midnight 25th/26th the enemy made a determined counter attack on the advanced position near HULLOCH Crossroads just before I had been put in a state of defence. The attack was pressed home in the endeavour to recapture the field Guns in GUN TRENCH. The enemy in the forward position gave way & Cheers of "GUN TRENCH & some even went back further than they were rallied by Officers of the Battalion, and the Brigade Major and taken back to help the men in GUN TRENCH. The enemy (enemy) attackers actually reached GUN TRENCH and were killed almost on the parapet while a good many others variously estimated at anything between 50 and 100 were killed in this attack which was taken	

WAR DIARY
or
INTELLIGENCE SUMMARY.
(Erase heading not required.)

Army Form C. 2118.

Hour, Date, Place	Summary of Events and Information	Remarks and references to Appendices
25/9/15	at HULLOCH Cross Roads was lost but all other ground gained by 20th Inf. Bde. during the day was held & consolidated before daylight.	
26/9/15	About 1 am information was received that the QUARRIES had been captured by the enemy. It was eventually made known that the enemy had not succeeded to their own line but still held the QUARRIES. At about 3am a counter attack was made on them by a Coy Battalion Inf. failed at Now & some other attempts was made till 5.30am. Our section 7 Brigade Bombers were sent to assist this attack which was fully partially successful. Major-General F Cappes KCMG, CB DSO. Commanding 17th Division was wounded during this attack and died later. During the day the Battalion was relieved in GUN TRENCH and took the place of the Royal Scots Fusiliers in BRESLAU AVENUE (Old German Communication Trench)	
27/9/15 to 31/9/15	The Battalion remained in BRESLAU AVENUE in Reserve until relieved on 1/10/15.	

E. Shrike Lieut. Colonel
Commanding 2nd Border Regt.

BATTALION OPERATION ORDERS.

OPERATION ORDERS BY
Lieut-Col E. de S. Thorpe
24th Sept 1915

1. The 20th Infantry Brigade will be formed up on the night of 24th-25th September on a front VERMELLES - HULLOCH ROAD - SAP 2. Preparatory to an attack on 25th September.
The 95th Field Coy R.E. and No 1 Trench Mortar Battery are attached to the Brigade. On the right of the 20th Infy Brigade is the 1st Infantry Brigade, 1st Division - on the left the 22nd Infantry Brigade 7th Division.

2. The Brigade will be distributed as follows:-
1st Line :- 2nd Gordon Highlders on the right (in four lines) HULLOCH ROAD to SAP 1.
8th Devons on the left (in four lines) SAP 1 to SAP 2.

2nd Line :- 2nd Border Regiment (in two lines)

3rd Line :- 1/6th Gordon Highlders

Brigade Reserve :- 9th Bn Devons Regt

3. 2nd Border Regt will occupy the following position:-

1st Line:- OLD SUPPORT TRENCH from CHAPEL ALLEY to FROG LANE as follows:-
From right to left:-
    1 Machine Gun
    B Company
    D   " -
    1 Machine Gun (on left of FOSSE WAY).

2nd Line:- CURLEY CRESCENT from CHAPEL ALLEY to 100 yards N. of FOSSEWAY as follows:-
From right to left
    1 Machine Gun
    C Company
    A   " -
    Headquarter Dug out
    Headquarter party } On N.side of
    1 Machine Gun } CURLEY CRESCENT.
Company Orderlies will join Battn Headquarters as soon as Coys are in position.

4. The Battn will move into the trenches by CHAPEL ALLEY and FOSSE WAY at X pm.

5. Order of March:-
   1 Machine Gun
   B Company
   D -"-   -"-
   1 Machine Gun
   I -"-   -"-
   C Company
   A -"-   -"-
   Head Quarters
   1 Machine Gun
   } At 10 minutes interval.

6. Great care must be taken during the concentration that the presence of troops in large numbers is not observed by the enemy. Troops must remain under cover and only move about by order of an Officer. Even this should be avoided in open places not usually occupied by troops. Lights will not be used. Bayonets will not be fixed, except at the last possible moment and they must not be allowed to show above the parapet.

7. Great coats will not be carried but will be stored, rolled in bundles of 20, in the last house in NOYELLES E side of the main road (L.17.b.6.8) at times to be notified later.

Packs will be worn & the following will be carried:-
- Waterproof Sheet
- Cardigan or extra vest
- 1 pair Socks
- 3 Sand Bags

8. One day's complete rations and the iron ration will be carried by all ranks.
The iron ration is not to be touched except by order of the O.C. Battalion. Water bottles are to be taken into the trenches filled and are not to be touched except by order of the O.C. Company.

9. Every man except Bombers will carry 200 rounds of S.A.A.
Advanced Reserve S.A.A. Store is situated at the corner of FOSSE WAY and 1ST. SUPPORT TRENCH.
Intermediate Reserve is situated in FOSSE WAY 100 yards W. of CURLY CRESCENT.
S.A.A. Carts will be concentrated at L.11.a by X-45 hrs.
Bomb Store is situated at corner of FOSSE WAY and CURLY CRESCENT.
Water is stored in FOSSE WAY at a point 100 yards W. of CURLY CRESCENT.

1st Line Transport and Tool Carts will be at LABOURSE

Baggage will be concentrated at FOUQUEREUIL by 6pm to-night.

Machine Gun Limbers to join SAA Carts at L.11.a by 2am 25/9/15

Advanced Dressing Stations - Eastern end of STANSFELD ROAD just W. of the railway and S of HULLUCH ALLEY in G.8.6. Each Company will have one stretcher and 4 bearers with it.

Divisional Collecting Station; VERMELLES.

Brigade Head Quarters: CHAPEL KEEP.
Battalion "   "   "   In CURLY CRESCENT in a dug-out just S. of FOSSE WAY.

10. Upkeep of trenches. The nearest troops will at once restore any damage done to trenches with as little noise as possible.

Badges. Wire cutters will wear a piece of rifle rag on the sleeve of the jacket on right forearm.

Bomb Carriers will wear a piece of rifle rag on the right shoulder strap.

P.2. B........ Lieut
Adjutant 2nd Border Regt

Operation Orders
by Lieut. Col. C. de S. Thorpe
24th Sept 1915

Information — Enemy defences consist of 2 well defined lines of trenches.
1st runs from FOSSE No 8 southwards to LOOS
2nd - 1500 yards to East running through HAISNES - CITE-ST-ELIE - HULLUCH
Both systems protected by wire.

Enemy troops holding this front is the 117th Re-constructed Division in following order from North:-
11th Reserve Regt, 22nd Res. Regt, 115th Res. Regt

Our troops are
1st Division (4th Corps) on right Eastwards
9th --- (1st ---) on left Southeast.
between HULLUCH and LOOS

Intention — In conjunction with the French the British Force will make an attack on 25th Sept.

The task of the 7th Divn is to clear the trenches in front, occupy HULLUCH - BENEFONTAINE - PUIT 13 - CITE ST. ELIE - from here on to line PONT-A-VENDIN - MEURCHIN seizing the Canal crossings about that place.

Task of 20th Inf. Bde.	The 20th Infy. Bde. will clear the trenches in front & occupy HULLUCH & BENEFONTAINE pushing on thence to PONT-A-VENDIN & seize canal crossings. After the 1st German trenches have been captured the O.C. 2nd Gordons will make a supporting point at Cross roads G.11.d.9.3. 8th Devons will do the same at point BRESLAU AVENUE crosses HAISNES ROAD.

Distribution	As stated in formation orders.
	 1st line. 2nd Gordons on right } to lead the
	      8th Devons " left } assault.
	 2nd line. 6th Gordons on right moving up
	      into position at time of assault
	      2nd Border Regt on left
	 3rd line. 9th Devons Regt
	      (time table will be issued later)

Artillery	On an obstruction being met & reported, the point will be bombarded by Artillery for ½ an hour the last 5 minutes intensive. Thus Officers will recognize when the bombardment is about to cease. In the case of small obstructions the bombardment will be for 10 minutes intensive. If this is not sufficient it will be repeated for another 10 minutes, intensive, if asked for.

Battalion Advance	The 2nd Border Regt will support the 8th Devons. As the 8th Devons vacate each line in their assembly formations the Battn will move forward line by line until the new fire trench is reached.
Work	The OC A Coy will detail 2 Platoons to dig a communication trench to connect the captured German trench with our FIRE TRENCH — one Platoon each way. This party must be pushed up FOSSE WAY & the Platoon to dig back will move forward as soon as the first German trench is occupied by 8th Devons and start their work. Each Coy will arrange to carry forward 1 bundle of 50 Sand bags.
Ammⁿ	Sergt Loughman will be in charge of the forward Reserve Ammⁿ. OC Coys will please detail 1 Sgt and 5 Ptes to report to him at that point. When the Battn moves Sgt Loughman will take forward 25 boxes to the German Fire Trench. Position of other Ammⁿ Units as notified
Prisoners of War	A collecting station for Prisoners will be established West of MALINGARBE – VERMELLES ROAD. in G.7.d.

Distinguishing Flags	7th DIVISION – Red and blue diagonal. 1st DIVISION – Red flag with white stripe. 9th " – Red & yellow diagonal.
Smoke Signals	Each Coy will be issued with 6 smoke candles. These are to denote the position of the leading Coy.
Vermorel Sprayers	The Battn will have no vermorel sprayers but should any be found they should be taken on. Bn. QM. Serjt should arrange to take forward a refill. Men must be cautioned not to enter hostile dugouts unless they have been sprayed.
Brigade Ammn Column	14th H.A. Brigade Ammn Column L.T. & 2 H.
R.E. Stores	Advanced Depots. Fallen tree North of VERMELLES. HULLUCH ROAD G.11.c.A.1. South of HAISNES ROAD G.11.d.8.0.
Visual Sig Station	Call up Battn N° Q5 for 2 minutes & then send message slowly repeating it 3 times in case wrongly can be seen owing to enemy seeing it. Serjt Greatorex is in charge of the Battn inter-communication & will make all necessary arrangements.

Battn Reserve Amm'n	The Regtl Sgt Major will be in charge of the Bn Reserve Ammn.
Liaison Offr.	Lt R Rawbarrn will report himself to the OC 8th Devons to keep up communication with OC 8th Devons & 2nd Border Regt on arrival in trenches.
Medical	Dressing Stations as notified
Personnel of RE Corps	Personnel of Nos 184 & 188 Special Coys RE will wear Red white & green brassards.
Water	Coy Commdrs will see that all ranks realize the importance of the water purifying tabloids & that they are carried. We must be on the look out for poisoned water. Even boiling will not mitigate the effects of this.
Correspondence	No orders, letters, or papers capable of giving the least information to the enemy are to be taken into the trenches or held
Battn HQrs	When 8th Devons advance the Bn HQ of 2/Border Regt will move to those vacated by 8th Devons

R.M. Burmann Lieut
Adjutant 2nd Border Regt

BRIGADE NARRATIVE OF EVENTS ON THE RECENT
                OPERATIONS.

Narrative of Events on the recent operations.

September. 24th.

On Saturday September 24th, the 20th Infantry Brigade Battle Station was established in CHAPEL ALLEY at 4.45 p.m. at which hour the Brigadier-General Commanding, Brigade Major and A.D.C. arrived.

The Brigadier-General went up to the front line and there met Colonels TUDOR and STANSFELD and watched the wire cutting. There still remained a certain amount of wire in between the two lines of trenches, and as it was too late for Artillery to cut this, it was decided to send out parties of men with wire cutters during the night. This would take place under cover of shrapnel fire.

No time as yet had been settled for the attack to begin but a message came from 7th Division at 7.15 p.m. that it was not likely that any decision would be come to on this matter until 2 hours before the attack was to take place.

The 7th Divisional Headquarters moved up to NOYELLES CHATEAU at 10 p.m. and about this hour the 20th Infantry Brigade began to concentrate in the trenches, some of which had been specially prepared for them.

The night was wet and very dark and there was no wind to speak of.

September. 25th.

By 2.30 a.m. the whole Brigade had concentrated, and a report to this effect was sent to 7th Division.

At 3.40 a.m. a message was received that the hour of attack would be 5.50 a.m., and that the actual assault would take place at 6.30 a.m., and orders were sent round to this effect.

The morning was drizzly and there was a slight wind from the South West.

The Brigadier-General went round and saw Commanding Officers of 2nd Battalion Gordon Highlanders and 8th Battalion Devonshire Regiment at 4.50 a.m. and found that everything was prepared for the attack. These two Battalions were the leading Battalions and it was arranged that they should issue to the assault at the same moment in five lines from their respective trenches. This was made possible by the placing of ladders and bridges in and across the trenches.

A report was received at 5.40 a.m. from the two leading Battalions that they were quite satisfied that all the wire on their front had been cut including that which had been cut by hand during the night.

At 5.50 a.m.

At 5.50 a.m. the attack began, and messages were continually received from Colonel TUDOR, Commanding 14th Brigade Royal Horse Artillery, who was watching the progress of the attack from his observation station and who was in telephonic communication with 20th Infantry Brigade Headquarters. These messages for the first 40 minutes were chiefly with reference to the effect of the smoke candles and concerning our own and enemy's artillery.

At 6.30 a.m. the Infantry left their trenches and advanced at a walk in line up to the enemy's trenches, and in 12 minutes were on the enemy parapet. In the meantime the remainder of the 20th Infantry Brigade was on the move and the 2nd Battalion BORDER REGIMENT and 6th Battalion GORDON HIGHLANDERS were already up in the front line trenches, and ready to advance in support of the two leading Battalions.

In 35 minutes from the hour of the assault the first line of enemy trenches in front of 20th Infantry Brigade had been captured with rather heavy losses, including Colonel GRANT and Major CARDEN of 8th Battalion Devonshire Regiment both killed and Colonel STANSFELD, 2nd Battalion GORDON Highlanders badly wounded.

Soon after 7 a.m. the Division reported that 22nd Infantry Brigade were held up by enemy in POPES NOSE Redoubt, and two sections of bombers were ordered up from 2nd Battalion BORDER REGIMENT to try and bomb down towards this obstruction.

At 7.25 a.m. the front system of enemy trenches opposite 20th Infantry Brigade had been captured, and both the 8th Battalion DEVONSHIRE REGIMENT and 2nd Battalion GORDON HIGHLANDERS were steadily advancing in spite of their losses.

The 6th Battalion Gordon Highlanders had shortly after 8 a.m. moved up past old GERMAN Line and were re-inforcing the 2nd Battalion. This was also being done by the 2nd Battalion BORDER REGIMENT who were supporting 8th Battalion DEVONSHIRE REGIMENT.

Shortly before 8 a.m. 7th Division reported that 22nd Infantry Brigade was still held up, and that the Artillery of 20th Infantry Brigade was to be used for its own support, as it was considered that if the success already obtained were to be further supported in this way, the result would be to automatically clear the right of the 22nd Infantry Brigade. For this reason at 8.15 a.m. Colonel JOHNSTONE Commanding 22nd Brigade Royal Field Artillery and Colonel TUDOR were ordered to Bring guns forward, the former, one battery and the latter one section. Colonel TUDOR placed his section immediately in rear of the old GERMAN Trenches, which gave effective support. The Battery of 22nd Brigade Royal Field Artillery was placed just in rear of the old BRITISH Line on South of VERMELLES - HULLUCH Road and eventually one more Battery of this Brigade was brought up to this same position and also another Section of "T" Battery joined the first section sent up.

At 8.5 a.m.

At 8.5 a.m. the Brigade Major was sent forward to report on the situation and reported at 8.20 a.m. that 4 Battalions had gone forward and that the 9th Battalion DEVONSHIRE REGIMENT were just about to leave the first line of trenches.

The first prisoners, a party of 24 passed Brigade Headquarters at 8.26 a.m., and at this hour a man from 8th Battalion DEVONSHIRE REGIMENT came and reported that his Battalion had reached "a big Colliery".

At this hour No. 1. Trench Mortar Battery under Lieutenant CARRIGAN, R.F.A. was ordered to advance to first GERMAN line of trenches, and then to act on his own initiative, bearing in mind the importance of getting as far forward as possible to deal with any houses which might hold up the advance.

Shortly before 9 a.m. two Companies of the BEDFORDSHIRE REGIMENT, of 21st Infantry Brigade were sent up to old BRITISH Front line, and a message was received from the Division at 9 a.m. to say that 21st Infantry Brigade would advance in support, as all the troops of 20th Infantry Brigade were engaged.

At this hour also, a man of 8th Battalion DEVONSHIRE REGIMENT came in and reported that his Battalion was at PUITS 13, and after it had been definitely ascertained from him that this was the case, it was reported to the Division. This was more or less confirmed by Officer Commanding 117th Battery who reported this Battalion near PUITS 13, and by a message written at 8.50 a.m. by Colonel THORPE, Officer Commanding 2nd Battalion BORDER REGIMENT.

This man also reported that a batch of 150 prisoners was on its way down.

The resistance of a party of the enemy about POPES NOSE still continued at 9.30 a.m. and the Division were most anxious to break this down; on his own initiative and before a message reached him, the Staff Captain seeing this resistance was affecting the advance organised a party of 2nd Battalion BORDER REGIMENT under Lieutenant Sutcliffe of that Regiment who led his men out with great dash and assisted by Captain Ostle with half a company, broke down the resistance and took the enemy in this place prisoners to the number of about 70. This set the example to the lines behind which came on and carried the advance forward to join the remainder of the Brigade.

The Cross Roads at H.7.c.4.4. were reached at 8.45 a.m. by 6th Battalion GORDON HIGHLANDERS who joined up with the 2nd Battalion and some of 8th Battalion DEVONSHIRE REGIMENT. About 9 a.m. a party of GERMANS estimated at 500 with a mounted Officer at their head marched into CITE St ELIE from a N.E. Direction. The 2nd Battalion GORDON HIGHLANDERS opened rifle and machine gun fire on them and broke the column in half in the main street of the village. The attack had now come to a standstill

for...

for want of further backing, and the position was, that a forward line East of HULLUCH Cross Roads on the points G.7.c.5.5., 5.2. 13.A.2.6. was held connecting up on the right with 1st Division, but with the left in the air. Behind this the GUN TRENCH was held with 8 enemy guns in it which was being heavily shelled.

At 10.50 a.m. General WATTS, 21st Infantry Brigade came up and two of his Battalions were ordered to reinforce 20th Infantry Brigade. One Company at least of BEDFORDSHIRE REGIMENT had previously gone forward but no forward movement from GUN TRENCH was possible as yet. Officer Commanding 22nd Brigade Royal Field Artillery was ordered to shell HULLUCH and PUITS No. 13, and the Division were asked to turn heavy guns ons to both these places later on about 12.50 p.m.

Some enemy were seen to be advancing from CITE St LEONARD on to CITE St ELIE about 1 p.m. and 22nd Brigade Royal Field Artillery were ordered to fire on them.

Meanwhile messages had been received that 4th Corps were to attack HULLUCH, and 21st Infantry Brigade were ordered to co-operate. So far as can be ascertained nothing came of this attack and the enemy continued to hold HULLUCH and CITE St ELIE, and were presumably getting more troops into both places. Reports came back to the effect, that the front houses in both these villages were strongly held by machine guns and in a few houses at least there were field guns, besides a trench with strong wire in front

At 2.15 p.m. the Brigadier-Generals of 20th and 21st Infantry Brigades went forward nearly up to GUN TRENCH to reconnoitre the position so as to be able to report the situation as it appeared to them to Divisional Headquarters.

An attack was ordered on CITE St ELIE for 4.45 p.m. but the views of the two Brigadier-Generals having been communicated to the Division this did not come off. It seemed that the greatest chance of success would be to attack HULLUCH in S.E. direction with two fresh Battalions as the outskirts of this place were reported to be held by 4th Corps.

At 4.30 p.m. the Division sent orders to consolidate positions gained. The position of units in 20th Infantry Brigade at 6.30 p.m. was as follows:-

2nd and 6th Battalions GORDON HIGHLANDERS about H.7.c.4.4. with a mixture of 8th and 9th DEVONSHIRE REGIMENTS. These were ordered to dig in and make the cross roads a strong point with the aid of two 1½ inch mortars under Lieutenant CARRIGAN who had his guns well forward.

2nd Battalion BORDER REGIMENT, some 8th and 9th Battalions DEVONSHIRE REGIMENTS and details of 21st Infantry Brigade in GUN TRENCH in touch on the right with 1st Division, and on left with 22nd Infantry Brigade, and the whole were ordered to dig themselves in, and R.E. were ordered to put out wire on their front.

At 8.10 p.m.

At 8.10 p.m. General CAPPER came up and talked over situation with Brigadier General Commanding 20th Infantry Brigade and then went back to see Brigadier General Commanding 21st Infantry Brigade who came up to Headquarters 20th Infantry Brigade to settle how best to deal with the advanced position at the HULLUCH Cross Roads. It was decided to hold these cross roads as an advanced post, connected up to the main line by an old German Communication trench. About 500 yards of new line had to be dug and Brigadier General Commanding 21st Infantry Brigade ordered up the ROYAL SCOTS FUSILIERS to do this while the wiring was to be done by the 2nd HIGHLAND FIELD COMPANY R.E. Brigadier-General Commanding 21st Infantry Brigade with his Brigade Major went up accompanied by Brigade Major 20th Infantry Brigade to start the work off.

Shortly before midnight 25th/26th the enemy made a determined counter attack on the advanced position near HULLUCH Cross Roads just before it had been put in a state of defence. This attack was pressed home in the endeavour to recapture the Field Guns in GUN TRENCH. The men in the forward position gave way and fell back on GUN TRENCH and some even went back further than this but were rallied by Officers in the 2nd Battalion BORDER REGIMENT and Brigade Major and taken back to help the men in GUN TRENCH.

The enemy's foremost attackers actually reached this trench and were killed almost on the parapet whilst a good many others variously estimated at anything between 50 and 100 were killed in this attack which was beaten off. Thus the advanced position at HULLUCH Cross Roads was lost, but all other ground gained by 20th Infantry Brigade during the day was held and consolidated before daylight.

September 26th

About 1 a.m. The Brigadier-General was informed that the QUARRIES had been captured by the enemy and a little later that some Germans had penetrated into their old line. On this information being received the Staff Captain was ordered to take 4th Battalion CAMERON HIGHLANDERS (at request of 21st Infantry Brigade) to turn them out of these trenches, and two Companies of ROYAL SCOTS FUSILIERS were sent to hold BRESLAU AVENUE in order to protect the left flank of the troops holding GUN TRENCH. It was eventually made known that the enemy had not penetrated to their old line but still held QUARRIES and about 3 a.m. General CAPPER informed Brigadier General that he was organising a counter attack on them by a fresh Battalion so the 4th Battalion CAMERON HIGHLANDERS were withdrawn to their former position.

The counter attack on QUARRIES failed at 7 a.m. and none other was attempted till 5.30 p.m. This was done by CARTERS DETACHMENT and 20th Infantry Brigade sent one Section of Bombers to assist. These men bombed down one of the
Communication

Communication trenches leading into the QUARRIES. This attack was only partially successful.

General CAPPER was wounded during this attack.

During this day the Battalions of the 20th Infantry Brigade held on to all the positions they had captured and so far as was possible collected their men together. Their line was taken over by 21st Infantry Brigade with the exception that of the 2nd Battalion BORDER REGIMENT who took the place of the ROYAL SCOTS FUSILIERS in BRESLAU AVENUE.

The remaining Battalions of 20th Infantry Brigade moved back to trenches in the old BRITISH Line East of CHAPEL KEEP.

Headquarters 20th Infantry Brigade moved to Battle Station of 21st Infantry Brigade, just East of VERMELLES railway crossing on HULLUCH Road, and after being in support till 29th instant, went back to billets in BEUVRY.

Bde. H.Qrs.

10th October, 1915.

Brigadier-general

Commanding 20th Infantry Brigade.

20th Inf. Bde.
7th Div.

2nd BATTN. THE BORDER REGIMENT.

O C T O B E R

1 9 1 5

WAR DIARY
or
INTELLIGENCE SUMMARY. — October 1915

Army Form C. 2118.

Hour, Date, Place		Summary of Events and Information	Remarks and references to Appendices
1/10/15		The Battalion was relieved in the Trenches and proceeded to billets at CAMBRIN	
2nd to 6/10/15	CAMBRIN	In Brigade Reserve Billets. Captain W.L. Manly and a draft of 50 Other Ranks joined the Battalion on 4th inst. Major Sir Arnold Hall, 2nd Lieutenant Chetham-Strode, 2nd Lt W. Kelly, 2nd Lieut C.J. Holland joined the Battalion on 6/10/15	
7/10/15	CAMBRIN	A draft of 32 O. Ranks joined the Battalion. The Battalion proceeded to Trenches at CUINCHY	
8/10/15		2nd Lieut Cuningham & a draft of 100 O. Ranks joined the Battalion	
9/10/15		The Battalion was relieved in trenches & proceeded to Billets at BEUVRY arriving about 6 p.m. Casualties 9-10/10/15 — 2 wounded	
10/10/15		In Billets. Casualties owing to billets being shelled. 1 Killed 2 wounded	
10/10/15 to 13/10/15	BEUVRY		
14/10/15	BEUVRY	The Battalion proceeded to Trenches R1 to the CAMBRIN – LA BASSEE Road relieving 2 Los Infantry Brigade	
16/10/15		The Battalion was relieved in the Trenches and proceeded to BETHUNE and billeted in Barracks (Casualties 14–16/10/15 — 2 killed)	
19/10/15	BETHUNE	The Battalion marched at 9.45 a.m. to L'ECLEME arrived at about 2 p.m. and billeted	

Army Form C. 21

WAR DIARY
or
INTELLIGENCE SUMMARY. — October 1915.
(Erase heading not required.)

Instructions regarding War Diaries and Intelligence Summaries are contained in F.S. Regs, Part II. and the Staff Manual respectively. Title pages will be prepared in manuscript.

Hour, Date, Place		Summary of Events and Information	Remarks and references to Appendices
18/10/15	L'ECLEME	In billets.	
19/10/15	"	The Battalion marched to billets near HINGES. 2nd Lieut R Rewcard joined the Battalion	
20/10/15	Near HINGES	The Battalion proceeded to trenches taking over the portion of the line between the SHRINE exclusive to A.3.c.2.3. N. of GIVENCHY	
21/10/15 to 23/10/15	"	In trenches. Casualties:- 3 wounded	
24/10/15		The Battalion was relieved in the trenches at about 2/am and proceeded to billets at BETHUNE	
25/10/15 to 28/10/15	BETHUNE	The Battalion remained in rest billets. 2nd Lieut 99 Sharp joined the Battalion on 27/10/15.	
29/10/15	"	The Battalion with other units of the 1st Corps was inspected by HM THE KING.	
29/10/15	"	A draft of 114 O.Ranks joined the Battalion	

B.Shute Lieut-Colonel
Commanding 2nd Bn Border Regiment.

20th Infantry Brigade.
7th Division.

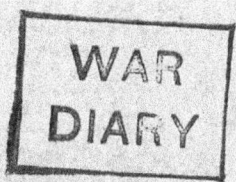

2nd BATTN. THE BORDER REGIMENT.

NOVEMBER

1915

WAR DIARY
or
INTELLIGENCE SUMMARY. November 1915

Army Form C. 2118.

Hour, Date, Place		Summary of Events and Information	Remarks and references to Appendices
BETHUNE	1/11/15	The Battalion proceeded to Trenches E of GIVENCHY	
HINGETTE	2/11/15		
E of GIVENCHY	3/11/15	The Battalion was relieved in Trenches & proceeded to Billets	
HINGETTE	4/11/15 to 7/11/15	at HINGETTE (Casualties 1-3/11/15 2 wounded). In Billets. Lieut B Hutton and Lieut F Bright joined the Battalion on 5/11/15	
HINGETTE	8/11/15	The Battalion marched to LE QUESNOY and billetted in Brigade Reserve Billets.	
LE QUESNOY	9/11/15	In billets.	
"	10/11/15	The Battalion proceeded to Trenches E of GIVENCHY.	
E of GIVENCHY	11/11/15	In trenches (Casualties 4 killed, 4 wounded)	
"	12/11/15	The Battalion was relieved by and Gordon Highlanders and proceeded to Brigade Reserve Billets at LE QUESNOY. 1 draft of 21 O.Ranks joined the Battalion	
LE QUESNOY	13/11/15	In billets.	
"	14/11/15	The Battn. proceeded to Trenches E. of GIVENCHY.	
E of GIVENCHY	15/11/15	The Battn. was relieved in Trenches & proceeded to billets at LE QUESNOY (Casualties:- 2Lt 2N Adamson killed 16/11/15 (wounded)	
LE QUESNOY	17/11/15	The Battalion marched to HINGETTE and billetted	
HINGETTE	18/11/15 to 22/11/15	In billets	
"	23/11/15	C and D Coys marched to RUE DE EPINETTE at 3pm and billetted. 1 draft of 23 O.Ranks A" B" and Head Q[r]s marched to LE HAMEL " about 3pm " " joined Bn on 23/11/15	
"	24/11/15	The Whole Battalion proceeded to Trenches E of FESTUBERT relieving 4th Middlesex. Lieut N.D. Nelson joined the Battalion.	

WAR DIARY
or
INTELLIGENCE SUMMARY.

(Erase heading not required.)

Army Form C. 2118.

Hour, Date, Place	Summary of Events and Information	Remarks and references to Appendices
25/11/15 to 30/11/15	The Battalion remained in Trenches (Casualties 5 Killed 7 wounded.)	

F.Hope. Lieut - Colonel
Commanding 2nd Bn Border Regiment

20th Infantry Brigade.
7th Division.

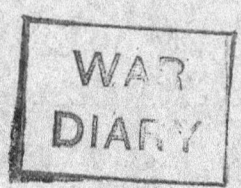

2nd BATTN. THE BORDER REGIMENT.

DECEMBER

1 9 1 5

Army Form C. 2118.

WAR DIARY
or
INTELLIGENCE SUMMARY. — December 1915
(Erase heading not required.)

Instructions regarding War Diaries and Intelligence Summaries are contained in F. S. Regs., Part II. and the Staff Manual respectively. Title pages will be prepared in manuscript.

Hour, Date, Place	Summary of Events and Information	Remarks and references to Appendices
1/12/15 E. of FESTUBERT.	The Battalion was relieved in the trenches by 1st Middlesex Regt. and proceeded to billets at LE HAMEL.	
2/12/15 LE HAMEL	The Battalion marched at 10.6 am to billets at GONNEHAM arriving about 12 noon.	
3/12/15 to 6/12/15 GONNEHAM 7/12/15 GONNEHAM	Lieut. M. Johnson joined the Battalion on 4/12/15. The Battalion marched at 1pm to LILLERS and entrained for SALEUX at about 3pm.	
8/12/15 SALEUX	The Battalion arrived at 1am and marched to billets at BREILLY.	
9/12/15 to 31/12/15 BREILLY (10 Km. West of AMIENS)	The Battalion remained in rest billets. Lieuts. R.F. Willard, P.R. Dowsing, and 2nd Lieuts. D. Strange & S.J. Russell joined the Battalion on 11/12/1915.	
	A draft of 45 Other Ranks joined the Battalion on 15/12/15.	
	" " " " " " " " " 28/12/15.	
	A draft of 149 Other Ranks " " " " 30/12/15	
	" 15 " " " " " " "	

[signature] Major for
Lieut. Colonel.
Commanding 2nd Bn. The Border Regt.

20th Brigade.

7th Division.

2nd BATTALION

BORDER REGIMENT.

JANUARY 1916.

Army Form C. 2118.

WAR DIARY
or
INTELLIGENCE SUMMARY. — January 1916
(Erase heading not required.)

Instructions regarding War Diaries and Intelligence Summaries are contained in F.S. Regs., Part II. and the Staff Manual respectively. Title pages will be prepared in manuscript.

Hour, Date, Place		Summary of Events and Information	Remarks and references to Appendices
1/1/16 to 3/1/16	BREILLY	The Battalions remained in rest billets	
4/1/16	BREILLY	The Battalion proceeded to billets at BUIGNY-L'ABBE at 9am. Arrived at 6pm and billeted	
5/1/16 to 27/1/16	BUIGNY-L'ABBE	The Battalion remained at rest billets. 2nd Lieut B. Meek and E.C. Shaw joined the Battalion on 13th January 1916. 50 Other Ranks joined the Battalion on 13th inst 20 " " " " " 14th " 2nd Lieut O.P. Lindsay and 6 Other Ranks joined the Battalion on 15th January 1916.	
28/1/16	BUIGNY-L'ABBE	The Battalion marched to billets at BREILLY at 9am. Arrived at 4pm and billeted.	
29/1/16 to 31/1/16	BREILLY	The Battalion remained in rest billets.	

J. Thorpe, Lieut. Colonel
Commanding 2nd Bn Border Regt

20th Brigade.

7th Division.

2nd BATTALION

BORDER REGIMENT

FEBRUARY 1916

WAR DIARY or INTELLIGENCE SUMMARY

Army Form C. 2118.

February 1916

16.L
4 sheet

Hour, Date, Place	Summary of Events and Information	Remarks and references to Appendices
BREILLY 1/2/16	The Battalion proceeded to POULAINVILLE at 9.30AM; arrived at 2pm and billeted	
POULAINVILLE 2/2/16	The Battalion proceeded to LA HOUSSOYE at 9.30AM; arrived at 1pm and billeted	
LA HOUSSOYE 3/2/16	The Battalion proceeded to BUIRE sur L'ANCRE; arrived 1pm and billeted	
BUIRE sur L'ANCRE 4/2/16	The Battalion proceeded to trenches Northly of FRICOURT, Square F3a. by Platoons at intervals, commencing at 10AM, relieving 11th Bn Queens Regt. 11th Bn Queens Regt were on left of the Battalion and 8th Devons Regt on right.	Was ALBERT 62d N.E. 1/40000
	Casualties 4/2/16 to 10/2/16 :- 2 Killed 7 wounded 2 missing. The Battalion was relieved in trenches by 2nd Bn Gordon Highlanders & proceeded to billets at MEAULTE	
MEAULTE 11/2/16		
MEAULTE 12/2/16	A draft of 22 Other Ranks joined the Battalion	
16/2/16	Lieut H.J. Sedgwick and 2Lieuts F.R.L. Bell and W.S. Iverson joined the Battalion	
MEAULTE 19/2/16	The Battalion proceeded to trenches North of FRICOURT, Square F3a. by Platoons at intervals, commencing at 8.45am relieving 2nd Bn Gordon Highlanders. 11th Bn Buffs Regt were on the left of the Battalion and 8th Bn Devons Regt on the right.	Was ALBERT 62d N.E. 1/40000

WAR DIARY or INTELLIGENCE SUMMARY

Army Form C. 2118.

Hour, Date, Place	Summary of Events and Information	Remarks and references to Appendices

22/2/16 TRENCHES

Between 5 and 5.15am at night the enemy opened a heavy fire with every description of artillery and trench mortar on our D3 Sector which was held by the Battalion. The heaviest projectiles came from N.N.E. and were mainly directed at the TAMBOUR salient on the right of the front line. Frontal fire was directed all along the whole of the front line French. The two Companies in the front line were "A" Company (left) and "C" Company (right). By 5.30am the bombardment was very intense and it was felt certain the enemy meant to attack.

At 5.40am it was found that communication between the right forward Company (C Coy) and Batn Head Quarters by telephone had been cut.

The bombardment continued until about 6.45am when the hostile guns lifted from the TAMBOUR but continued on the trenches further back.

At 7.25am a report was received that the enemy had attacked the TAMBOUR. Two enemy parties succeeded in getting into the front line in two places but were driven out.

At about 8.40am the hostile artillery fire slackened and by 9am had always quieted down. The estimated number of Germans who attacked were some 80 all ranks of whom 29 dead were counted from our fire trench next day.

The enemy succeeded in throwing a bomb down one of our disused mine shafts before they were turned out and in their flight they left behind a lot of bombs and 3 pairs of wire cutters.

A German Corporal was taken prisoner and on being questioned he stated that they had moved forward in three parties of about 28 Other Ranks each. One between the two southern craters and two round the North of them. The bomb parties had orders to take trenches. The inner eye to destroy mine heads by throwing them with special large bombs. The prisoner belonged to the 99TH Reserve Regiment.

WAR DIARY
or
INTELLIGENCE SUMMARY.

Army Form C. 2118.

(3)

Hour, Date, Place	Summary of Events and Information	Remarks and references to Appendices
22/2/16 (continued)	Our Artillery retaliation seemed slovenly and was most effective. The casualties sustained by the Battalion were:- KILLED:- 2nd Lieut U.R. Bell and 11 Other Ranks WOUNDED:- 26 Other Ranks MISSING:- 9 Other Ranks Other casualties from 19/2/16 to 26/2/16:- 4 Killed, 11 Wounded Captain L.A. NEWTON joined the Battalion on 24/2/16. A draft of 20 Other Ranks joined 26/2/16	
27/2/16	The Battalion was relieved in the trenches by 2nd Bn. Gordon Highlanders. A & C Coys proceeded to billets at BECORDEL. B & D Coys to billets at MEAULTE	
28th & 29/2/16	In billets.	

B. Stephen Lieut. Colonel.
Commanding 2nd Bn. The Border Regt.

A.
C.
D. Companies   21st Sept 16

I have received a report that a portion
of the front line trench has been blown
in between the two forward companies.
The following precautions are to be taken

I. Ole Sow lanes for certain observation
posts to watch the ground in front of
this part of the line very carefully, especially at dusk & after dark until it is
cleared so as to prevent any chance of a
hostile entrance into our trench system.
These lookouts should be found by very
reliable men.

II. O.C. D Company in Surrey Street will also
post a special sentry to watch the above
portion of the line. — He will also have
at least two Platoons of his company ready
to move up at once & reinforce the line
in case of an attack. The best line of
advance, with alternative lines, to be re-
connoitred immediately.

III. All companies will have their runners ready
to bring any message to Bn. H. Qrs. in the event
of telephone lines being cut.   E. Thorpe Lt Col

D.O.

Dear Colonel

Had hoped to get over & call on you today to let you know verbally what was going on in this Sector but have been unable to do so. —

We had a fairly good shelling today which rather spoilt the look of our trenches & caused just a very few casualties. — We are hard at work repairing our parapet tonight. — I don't know if by any chance the bombardment was intended as a preparation for an expedition on the Hun's part or not but all arrangements have been made to receive them as far as we can do so & the guns warned. I let you know this in case you should think it desirable to warn your people to be ready to cooperate in case anything should happen. I don't anticipate anything but consider it is better to try to be ready for any eventuality. —

Yours truly
E. Thorpe Lt Col
Comdg 2nd Border R. (Sector D.3.)

21st Feby 16

To O.C. 7th The Buffs.
Sector E.1.

Dear Colonel,

Very many thanks for your note. We also have made preparations for anything that might happen, as far as possible, and are keeping ready for the night.

My Right Company has been ordered to keep in constant communication with your Left Co'y. We have a M.G. in position to fire across the front of your GUILDFORD salient.

Our Artillery is also warned.

Yours truly
R. P. Birch Major
Command'g 7th Batt'n The Buffs
(Sector E 1.)

21-2-16.

Reply.

The Brigade Major
20th Infy Brigade

In a careful inspection I made of the fire trench in Sector D.3. after the bombardment this afternoon I found the following:—

I. Trench 106 to PURFLEET (inclusive) slightly damaged & in consequence very untidy.—

II. PURFLEET ditto on north side, East side badly damaged particularly the southern end of this face.—

III. Round Pt 99 the fire trench has absolutely disappeared for a distance of some 25 yds.—

IV. Pt 99 to 98 fire trench more or less badly damaged & untidy.

V. The TAMBOUR, badly damaged, trenches in places particularly on the south-east (Pt 96 to 95). Several passages damaged & blocked.

VI. Damage to other trenches not severe.

Extra working parties have been sent up from the Reserve Company to assist in remaking the parapet. This last however & the ordinary carrying fatigues reduces the available reserve at QUEEN'S REDOUBT to a minimum.

All ranks have been warned to keep a careful look-out & both machine guns & artillery have been warned to be prepared for instant action.

E. Thorpe Lt. Col.
Comdg 2nd Border R.

21st Feby /16

To Adjutant
 2nd Border Regt.

forward
Herewith report on hostile attack
on the evening 22/2/16 for information.

G.P.S. Drake-Brockman
Capt
O.C. "A" Coy

22/2/16

(1)

To Adjutant
2nd Border Regt

With reference to the hostile attack made by the enemy on the sector D3 on the night 22/2/16 I beg to submit the following report.

At about 5.30pm 22/2/16 I was sitting in Coy HQrs left half D3 when the enemy opened a very vigourous bombardment of our front line trenches, the fire increased in intensity; most of the fire appeared to be concentrated on the TAMBOUR, but a fair amount was directed against PURFLEET. The majority of the shells appeared to come from the left flank, thus enfilading our trenches. I directed 2/Lt E.R. Chetham Strode to go down to extreme right flank of the company with orders to assist 2/Lt W.L. Johnson to keep in touch with "C" Coy & ensure that the men kept a good look

(2)

out. I at once got in touch with "T" battery R.H.A and gave the S.O.S signal. Shortly afterwards I received a telephone message from Capt Sutcliffe to the effect that the telephonic communication between the "TAMBOUR" and TANGIER had broken down. I also received a message from the Commanding Officer telling me to keep in touch with "C" coy. I then sent an orderly to Capt Wright with a message to the effect that I was keeping in touch with his Left flank. I received an answer, timed 7.10 p.m that matters were progressing favourably. Meanwhile the enemy opened very heavy rifle and machine gun fire on our parapet.

About this time the shell fire on the trenches of No 4 Platoon was particularly heavy and for a length of about 15' was blown in on the extreme left of "C" coy burying the personnel of a bombing post, belonging to the same company, thus forming

(3)

a gap between the two companies of about 50x. This gap was patrolled under very heavy shell fire by 2nd Lt W.L. Johnson, who then kept up connection. It was during this time that a party of five Germans endeavoured to enter our trenches at this point. They were seen by some men of "C" Coy who threw some bombs at them, four of them retreated, two of them wounded according to subsequent prisoners statements. The fifth man, a corporal of the 99th Res. regiment reached the trench where he was captured by 2nd Lt Johnson. Shortly afterwards 2Lt Chetham-Strode closed the gap with 12 men of C Coy & later No 16 platoon came up, No 13 having previously reinforced No 14. Just previous to this enemy lifted his fire, but the star shells sent up did not show any signs of the enemy leaving his trenches opposite my company. About 7.45 p. the shell fire died down & finally ceased about 8 p.m. I at once reorganised

(4)

my line and sent out a patrol to examine the wire, which was reported to have been smashed in places. No enemy killed or wounded were reported near our wire. I should like bring forward the names of 2nd Lt E.R. Chettam Strode for the aid rendered by him in keeping the firing line on the night steady in bad trenches under very heavy shell fire, also 2nd Lt W.L. Johnson for the splendid way in which he kept in touch with "C" coy at an extremely critical time. I should also like to call attention to the fact that all the N.C.Os + men were very steady + that a good lookout was kept by all in spite the heavy bombardment.

G.P.L. Drake-Brockman
Capt
O.C "A" coy
2nd Border Regt

25/2/16

I further beg to submit the following names of men whose conduct was noteworthy.

No 2468 Pte McLean, William. "Kept a good lookout all the time under very heavy shell fire, till wounded in the head by shrapnel"

✓

"C" coy
No 5060

Pte Cowan, John was in charge of a bombing post on the left of "C" coy. His trench was blown in & the two men with him were buried. He extricated them & reported to 2Lt Johnston. He afterwards did valuable work as orderly carrying messages along the coy under shell fire.

✓

No 6904
Sgt Fletcher, Thomas "D" coy

Brought his platoon along Shuttle lane under heavy fire & reinforced "A" coy. He did rendered valuable aid by man-

✓

...taining steadiness among the men under heavy shell fire

Arnold
Pte Hayton (Lewis Gunner) Acted as
No 18091 sentry during the whole bombardment keeping a sharp look out all the time.

G. P. L. Drake-Brockman
Capt

2nd Border Regt.   O.C. A coy

25/2/16

The Brigade Major
20th Infantry Brigade.

Sir,
At between 5 p.m. & 5.15 p.m. on the 22nd Feby 16 the enemy opened a heavy fire with every description of artillery & trench mortar on D.3 Sector.

The heaviest projectiles came from the N.N.E. the direction of CONTALMAISON & was mainly directed at post on the CHORD of the TAMBOUR, the southern portion of TANGIER TRENCH & southern portion of SURREY STREET & on KING'S AVENUE.

A frontal fire from the direction of FRICOURT was directed all along the front line, principally on the TAMBOUR portion & trenches immediately on either side of it, by light field guns & trench mortars (Sausages) also aerial torpedoes.

At about 5.15 p.m. the O.C. of my right forward company asked for artillery retaliation.

At 5.25 p.m. the above officer sent round the S.O.S. signal.

By 5.30 p.m. the bombardment was very intense & it was felt certain the enemy meant to attack. Gas shells were burst over us at this time.

At 5.40 p.m. it was found that communication between the right forward company & Bn Hd qrs by telephone had been cut. Runners had then to be used from O.C. TAMBOUR to telephone at KINGS CROSS & to the telephones right (DEVON Regt) & left to "A" Co.

II

2nd Border Regt.—

The heavy & intense bombardment continued to about 6.45 p.m. the hostile guns lifted from the TAMBOUR but continued on the other trenches & further back along KING'S AVENUE right up to QUEEN'S REDOUBT.—

At 7.25 p.m. a report was received that the enemy had attacked the TAMBOUR. They succeeded in getting into the front line in two places. A few of them got in between the TAMBOUR & PURFLEET, numbers about 3 men. Also a few were seen near Pt 96 in the TAMBOUR. These parties were driven out.—

The following action was taken. At about 5.15 p.m. the whole Bn stood to arms the men being kept under cover as much as possible from the effect of the hostile artillery fire. In the TAMBOUR the miners & R.E. also stood to arms under the OC. TAMBOUR.

A little later two working parties of the 2nd Gordon Highlanders. 2 officers & 100 men were put into QUEEN'S REDOUBT as also a party of the 9th Devon Regt, 3 officers & 110 men.—

From this time bombs & ammunition & sandbags etc were pushed forward to KING'S CROSS to form an advanced store. From here they were sent up to front line as required.—

By about 5.45 p.m. the Bn Hd Qrs in D.3. sector had established telephone communication with Bn Hd Qrs in Sectors D.2 & E.1. direct. Communication with 20th Brig. Hd Qrs. the R.A. & all companies 2nd Border R.

III

except the one in the TAMBOUR held good the whole time. With the TAMBOUR it was maintained by newness.—

At between 6.45 pm & 7 pm reinforcements were pushed forward by platoons from SHUTTLE STREET & TANGIER TRENCH, being replaced from SURREY STREET which again was replaced by the Company 2nd Border Regt & H.Q. Platoon. The grand QUEENS REDOUBT party 2nd GORDONS & 9th Devons being kept in QUEENS REDOUBT as a reserve.

About 8.40 pm the hostile artillery fire slackened & by shortly after 9 pm had almost quieted down. From this time onwards the work of reorganizing & repairing damage etc was commenced.

Our artillery retaliation seemed splendid & most effective. — All ranks in the TAMBOUR are loud in praise of the Mining Coy. R.E. who assisted them magnificently. — All ranks of the Battalion were very cool & keen on making the enemy pay as heavily as possible for their attempt on the TAMBOUR.

At present the casualty list shows:-
Killed: 1 officer & 8 men. (amended to 11 men)
Wounded: 22 men.   (one since died)
Shell shock: 4 men.   (admitted to hospital)
Missing: 12 men.   (amended to 9 men)

Of these last everyone is convinced that none were taken prisoners but were either blown to pieces or buried in the bombardment.

The enemy succeeded in throwing a bomb down one

IV

raised mine shaft, before they were turned out. In their flight they left a lot of bombs & two pairs of wire cutters behind. — The estimated number of Germans who attacked are some 80 all ranks of whom 20 dead have been counted from our fire trench.

A corporal who was taken prisoner stated to me that they moved forward in three parties. One between the two Southern craters & two round the north of them. Each party consisted he thought of twenty eight all ranks. The flank parties had orders to take prisoners, the inner one to destroy the mine head by bombing them with specially large bombs. The prisoner belonged to the 99th Reserve Regt.

A separate report of gallant actions performed by certain officers N.C.Os & men will be submitted as soon as certain facts in connection with their actions are established.

I much regret the delay in submitting this report.

E. Thorpe
Lt Col
Comdg 2nd Bn Border R.

24th Feby 1916

Report on Attack on night of 22nd inst

The line held by 'C' Company 2nd Border Regt. was from Right of TAMBOUR No 96 to No.100 point, inclusive consisting of small detached posts, with 2 Lewis Gun positions. The Bombardment commenced at or about 5-10 pm. I asked for retaliation which was given quickly. Shortly after I noticed the smell of Gas shells I gave the S.O.S. signal & gave orders that smoke helmets were to be worn. I then found my telephone line had been cut & as reinforcements were urgently required No 8601 L/Cpl. H. Nicholls volunteered to go back with message to support line. He succeeded in reaching this line under heavy shell fire. I then gave the men immediately under my command the orders to man the fire trench. I ordered ft. Dowding to distribute the ammunition & bombs from various stores along the line. I then took up my position in the centre of company line, where I found 2/Lt Russell getting the men & Lewis Gun into position. At the same time 2/Lt Louson with a grenadier proceded to the sap in trench 99 followed by grenade party with supply of 'mills'. The enemy attacked this post & were repulsed with the exception of one man who got into the trench but was captured by 2/Lt Johnson.

2.

Meanwhile a small party attacked my position & they were driven off leaving one man wounded who was taken prisoner but died shortly afterwards. I sent his smoke helmet to Battn Head Qrs. & also identification disc. He bore no other distinguishing marks. During this attack reinforcements had arrived strengthening my line. I got into touch with the companies on my Right & Left flanks & found the line intact. I had by this time received a fresh supply of grenades & Very's lights. The fire decreased & I sent out a patrol & wiring party.

The patrol reported that our wire was broken in places & that the enemy was repairing his own trenches. The men received hot tea about 2 A.M. 23rd inst.

The Attack on Tambour.

In the TAMBOUR 4 posts were held by two Platoons, the two on the Right by No 9 Platoon under Sergt. Morgan & those on the Left by No 10 Platoon under Lt. Holland. At the commencement of Bombardment these posts were manned & cover was taken. The posts on the Right being heavily shelled, the men moved along the trench towards the 8th Devonshire Regt & took up firing positions. On the fire being lifted to support line

3.

Sergt Morgan again moved his men to the saps. The enemy were not seen at these two points, but a collection of unexploded grenades being found in sap No 2. on the Left. it was evident that enemy had been in there and had retired on hearing our grenadiers returning to their posts. Some of the men in this sap had evidently taken cover in the mine shaft half way down the sap, & probably buried by shell fire. Nothing was heard or seen of the enemy in sap No 1. on Right.

From all information gathered this was the only point entered by the enemy in the TAMBOUR.

It is well known that the missing men were extremely good soldiers & would fight to the last to avoid capture.

I recommend that mention be made of 2 Lt. Russell who showed great courage & forethought in getting his men & Lewis Guns into positions, also of No. 8601 L/Cpl H. Nicholls who carried back a message at great risk under heavy shell fire.

In the Field
23/2/16

A Wright Capt.
Comdg 'C' Company.
2nd Border Regt.

20th Brigade.

7th Division.

2nd BATTALION

BORDER REGIMENT

MARCH 1916

Army Form C. 2118.

WAR DIARY

INTELLIGENCE SUMMARY.
(Erase heading not required.)

Reference Map ALBERT, 57DSE and 62DNE 1/40000

Instructions regarding War Diaries and Intelligence Summaries are contained in F. S. Regs., Part II. and the Staff Manual respectively. Title pages will be prepared in manuscript.

Place	Date	Hour	Summary of Events and Information	Remarks and references to Appendices
MEAULTE	8/3/16		The Battalion remained in billets in Brigade Reserve	
-"-	9/3/16	8.30AM	The Battalion proceeded to trenches (X26.c. to E.3.c) relieving 2nd Bn Gordon Highlanders. The 11th Bn Border Regt were on the left and 8th Bn Devons on right of the Battalion	
	11/3/16		A draft of 147 Other ranks joined the Battalion (Casualties 3rd to 10th March :- 1 Killed 12 wounded)	
Trenches	10/3/16		The Battalion was relieved in trenches by 2nd Bn Gordon Highlanders and proceeded to billets in Brigade Reserve (A and C Coys and Battn HdQrs to MEAULTE, B and D Coys to BECORDEL)	
MEAULTE	11/3/16		A draft of 31 Other Ranks joined the Battalion	
	12/3/16		B and D Coys rejoined the Battalion in MEAULTE	
-"-	14/3/16 15/3/16		In billets	
-"-	16/3/16	8.30am	The Battalion proceeded to trenches (X26c to E3c) relieving 2nd Bn Gordon Highlanders. The 11th Bn Border Regt were on the left and 8th Bn Devons on right of Battalion	
	21/3/16		A draft of 27 Other Ranks joined the Battalion (Casualties 16/3/16 to 21/3/16. (3 Killed, 12 wounded)	
	22/3/16		The Battalion was relieved in trenches by 2nd Bn Gordon Highlanders and proceeded to billets in Brigade Reserve (B and D Coys and Battn HdQrs to MEAULTE, A+C Coys to BECORDEL)	

Army Form C. 2118.

WAR DIARY
INTELLIGENCE SUMMARY.
(Erase heading not required.)

Place	Date	Hour	Summary of Events and Information	Remarks and references to Appendices
MEAULTE	24/3/16		A draft of 59 Other Ranks joined the Battalion	
-"-	25/3/16		"A" and "C" Companies relieved the Battalion in billets at MEAULTE.	
-"-	26.3.16		In billets	
-"-	27.3.16		The Battalion proceeded to trenches (X2bc to E.3.c. relieving 2nd Bn Gordon Highlanders	
-"-	28/3/16		The 11th Border Regt were on the left and 8th Bn Devons on right of Battalion. (Casualties 1 Killed, 4 wounded.)	
	29, 30, 31.3.16.		In trenches	

MWural Major for
Lieut. Colonel.
Commanding 2nd Bn The Border Regt.

20th Brigade.
7th Division.

2nd BATTALION

BORDER REGIMENT

APRIL 1916

Army Form C. 2118.

WAR DIARY
or
INTELLIGENCE SUMMARY.
(Erase heading not required.)

Instructions regarding War Diaries and Intelligence Summaries are contained in F.S. Regs., Part II. and the Staff Manual respectively. Title pages will be prepared in manuscript.

Place	Date	Hour	Summary of Events and Information	Remarks and references to Appendices
TRENCHES X26 c 16 E2c 2	1/4/16 to 3/4/16		In trenches. Casualties 1st & 2nd Mob:- 2 Killed 5 Wounded	
-"-	3/4/16		The Battn was relieved in the trenches by 2nd Gordon Highlanders. A and C Coys and Battn Head Quarters to billets in MEAULTE and B & D Coys to billets in Brigade Reserve at BECORDEL. A draft of 14 Other Ranks joined the Battalion	
MEAULTE and BECORDEL	3/4/16 to 5/4/16		The Battn less B & D Coys in billets	
-"-	6/4/16		The Battn less B & D Coys moved to billets at BRAY by platoons commencing at 2pm. B & D Coys joined the Battalion in billets at BRAY. A draft of 34 Other Ranks joined the Battn.	
BRAY	8/4/16			
-"-	8/4/16 to 12/4/16		The Battn remained in billets in Divisional Reserve coming under the command of C.O.G. 91st Infantry Brigade	
-"-	13/4/16		The Battalion proceeded to trenches on Square File relieving 9th Bn Devons Regt	
TRENCHES F.11.C.	14/4/16 to 18/4/16		During this period the enemy artillery was very active and fair apparently registering on our trenches. An attack was expected and the fullest arrangements were made for the defence of all lines	
-"-	19/4/16		At 7.25pm on 19/4/16 the enemy opened a violent bombardment on B2 Subsector which the Battalion held. The front support and reserve lines were all shelled. The bombardment was most intense on the front from MANSEL COPSE to junction F10.1 and F.10.2. It continued between 8.15pm and 8.30pm the barrage was lifted	

Army Form C. 2118.

WAR DIARY
or
INTELLIGENCE SUMMARY. (Page 2)
(Erase heading not required.)

Place	Date	Hour	Summary of Events and Information	Remarks and references to Appendices
	19/4/16 (Continued)		Between MANSEL COPSE and 71 Street and a party of the enemy approached our line at the head of BLOOD ALLEY. They did not succeed in entering our trenches they being driven back by bombs. They then appeared to have moved towards F.11.8. and they entered our front line trench somewhere in this Subsector. A number of unexploded enemy bombs were found in our trench. It is believed that the enemy left 12 of her dead near MANSEL COPSE. The trenches were severely damaged in many places both front line, support line and communication trenches being blocked. Our casualties were 1 Officer and 18 Other Ranks Killed (Officer:- 2nd Lieut W. N. Bluison) 2 Offrs and 42 Other Ranks wounded (Officers Lieut V. H. Hodgson, 2nd Lieut W. G. Lindsay.) * 9 Other Ranks:- Missing * Lieut V. N. Hodgson - Died of Wounds 20/4/16.	
	20/4/16		At 8.30 pm on 20/4/16 the enemy opened a very violent bombardment on much the same front as was shelled the previous night but the bombardment was not nearly so long. A party of the enemy approached our line at the head of BLOOD ALLEY and threw bombs into the trench. We replied with Mills' Grenades. After a short fight the enemy were over and attacked the line about the centre of F.11.8. Here they were again driven off by our bombers. The party appeared to consist of 20 men. No enemy bodies were seen in front of our trenches the next morning, but judging from cries which were heard that night have suffered casualties. Our Artillery retaliated with good effect.	

* On 21 May 11th the Teasans 5 (Aerials) (1) If there wounded men were recovered by the relieving party during the clearing of the Trenches but so shattered by shell fire that identification of the bodies was impossible.

Army Form C. 2118.

WAR DIARY
or
INTELLIGENCE SUMMARY. (Page 3)
(Erase heading not required.)

Instructions regarding War Diaries and Intelligence Summaries are contained in F. S. Regs., Part II. and the Staff Manual respectively. Title pages will be prepared in manuscript.

Place	Date	Hour	Summary of Events and Information	Remarks and references to Appendices
	20/4/16 (Continued)		later at 10.15 p.m. and 10.45 p.m. our Heavy Artillery retaliated on the enemy front line between the Craters and BLACK HEDGE with field Guns co-operating, this retaliation was very successful the enemy trenches being blown in in many places. Our casualties were :- 1 O.R. Killed 6 O.R. Wounded. (Total Casualties 13/4/16 to 21/4/16 :- Killed 1 Offr + 20 Died of Wounds 1 Offr + 5 O.R. Wounded 1 Officer and 61 O.R.- Missing " 9 O.R. The Battalion was relieved at night by 9th Bn Devons Regt and proceeded to billets at BRAY. 2nd Lieut. F. Argles and 30. O.R. joined the Battalion	(Sketch of Bn Sub-sector attached)
TRENCHES	21/4/16			
BRAY	22/4/16			
"	23-4-16 }		The Battalion proceeded to rest billets at CORBIE	
CORBIE	26-4-16 }		in rest billets at CORBIE	
"	27/4/16		The Battalion proceeded to billets at VAUX sur SOMME	
VAUX	28/4/16		A Draft of 62 O.R. joined the Battalion	
"	29-4-16 } Y 30-4-1 16 }		in billets at VAUX sur SOMME.	

(Worrall) Major for
Lieut. Colonel,
Commanding 2nd Bn The Border Regt

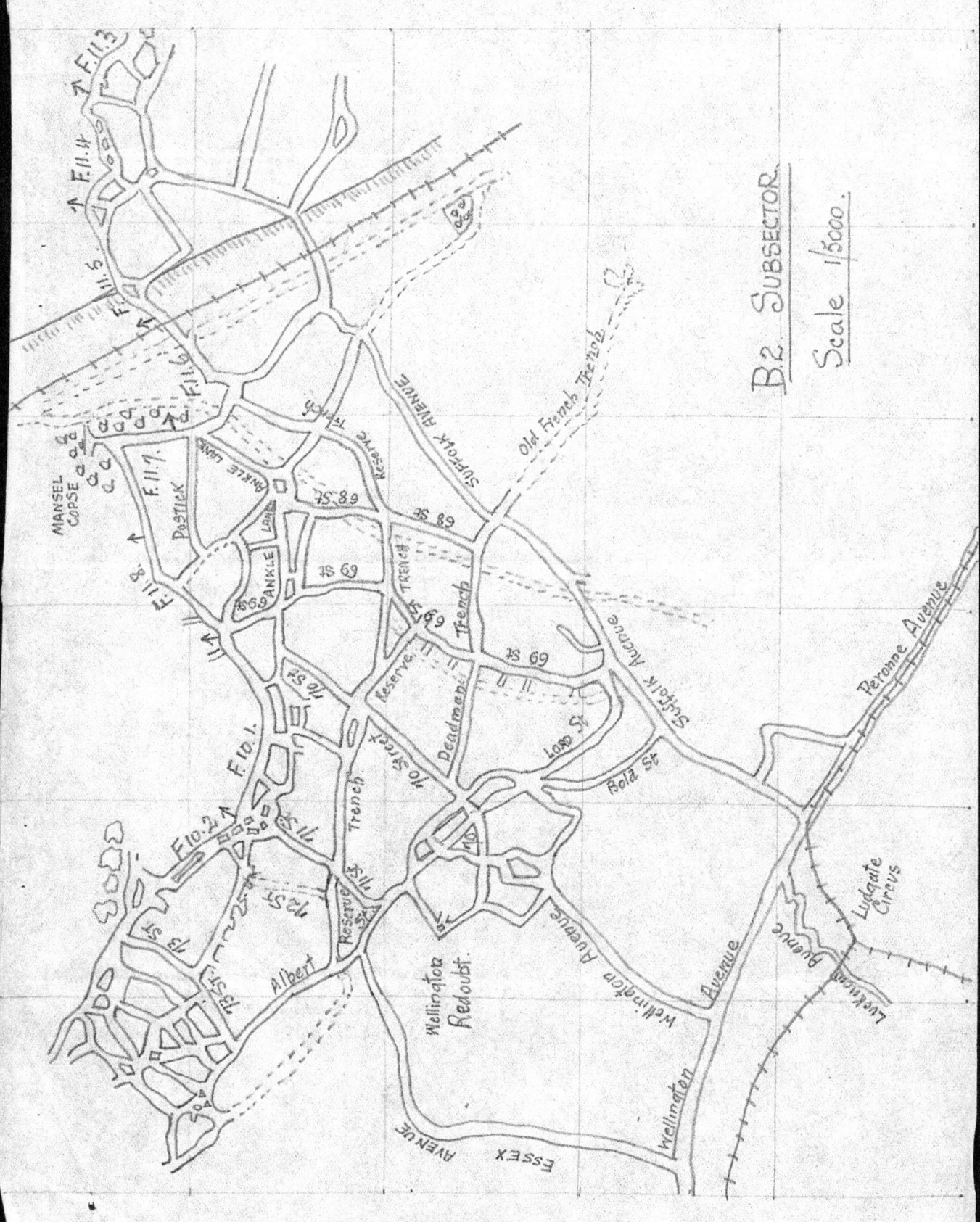

20th Brigade.

7th Division.

2nd BATTALION

BORDER REGIMENT

M A Y   1 9 1 6

2 Border Regt 7
May 1916 Vol 16

WAR DIARY
INTELLIGENCE SUMMARY
(Erase heading not required.)

Army Form C.2118

Place	Date	Hour	Summary of Events and Information	Remarks and references to Appendices
VAUX-SUR-SOMME	1/5/16 to 5/5/16		The Battalion remained in billets	
— " —	6/5/16		The Battalion proceeded to shelters at BOIS DES TAILLES arriving about 4pm	
BOIS DES TAILLES	7/5/16 to 10/5/16		The Battalion remained in billets. 2nd Lieut B. Cumbston joined the Battn on 9/5/16.	
— " —	11/5/16		A draft of 50 Other Ranks joined the Battn on 13/5/16. 2nd Lieut 2 Companies and Battn Head Quarters proceeded to shelters at GROVETOWN - A & C Companies proceeded to shelters at GRANTOWN	
GROVETOWN GRANTOWN	18/5/16 to 21/5/16		Lieut T.T. Wilson & 2nd Lieut's Gilmour & 2d Gillespie joined the Battn.	
GROVETOWN	22/5/16		B and D Companies and Battn Head Quarters proceeded to shelters at BOIS DES TAILLES A and C Companies joined Band D Coys in shelter at BOIS DES TAILLES.	
GRANTOWN	23/5/16			
BOIS DES TAILLES	24/5/16 to 31/5/16		2nd Lieut H. Croft and a draft of 83 Other Ranks joined the Battalion on 25/5/16 2nd Lieut's O.G. Lucas, W.R. Hinton & March joined the Battalion on 28/5/16 Lieut G.W. O'Brien and 2Lieut D.R. Logan joined the Battalion on 29/5/16	

B. Rhodes Lieut. Colonel
Commanding 2nd Bn The Border Regt

20th Brigade.

7th Division

2nd BATTALION

BORDER REGIMENT

JUNE 1916

2 Border Regt
Army Form C.
20/L
7 sheets

WAR DIARY
INTELLIGENCE SUMMARY
(Erase heading not required.)

Pt 17

Place	Date	Hour	Summary of Events and Information	Remarks and references to Appendices
	9/6/16		The Battalion was employed during this tour on work in connection with railway construction.	
	10/6/16		2nd Lieut J Ellis & 110B Others joined the Battn on 11/6/16. Lieut Ed Shaw joined the Battn on 26/6/16. 110 B Others joined the Battn on 29/6/16. The Battalion accepted 10 touches in 8a Character returning 10 B Sask Stafords Regt. A draft of 16 Other Ranks joined the Battalion on 14/6/16	
	12/6/16 14/6/16		2 Francisco (Casualties) 4 Killed 9 Wounded. A draft of 1 Other Ranks joined the Battn on 16/6/16. 2nd Lieuts W Harrison Cape, H Gothie & O Sergeston joined the Battn on 17/6/16. Maj C Robbins + 2nd Lieut Bath joined the Battn on 29/6/16. Capt A Hennessey (who was wounded at Ypres) & 2nd Lt Andrew McKinnon	
	18/6/16		The Battalion was relieved in trenches by 2nd Bn Gordon Highlanders succeeded by Kielters at GRAN TOWN	
	20/6/16 21/6/16		1 Other Ranks joined the Battalion on 2/6/16	

WAR DIARY
or
INTELLIGENCE SUMMARY.
(Erase heading not required.)

Army Form C. 2118.

Place	Date	Hour	Summary of Events and Information	Remarks and references to Appendices
GRAN TOWN	24/6/16		Battalion proceeded to billets at MERICOURT	
	25/6/16		Battalion in billets	
MERICOURT	25/6/16		Battalion proceeded to billets at MORLANCOURT	
MORLANCOURT	26/6/16		Maj. C. Reilly Barnett and 4 Other ranks joined the Batln on 25/6/16. 12 Other Ranks joined the Battn on 26/6/16. Parties were dispatched by the Battalion at the request of 2nd Battn & 29th Wilts to cut the wire on the main Bn Sub sector preparatory to an attack on 1/7/16. Casualties - 25/6/16. Killed 2Lieut W.A. Jones 3 O.R. Wounded 6 O.R.	
	28/6/16		" 29/6/16. Killed - 3 O.R. Wounded 6 O.R.	
	30/6/16		Battn Head Quarters and B Company proceeded to trenches in Bn Sub sector. D. Company relieved B. Crawford in trenches - B Coy remaining in billets at MORLANCOURT	
	30/6/16		Casualties 29/6/16. Killed 1 O.R. Wounded Capt W.D. Cheetham - Steede & 1 O.R. A & C Coys proceeded to trenches in Bn Sub sector taking up assembly position for the attack. Casualties 30/6/16 - Killed 1 O.R. Wounded 5 O.R.	

E. Thompson, Lieut. Colonel,
Commanding 2nd Bn The Border Regt.

Operation Order by
Lieut. Col. E. Thorpe.
Commanding 2 Bn Border Regt.

Maps referred to:
FRICOURT - 1/5000.
Brigade Trench
Map - 1/5000.

France
26th June 1916.

1. In conjunction with the FRENCH who are operating from MARICOURT Southwards, the FOURTH Army is about to assume the offensive.
The attack will be developed to the North and South of FRICOURT VILLAGE and FRICOURT WOOD by the 21st and 7th Divisions respectively with the object of isolating the triangle formed by these localities, which will be afterwards dealt with in a subsidiary operation.

The task of the 7th Division is to clear the trenches in front and seize and occupy the Spur from the track at S.25.b.5&32. to WILLOW AVENUE at X.29.b.5.6. Immediately on the right of the 7th Division the left Brigade of the 18th Division will advance simultaneously and prolong the 7th Division line towards MONTAUBAN.

On the left of the 7th Division advancing on the North side and clear of FRICOURT VILLAGE and WOOD will be the 50th Inf. Brigade attached to the 21st Division with their right on FRICOURT FARM. That Brigade will join hands with the 7th Division at WILLOW AVENUE and prolong the line Northwards.

7th Div. Plan.
2(a) The Division will be distributed as follows:-
Right :- 91st Infantry Brigade.
Centre :- 20th Infantry Brigade.
Left :- 22nd Infantry Brigade less 2 Battalions and 2 Sections of M.G. Company.

(b) Main Attack.
The main attack of the 7th Division will be carried out by the 91st and 20th Infy Brigades.

(c) Subsidiary Attack.
The subsidiary attack will be carried out by the 22nd Infy Brigade who will clear the German trenches North of BOIS FRANCAIS at an hour to be decided later, when the main attack has reached the final objective. This operation will take place in conjunction with the two Battalions of the 50th Infy Brigade who will clear FRICOURT VILLAGE and WOOD.

20th Infy Bde
objective
3. The object of the 20th Infy Brigade will be to form a defensive flank facing NORTH-WESTWARDS to cover the advance of the 91st Infantry Brigade. Its objective

objective is the line from the bend of BUNNY TRENCH F.5.c.35.90 (road inclusive) along BUNNY TRENCH to "M" in BM 90.0 - thence along SUNKEN ROAD to the junction of ORCHARD TRENCH NORTH with ORCHARD ALLEY - ORCHARD ALLEY to junction with APPLE ALLEY - then along APPLE ALLEY to the small salient in our present line at F.10.c.7.4.

Object of 2nd Border Regt (4. The special object of the 2nd Bn Border Regt is APPLE ALLEY from the junction with ORCHARD ALLEY to the present German front line.

Bombardment 5. A very heavy bombardment of the hostile line by guns and mortars of all description will take place for X days previous to the assault.

Assembly Positions 6. For the assault the Brigade will be formed up as follows - each Battalion in four lines.

Right   -   2nd Gordons.
Centre   -   9th Devons.
Left   -   2nd Border.
Reserve   -   8th Devons.
Rear   -   95th Field Coy. R.E.

Reference to the above, the BORDER REGT will assemble by   on the   June. 1916 in the following trenches:-

"A" Company. { FIRE TRENCH - 2 platoons from the junction of F.11.8 & F.10.1 to point by the "10" of F.10.1 on the Trench map.
              { SUPPORT TRENCH:- 2 platoons from 70 STREET to a point in rear of the F. of F.10.1 on the Trench map.

"C" Company. { FIRE TRENCH :- 4 platoons from left of "A" Company to left of F.10.2

"B" Company:- { RESERVE TR:- 70 to 71 Street.

"D" Company:- { RESERVE TR:- 71 Street along ALBERT STREET as far as necessary.

Battn. Head Qrs:- 71 STREET between SUPPORT and RESERVE TRENCHES.

Routes to the Assembly Positions 7. "A" & "B" Companies will move into position via ESSEX AVENUE and 71 STREET with "A" Company leading.
"C" & "D" Companies move via ESSEX AVENUE & 73 Street.
Battn. HdQrs will follow "A" & "B" Companies.

20th Inf.Bde.
7th Div.

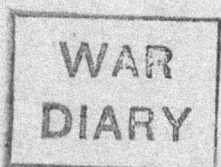

2nd BATTN. THE BORDER REGIMENT.

J U L Y

1 9 1 6

WAR DIARY.

2ND. BATTN. BORDER REGIMENT.

1ST - 31ST JULY 1916.

WAR DIARY
INTELLIGENCE SUMMARY.
(Erase heading not required.)

Army Form C. 2118.-

Place	Date	Hour	Summary of Events and Information	Remarks and references to Appendices
	1/7/16		On the night of the 30th June/1st July 1916 the Battalion moved up from MORLANCOURT & took up a position in B.2. Sub-sector of the trenches. The move was completed at about 1-30am on 1st July 1916. The Battalion was formed up as follows:-	

1ST. LINE.
{
RIGHT:- "A" Company under Lieut G.M.F. PRYNNE occupying RESERVE TRENCH from 70 Street to 71 Street
LEFT:- "C" Company under Capt L.A. NEWTON occupying RESERVE TRENCH from 71 Street up to about 72 Street in ALBERT STREET.
}

2ND. LINE.
{
RIGHT:- "B" Company under Lieut R.F. MILLARD having 2 Platoons in ALBERT STREET on N.W. of 70 Street & 2 Platoons in WELLINGTON REDOUBT.
LEFT:- "D" Company under Lieut P.N. FRASER having 2 Platoons in ALBERT STREET from junction of WEBB STREET to the left. 2 Platoons in WELLINGTON REDOUBT.
}

Battalion Head Quarters } WELLINGTON
Head Quarter Bombers } REDOUBT
Signallers, 2 Lewis Guns in Reserve,
Battalion Aid Post.

Whilst the Artillery Bombardment of the hostile line continued the Battalion was subjected to a heavy bombardment in retaliation from the enemy but as this

WAR DIARY or INTELLIGENCE SUMMARY.
(Page 2.)

Army Form C. 2118.

was mostly directed at our front and support lines little damage was done.
At 1-27am. the Battalion advanced in 4 lines from our trenches in the following order:-

1ST. LINE. Right:- 2 Platoons of A Company. Left:- 2 Platoons of C Company.
2ND. LINE. Right:- 2 Platoons of A Company. Left:- 2 Platoons of C Company.
          Three Lewis Guns.
3RD. LINE. Right:- 2 Platoons of B Company. Left:- 2 Platoons of D Company.
          Three Lewis Guns.
4TH. LINE. Right:- 2 Platoons of B Company. Left:- 2 Platoons of D Company.
or Reserve. Two Lewis Guns.

Just as our first line had cleared our front the head of the subway from Y Street towards DANUBE TRENCH was blown-in. Zero hour.
The Battalion now moved forward until it reached its first objective DANUBE SUPPORT TRENCH when the left wheel was commenced.
Up till now the casualties were small in the first and second lines and were caused by a machine gun firing from our right in the direction of SAP "A" in Nettle Trench & also from our re-en left in DANUBE SUPPORT. The wheel was now gradually completed & the advance continued towards our objective, APPLE ALLEY which was reached by our 1st Line at about 8.30 a.m. During this

WAR DIARY
or
INTELLIGENCE SUMMARY.

(Page 3)

Army Form C. 2118.

Place	Date	Hour	Summary of Events and Information	Remarks and references to Appendices

advance our line was broken up into a line of Groups bombing & bayoneting the enemy, who when they found that their line had been entered, forged a new front to in Shell holes & communication trenches facing us thus checking our advance.

On reaching SHRINE ALLEY the Battalion was temporarily checked through coming under heavy indirect machine gun fire from FRICOURT and enfilade fire from MAMETZ, but on the 1st & 2nd lines being reinforced by the 3rd Line the advance was continued to HIDDEN LANE. Here the line was again temporarily held up by fire from a machine gun & hostile party in HIDDEN WOOD & another party at about the junction of KIEL SUPPORT & BOIS FRANCAIS SUPPORT. The latter were bombed out without very much difficulty by our party working along KIEL SUPPORT but the former had to be attacked across the open as well as down HIDDEN LANE. This was done by a party organised & led by 2nd Lieut S.V.C. RUSSELL. The advance was now continued to APPLE ALLEY by parties being pushed forward by the 1st & 2nd Lines whilst the 3rd Line consolidated HIDDEN LANE.

At this time the right of the 11th Line moved up to HIDDEN WOOD so as to strengthen that flank as it was found that the DEVON REGT had not kept up with the advance of the Battalion & this flank was very exposed. The left of the 11th Line was still in Reserve in KIEL TRENCH, close up to the junction of HIDDEN LANE. The Battalion was now checked in HIDDEN LANE with posts forward in APPLE ALLEY

WAR DIARY
or
INTELLIGENCE SUMMARY.
(Erase heading not required.)

(Page 4.)

Army Form C. 2118.

Place	Date	Hour	Summary of Events and Information	Remarks and references to Appendices

at junction of it & PEAR TRENCH - ditto BOIS FRANÇAIS SUPPORT & also BOIS FRANÇAIS TRENCH. At 2.30 P.M. the 20TH MANCHESTER REGT. advanced across our front and bombing parties of the BORDER REGT. worked along APPLE ALLEY without any opposition. At about 5 P.M. APPLE ALLEY was occupied by A and C Coys of the BORDER REGT with a party of 8TH DEVON REGT on the right. B and D Coys BORDER REGT held HIDDEN LANE as a support line. Head Quarters were established in an old Company dugout in SUPPORT TRENCH at its junction with 76 Street.

This position was maintained until 8 a.m. on 3rd July when the Battalion changed its position to BOIS FRANÇAIS SUPPORT which was held by B and D Coys with A and C Coys in BOIS FRANÇAIS TRENCH - Battn Head Quarters remaining in the same position. Here the Battn remained until the evening of 3rd July when it moved down to POST 91 SOUTH in Reserve.

The casualties in the attack were not as heavy as they might have been owing, firstly to the splendid way they were had been cut by T Battery R.H.A. & secondly to the fact that the advance was very low behind the artillery barrage the whole time. During the latter half of the attack the Battn was subjected to a heavy sprinkling of hostile shrapnel which in addition to rifle and machine gun fire & bombs caused the casualties mentioned.

The whole Battalion behaved with their usual steadiness & coolness under fire & all orders were strictly carried out. No mistake was made in the advance

Army Form C. 2118.-

WAR DIARY
or
INTELLIGENCE SUMMARY.

(Page 5)

(Erase heading not required.)

Place	Date	Hour	Summary of Events and Information	Remarks and references to Appendices
			& the object was carried out without any gabs being left in the line, which is entirely due to the care taken by all Officers in instructing their NCO's & men in all points regarding the operation and the orders taken by all ranks in it. The Battalion captured 3 Machine Guns, 2 Trench Mortars, 1 Projector, 5 Canister Throwers. The casualties were:- Officers:- 3 Killed, 6 Wounded, 1 Died of Wounds. Other Ranks:- 19 Killed, 210 Wounded, 10 Died of Wounds, 4 Missing.	
	3/7/1916		The Battalion was relieved on the night of 3rd July & proceeded to dugouts & shelters at the CITADEL.	
	4/7/1916 5/7/1916		The Battalion remained at the CITADEL.	
	10/7/16 to 12/7/16		The Battalion marched to billets at RIBEMONT. In billets	
	11/7/16		The Battalion marched to bivouacs near MINDEN POST	
	13/7/16		At 10pm on 13th July the Battalion moved and was in its position of deployment in CATERPILLAR WOOD by 1-15am on 14th July 1916. During the latter part of the march to WILLOW VALLEY & when in position the Battalion was subjected to a bombardment by hostile field guns & 10.5cm howitzers firing High Explosive & Shrapnel	

Army Form C 2118.

WAR DIARY
or
INTELLIGENCE SUMMARY. (Page 6)
(Erase heading not required.)

Place	Date	Hour	Summary of Events and Information	Remarks and references to Appendices
			The objective of the 20th Infantry Brigade was BAZENTIN-LE-GRAND WOOD with a small portion of the German 2nd line heyeh to EAST and West of it. The Battalion had the left of the 1st line with the 8th DEVON REGT. by the right. The dividing line between these 2 Battalions was a portion of the German trench which jutted out & was known by the name of the SNOUT. The 2nd BORDER REGT. was to open to four lines, the fourth one being the Reserve in	
CATERPILLAR WOOD.				
		2.20 a.m.	the advance was ordered so as to move in conjunction with the 8th DEVON REGT. The Battalion moved as follows:-	
			1st & 2nd. LINE:- { LEFT:- D Company under Captain A. WRIGHT 2 Platoons in each line RIGHT:- B Company under Captain R.F. NEWDIGATE 2 Platoons in each line	
			3RD LINE:- A Company under Lieut. P.R. DOWDING in line of Platoons ready to support either Front Companies.	
			4TH LINE, RESERVE:- C Company under Lieut E.L. HOLLAND	
			Lines advanced at 150 yards distance. Owing to the night through moonlight being cloudy the 1st line was able to move straight on to the Southern edge of FLAT-IRON COPSE covered by Scouts & the others to their positions in rear of this line. This stage was reached by about 2.35 a.m. From this position the Battalion crawled forward to some 30 yards	

Army Form C. 2118.

WAR DIARY
or
INTELLIGENCE SUMMARY.
(Erase heading not required.)

(Page 7)

Place	Date	Hour	Summary of Events and Information	Remarks and references to Appendices
			from the hostile trenches & awaited the lift of the artillery bombardment at 3.25am. If 3.25am the Battn again advanced & the first hostile line was captured. Here another halt had to be made until the artillery barrage lifted off the WOOD. At 4.25am the Battn again advanced & pushed through the wood to its final objective which was reached at 4.40am. The order had been given that the north side of the wood should be consolidated but it was found that if this were done there would be very considerable delay in obtaining cover owing to the ground being thickly strewn by the branches of trees so advantage was taken of a good bank which ran parallel with the edge of the wood and some 30 to 50 yards from it, & the position was consolidated. It was soon found that owing to casualties & other causes the 2 Companies were insufficient to hold the line so the 3rd line, 'A' Company, was absorbed into the general line. Just previous to the actual assault at about 3.15am 2 Platoons of the Reserve Company had been advanced as far as FLATIRON COPSE so as to be closer in case reinforcements were necessary. The remaining 2 Platoons of 'C' (Reserve) Company remained in their place in CATERPILLAR WOOD as also did Battn Head Quarters.	

Army Form C. 2118.-

WAR DIARY
or
INTELLIGENCE SUMMARY.
(Erase heading not required.)

(Page 8)

Place	Date	Hour	Summary of Events and Information	Remarks and references to Appendices
			In this attack the casualties were few amounting to:- Officers:- Killed 2. Wounded 1. Other Ranks:- Killed 23. Wounded 136. Missing 58. All ranks behaved with their usual coolness and the advance was very steadily carried out. During the night the Battalion remained in the captured position. On the afternoon of 15th inst the Battalion was withdrawn & proceeded to POMMIERS REDOUBT in Reserve where it remained until 19th July.	
	20/7/16		On the night of 19th July the Battalion moved from POMMIERS REDOUBT in old 20th German line to CATERPILLAR WOOD at 10 p.m. being in position at 12.30 a.m. 20th July. The Battalion was in Brigade Reserve all day & never came into action. With the exception of a certain amount of hostile shelling which caused few casualties owing to the Battn. being well entrenched there is nothing to report.	
	22/7/16		The Battalion moved back at night & rested in a field near DERNANCOURT. The Battalion entrained at MERICOURT Station at about 2 p.m. and detrained at HANGEST and marched to billets at BREILLY.	
BREILLY	23/7/16 to 31/7/16		In billets.	

WAR DIARY or INTELLIGENCE SUMMARY

Army Form C. 2118.
(Page 9)

Summary of Events and Information

The undermentioned Officers became Casualties during the month.

KILLED 1/11/1916. Lieut. P.W. Fraser, 2 Lieut. W. Robertson, Lieut. D.H. Logan

WOUNDED 1/11/1916. Capt. L.A. Newton, Lieut. B.J. Millard, Lieut. G.H. O'Brien
2 Lieut. G.H. Sharp, 2/Lieut. J. Argles, 2 Lieut. J. Ellis

DIED OF WOUNDS 6/11/1916. 2nd Lieut. W. Lucas

WOUNDED 12/11/1916. 2 Lieut. S.C. Russell

KILLED 14/11/1916. 2 Lieut. M.S. Towson, Lieut. W.R. Hinton

WOUNDED 14/11/1916. Capt. R. Wright

The following reinforcements joined the Battalion during the month.

JOINED 1/11/1916.: 7 Other Ranks
  -"- 9/11/1916.: 45 "
  -"- 9/11/1916.: 239 "
  -"- 10/11/1916.: 132 "
  -"- 19/11/1916.- Lieut. R.H. Ehrenborg, Lieut. R.G. Newroy, Lieut. D. Elliot, Lieut. J.A. Walker,
    2/Lieut. D.W.P.T. Slack, Lieut. B.P. Beeth, 2 Lieut. J. Martindale,
    2/Lieut. J.J. Beaty-Pownall, Lieut. K.D. Tees.
  -"- 21/11/1916.- Lieut. C.H.E. Ingledew, 2/Lieut. R.B. Wood, Lieut. H.G. Montgomerie.

Army Form C. 2118.

WAR DIARY
or
INTELLIGENCE SUMMARY.
(Erase heading not required.)

(Page 10)

Place	Date	Hour	Summary of Events and Information	Remarks and references to Appendices
			JOINED 21/11/16 :- 2nd Lieut S.B. Beadle, 2 Lieut W.B. Stoat, -"- 23/11/16 :- 2 Lieut D.M. Nill. [signed] E. Thorpe Lieut Colonel, Commanding 2nd Bn The Border Regt.	

7th Division No G.1/444.

SECRET

Officer Commanding,
~~8th Devon Regt.~~
9th Devon Regt.
2nd Border Regt.
~~2nd Gordon Highlanders.~~

S/99

20/BM/647.

Herewith copy of "Narrative of Operations for period 1st - 20th July, 1916.

3rd August, 1916.

Major.
Brigade Major.
20th Infantry Brigade.

"A" Form. Army Form C. 2121
MESSAGES AND SIGNALS.

TO: OC Companies & Specialists

Day of Month: 10/8/16

AAA

The attached 7th Division Narrative of Operations from 1st to ~~5th~~ 20th July 1916 is forwarded for your information. Please initial & pass quickly last named to return to this office.

INITIALS
A FRD
B DA
C

Adjt. 2nd Border Regt.

SECRET

7th Division.

NARRATIVE OF OPERATIONS FROM 1ST to 5TH JULY, 1916.

Reference -
Sheets 1/20,000 and MONTAUBAN.

During the night 30th June/1st July the infantry moved to their assembly trenches. The assaulting troops of the 20th Infantry Brigade were moved to a position of readiness in the support line and were ordered to assault at 2 minutes before ZERO. This alteration in venue was rendered necessary owing to the damage done to our front line, from MANSEL COPSE to the Craters, by the enemy's artillery and Mortars.

July 1st. Heavy fire was maintained during the night by all arms, a concentrated bombardment lasting for one hour and 5 minutes being opened at 6.25 a.m.

At 7.30 a.m. the Division moved to the assault. The 22nd Bn. Manchester Regiment on the right, in close touch with the 1st Bn. South Staffordshire Regiment, had little difficulty in passing over the first line of German trenches.

In the centre, the 2nd Bn. Gordon Highlanders, in touch with the 1st Bn. South Staffordshire Regiment, came under very heavy Machine gun fire after crossing "NO MAN'S LAND", but succeeded in advancing, with the exception of their left company, who were held up by uncut wire.

At 7.50 a.m. the road running N.E. from the HALT was occupied, close touch being continuously maintained on the right. On the left, however, the 9th Bn. Devonshire Regiment failed to keep touch. This Battalion on reaching our front line near MANSEL COPSE suffered very heavily from Machine gun and Artillery fire, the leading companies losing all their officers. They remained near TIRPITZ Trench and SHRINE ALLEY and failed to establish touch either to the right or left, or to clear the dug-outs in the wooded bank West of the Railway, this task being carried out by one company of the 8th Bn. Devonshire Regiment who were sent forward from Brigade Reserve to assist the 2nd Bn. Gordon Highlanders. In the meanwhile the 2nd Bn. Border Regiment had reached DANUBE SUPPORT with but little trouble, and wheeled to the left, as ordered; reaching their final objective, but not consolidating it, by 9.30 a.m. During its advance the Battalion was temporarily held up at SHRINE ALLEY and again at HIDDEN LANE by indirect and enfilade Machine gun fire from FRICOURT and MAMETZ respectively. Small parties of the enemy were disposed of by bombing parties in KEIL SUPPORT and by direct attack across the open. The advance was then continued, APPLE ALLEY and HIDDEN LANE being consolidated. On the right a defensive flank, rendered necessary owing to the inevitable failure of the 9th Bn. Devonshire

Regiment/

page 2.

Regiment to maintain touch, was established.

Meanwhile the 91st Infantry Brigade had continued its advance with varying success. The 22nd Bn. Manchester Regiment took BUCKET Trench and entered DANTZIG ALLEY at 8.15 a.m, the 1st South Staffordshire Regiment having entered the outskirts of MAMETZ at 7.45 a.m, where they were held up by Machine gun fire from houses. During these operations casualties were very heavy and two companies 21st Bn. Manchester Regiment were sent up in support.

On the right a counter-attack from FRITZ Trench drove the 22nd Bn. Manchester Regiment out of DANTZIG ALLEY. It was therefore impossible to launch the 2nd Bn. "Queens" Regiment to their objective. This Battalion had occupied a position of readiness in our old front line when the assaulting troops moved to the attack. The General Officer Commanding 91st Infantry Brigade at once ordered one company 21st Bn. Manchester Regiment to support the 22nd Bn. Manchester Regiment in an attack on DANTZIG ALLEY, so as to enable the 2nd Bn. "Queens" Regiment to advance through FRITZ Trench, to their final objective, the necessary artillery barrages being arranged.

At 12.0 noon the XV Corps reported that the whole of MONTAUBAN had been captured, and that the enemy were in full retreat to BAZENTIN-le-GRAND. In view of this information the Divisional Commander ordered the 91st Infantry Brigade to attack as soon as possible and the times of barrages were adjusted as necessary.

At 1.0 p.m. the situation was approximately as follows :-

On the right, the 22nd Bn. Manchester Regiment after very severe fighting had been reinforced by one company of the 21st Bn. Manchester Regiment and were moving into DANTZIG ALLEY, which they occupied at 1.30 p.m. The 1st Bn. South Staffordshire Regiment supported by 2 companies 21st Bn. Manchester Regiment were holding the line of DANTZIG ALLEY through MAMETZ and were in touch with the 2nd Bn. Gordon Highlanders. The 2nd Bn. "Queens" Regiment in support had two companies in our original front line and two companies in that of the enemy's in readiness to move to their final objective as soon as MAMETZ was won.

In the centre, the 2nd Bn. Gordon Highlanders with 2 Stokes Mortars were held up in front of MAMETZ, in touch with the 91st Infantry Brigade but not in touch with the 9th Bn. Devonshire Regiment who had been unable to advance and had suffered heavy casualties. The 2nd Bn. Border Regiment had reached, but had not yet consolidated, their final objective, as they were waiting for the 9th Bn. Devonshire Regiment to come up on their right flank.

On the left, the 22nd Infantry Brigade were in a position of readiness preparatory to their subsidiary attack at 2.30 p.m.

Orders/

page 3.

Orders for the Advance.
The 91st Infantry Brigade carried out the instructions previously issued. The General Officer Commanding 20th Infantry Brigade ordered two companies of the 2nd Bn. Royal Warwickshire Regiment already attached to him, to report to Officer Commanding 2nd Bn. Gordon Highlanders and to attack and capture MAMETZ. The Officer Commanding 9th Bn. Devonshire Regiment was ordered to gain touch with the 2nd Bn. Border Regiment and to capture the trench near HIDDEN WOOD and to press on to his objective. The Officer Commanding 2nd Bn. Border Regiment was ordered to consolidate APPLE ALLEY and to co-operate with the 22nd Infantry Brigade. The 8th Bn. Devonshire Regiment was moved up in support, by HIDDEN WOOD to PLUM LANE. The 22nd Infantry Brigade was ordered to move to the attack at 2.30 p.m.

At 2.0 p.m. the 2nd Bn. "Queens" Regiment in touch with the 54th Infantry Brigade (18th Division) began their advance towards their final objective and reached the eastern edge of FRITZ Trench at about 4.0 p.m. On their left the 22nd Bn. Manchester Regiment, reinforced by one company of the 21st Bn. Manchester Regiment, advanced on the western half of FRITZ Trench and on BRIGHT ALLEY; the 1st Bn. South Staffordshire Regiment advancing simultaneously on the N. and N.E. corner of MAMETZ. This line was taken and touch established with the 20th Infantry Brigade by 5.0 p.m.

In the Centre, the 20th Infantry Brigade carried out their orders, and, as soon as the 2nd Bn. Royal Warwick Regiment advanced to support the Gordon Highlanders, 600 of the enemy at once surrendered and at 4.5 p.m. the N.W. corner of MAMETZ was occupied. By 5.0 p.m. the work of consolidating the day's objective was started. The remaining two companies 2nd Bn. Royal Warwickshire Regiment were attached and formed the Brigade Reserve near SHRINE ALLEY.

At 2.30 p.m. the 20th Bn. Manchester Regiment, 22nd Infantry Brigade, advanced to the attack and captured BOIS FRANCAIS SUPPORT and SUNKEN ROAD Trench with little difficulty. Their supports, however, suffered heavy casualties by Machine gun fire from the RECTANGLE SUPPORT and FRICOURT, which held up the advance. The Officer Commanding the left company moved to his right to gain touch with the troops in BOIS FRANCAIS SUPPORT and at once organised a bombing party which advanced down ORCHARD ALLEY and made a block in LIME Trench. It was, however, held up at PAPEN Trench and forced back to BOIS FRANCAIS SUPPORT. At about 3.30 p.m. touch was established with the 20th Infantry Brigade and during the rest of the afternoon there was a considerable amount of Bomb fighting round the RECTANGLE and the adjoining trenches. The situation was eventually cleared up by a company of the 1st Bn. Royal Welsh Fusiliers who consolidated the RECTANGLE-SUNKEN ROAD Trench- BOIS FRANCAIS SUPPORT and part of ORCHARD ALLEY.

As the 21st Division, and the 50th Brigade, (17th Division), had found it impossible to advance and

to/

to maintain touch on our left at the N.E. corner of FRICOURT WOOD, and at WILLOW Trench respectively, a defensive flank was consolidated and wired from our original line South of FRICOURT to the ORCHARD. At nightfall the situation was as follows :-

On the right, the 2nd Bn. "Queens" Regiment held FRITZ Trench with one company of the 21st Bn. Manchester Regiment on their left. The 22nd Bn. Manchester Regiment with one company 2nd Bn. Royal Irish Regiment, who had been sent up to strengthen the line, were in BRIGHT ALLEY and the 1st Bn. South Staffordshire Regiment in BUNNY Trench with two companies 2nd Bn. Royal Warwickshire Regiment in BUNNY ALLEY.

In the centre, the 2nd Bn. Gordon Highlanders occupied the S.W. portion of BUNNY Trench and the SUNKEN ROAD as far as ORCHARD Trench. The 8th and 9th Bns. Devonshire Regiment held the line from that point along SUNKEN ROAD to ORCHARD ALLEY, to its junction with APPLE ALLEY, with the 2nd Bn. Border Regiment in APPLE ALLEY.

On the left, the 20th Bn. Manchester Regiment with one company of the 1st Bn. Royal Welsh Fusiliers on their flank held BOIS FRANCAIS SUPPORT up to the RECTANGLE inclusive.

Information was received at midnight that the 17th Division would attack FRICOURT and FRICOURT WOOD at 12.15 p.m. and that the 7th Division would co-operate on their right flank. Information was also received that the 18th Division had advanced to their final objective. *July 2nd. Information.*

Patrols were sent forward during the night July 1st/2nd by the 22nd Bn. Manchester Regiment to QUEEN'S NULLAH which they found unoccupied; and by the 1st Bn. Royal Welsh Fusiliers with orders to bomb as far as WING CORNER; also by the 2nd Bn. Royal Irish Regiment into FRICOURT, which they reported clear. *Patrols.*

In view of the above information the General Officer Commanding, 91st Infantry Brigade was ordered at 7.30 a.m. to advance to his final objective. At 11.0 a.m. two companies of the 2nd Bn. "Queens" Regiment with two Machine guns moved forward via BEETLE ALLEY and WHITE Trench, reaching QUEEN'S NULLAH at 1.16 p.m. and capturing a few prisoners and one machine gun. *Orders for Advance.*

The 21st Bn. Manchester Regiment advanced at 12.40 p.m. up VALLEY Trench and BRIGHT ALLEY and established touch with the 2nd Bn. "Queens" Regiment at 1.20 p.m.

In the centre, the 8th Bn. Devonshire Regiment at 6.0 a.m. had advanced up ORCHARD Trench NORTH, and consolidated, and wired this position, the work being completed by noon.

On/

5.

On the left, the 1st Bn. Royal Welsh Fusiliers who had advanced during the night up SUNKEN ROAD TRENCH to WING CORNER were ordered to withdraw to enable the artillery to bombard FRICOURT, preparatory to an advance by the 17th Division. It was, however, evident from the report of patrols that the place was being rapidly evacuated. The bombardment was cancelled and patrols were at once pushed forward. The 20th Bn. Manchester Regiment moved down ORCHARD ALLEY to PAPEN TRENCH gaining touch with the 20th Infantry Brigade. The 1st Rl. Welsh Fusiliers cleared ZINC TRENCH, RECTANGLE SUPPORT and ROSE ALLEY capturing 25 prisoners. Patrols were pushed into FRICOURT: they met with no opposition, and by 12 noon the 17th Division had begun to advance. The line was then organised and consolidated as follows:-

On the right QUEEN'S NULLAH was held by the 2nd Bn. "The Queen's" Regiment: VALLEY TRENCH and North part of BRIGHT ALLEY by the 21st Bn. Manchester Regiment. The 22nd Bn. Manchester Regiment and 1st Bn. South Staffordshire Regiment were in support, two companies of the 2nd. Bn. Royal Irish Regiment having rejoined the 22nd Infantry Brigade.

In the centre, the 2nd Bn Gordon Highlanders held the N.W. Corner of MAMETZ, with the 8th Bn. Devonshire Regiment on their left along SUNKEN ROAD - B.H.90 - ORCHARD TRENCH North - ORCHARD, and touch was established with the 17th Division at WILLOW TRENCH at 7-0 p.m. The remaining battalions, the 9th Bn. Devonshire Regiment and the 2nd Bn. Border Regiment, were in Brigade Reserve, the 2nd Bn. Royal Warwickshire Regiment having rejoined the 22nd Infantry Brigade.

On the left, the 1st Bn. Royal Welsh Fusiliers held ROSE ALLEY which they consolidated, the remainder of the Brigade being in Divisional Reserve.

Consolidation.   The whole of the line was consolidated and strongly wired.

July 3rd.   During the early morning a patrol was sent out by the 21st Bn. Manchester Regiment to BOTTOM WOOD which was reported unoccupied. This report only reached Brigade Headquarters at 8-45 a.m. The WOOD was then being heavily bombarded previous to an assault by the 17th Division. As soon as the barrage lifted the WOOD was immediately occupied by the 21st Bn. Manchester Regiment who captured three Field Guns, and held the N.E. edge of the WOOD which they at once proceeded to consolidate. A company of the 1st Bn South Staffordshire Regiment moved up on their right and established touch between them and the 2nd Bn. "The Queen's" Regiment. This line was consolidated during the rest of the day. Touch was established at about 5-0 p.m. with the 17th Division on the N.W. corner of BOTTOM WOOD.

The/

The 20th Infantry Brigade front, constituting a Divisional Supporting line, was held by the 8th Bn. Devonshire Regiment: the remainder of the Brigade being withdrawn to the CITADEL while the 22nd Infantry Brigade were concentrated between CAFTET WOOD and MANSEL COPSE, the latter operation being completed by 9-0 a.m.

At night the 2nd Bn. Royal Irish Regiment and the 1st Bn. Royal Welsh Fusiliers were ordered to consolidate a line South edge of MAMETZ WOOD to STRIP TRENCH, Northwards along STRIP TRENCH, WOOD TRENCH, QUADRANGLE TRENCH to its junction with BOTTOM ALLEY. The guide for the 1st Bn. Royal Welsh Fusiliers lost his way and the battalion did not arrive until daylight was breaking. The 2nd Bn. Royal Irish Regiment penetrated into MAMETZ WOOD, and killed some 50 Germans and removed the breech blocks from two Field Guns. Orders however, having been received from higher authority that the Division was not to become heavily engaged at this point, the battalions concerned were withdrawn to their bivouacs near MANSEL COPSE.

Throughout the day the Division was engaged in collecting the arms, ammunition and equipment abandoned by the enemy, and in burying the dead.   <u>July 4th.</u>

At 12-0 noon orders were received that the line allotted to the 1st Bn. Royal Welsh Fusiliers and the 2nd Bn. Royal Irish Regiment on the previous night was again to be attacked and consolidated.

The Artillery Brigade to whom the duty of cutting the wire in front of WOOD TRENCH was allotted, failed to fulfil its task. This was not reported until 6-45 pm and the 35th Brigade R.F.A. under very adverse conditions, worked at the highest pressure to clear the wire.

The assault took place at 12-45 a.m. after very   <u>July 5th</u>
heavy rain. The left company 1st Bn. Royal Welsh Fusiliers in touch with the 7th Bn Northumberland Fusiliers (17th Division), entered QUADRANGLE TRENCH and sent a bombing party to their right. The right company lost touch and was held up by wire: two platoons were sent up to close the gap and entered the trench.

Meanwhile, the 2nd Bn. Royal Irish Regiment attacked WOOD TRENCH across the open, and bombed up STRIP TRENCH for about 150 yards. The company attacking WOOD TRENCH was held up by wire and enfiladed by Machine Gun fire, while a heavy counter-attack drove back the bombing party. Two further attacks launched by the O.C. 2nd Bn. Royal Irish Regiment were held up by wire in the same way. By this time (5-0 a.m.) the 1st Bn. Royal Welsh Fusiliers were firmly established, and the 2nd Bn Royal Irish Regiment was withdrawn under cover of artillery fire and a Smoke barrage. The 1st Bn. Royal Welsh Fusiliers secured QUADRANGLE TRENCH and cleared QUADRANGLE ALLEY to the trench junction half-way to QUADRANGLE SUPPORT, where they made a block, and successfully repelled two counter-attacks.

During the afternoon and evening the Division was relieved by the 38th Division and moved to rest billets at HEILLY, RIBEMONT, BUIRE and TREUX.

Artillery/

Page 7.

Artillery. The services rendered by the Divisional Artillery were admirable throughout the operations. The wire was very well cut, although in places it presented exceptional difficulties. The fact that the wire was so thoroughly cut, contributed very materially to the successful advance of the Division. Very close co-operation was constantly maintained by F.O.O's. with the advancing infantry. The evidence of prisoners proves conclusively the extreme accuracy of our Artillery fire.

R.E. Field Companies were admirably handled. They were not sent up until the position to be consolidated had been definitely secured by the advancing infantry, and in consequence suffered very few casualties, while they rendered invaluable service in constructing strong points, in opening roads and in wiring the line. Shallow Mine Tunnels constructed by the Tunnelling Companies, proved of the greatest service, both as communication trenches, and as shelter for telephone wires.

Medical Services. Were admirably carried out, the evacuation of our own and the enemy's wounded proceeding without a hitch throughout the operations. The German prisoners very readily offered themselves as stretcher bearers.

Supply. The supply services were excellent in every way. Rations reached the most advanced troops by 1-0 a.m. on the night 1st/2nd July, and the flow of ammunition and bombs was constantly maintained.

Prisoners. During the operations about 1,600 prisoners, including 25 Officers, were captured by the Division.

Booty.
4 Field Guns.
1 Naval Gun.
10 Machine Guns.
7 Automatic Rifles.
6 Trench Mortars.
4 Minenwerfers.
6 Canister throwers.
besides a large number of rifles, were captured.

A great amount of ammunition, bombs, and stores of clothing and food, fell into our hands. In addition the breech blocks were removed from two Field Guns at the South end of HAMETZ WOOD.

General. From the evidence of prisoners there can be no doubt that the enemy's morale has been very severely shaken. They have been unanimous in stating that, had it not been for their deep dug-outs, it would have been impossible for them to hold the line in the face of our sustained bombardment.

"P" Bombs were of great service both during the preliminary bombardment and at the moment of assault. They proved far more serviceable than MILL'S Grenades in clearing deep dug-outs: they were also used very successfully in covering the retirement of bombing parties and patrols.

Casualties. The total number of casualties for the Division were:-

Officers	Other ranks.
151	3,873

7th Division.
======================

NARRATIVE OF OPERATIONS FROM 11TH TO 20TH JULY, 1916.
****

Reference
    Trench Maps 1/20,000 and MONTAUBAN and MARTINPUICH Sheets.

          On July the 9th the Divisional Commander moved to
GROVETOWN to direct the operations of the 38th Division
against MAMETZ WOOD which was finally captured and
consolidated, after severe fighting, on the night of the 11th.
On that day, after a week's rest at TREUX, Divisional
Headquarters were moved to MINDEN POST. Brigade Headquarters
were established as follows:-

        20th Infantry Brigade - POMMIERS REDOUBT

        22nd Infantry Brigade - Near WHITE TRENCH, point
                                    S.25.b.8.6.
        91st Infantry Brigade - At the HALT, point F.10.b.
                                    05.65.

          A portion of MONTAUBAN VALLEY was taken over from
the XIII Corps, and was held by the 2nd Gordon Highlanders
and six guns of the Brigade Machine Gun Company. In addition
to this, the Division took over from the 38th Division, the
front from the East of MAMETZ WOOD (exclusive) - CATERPILLAR
WOOD - MARLBOROUGH WOOD (inclusive). This line was held
by the 9th Bn. Devonshire Regt.

          CATERPILLAR WOOD itself proved to be untenable
owing to very heavy shell fire, and the battalion therefore
established itself on the Northern Bank of CATERPILLAR
VALLEY with a line of outposts on the slope above the
bank, and with one platoon and two machine guns in
MARLBOROUGH WOOD.

          On the night of the 12th orders were received that
the Fourth Army would co-operate with the French to the
South, and the Reserve Army to the North, in an attack on
the enemy's second line to take place at dawn on the 14th.

          To the XV Corps was allotted the enemy's line
from S.15.c.15.40. to the South-west corner of BAZENTIN-le-
PETIT WOOD; the front from S.15.c.15.40. to S.14.a.7.3. was
apportioned to the 7th Division, with the 21st Division on
its left and the 3rd Division, XIII Corps, on its right;
the bounderies being, on the right, S.20.d.90.35.- junction
of roads S.14.d.90.15.- East edge of BAZENTIN-le-GRAND WOOD -
N.E. Corner of CEMETERY inclusive, on the left, S.19.central
- Road from East corner of MAMETZ WOOD S.20.a.1.8.- Road
junction S.14.b.1.5.- Road along East of BAZENTIN-le-PETIT
WOOD towards MARTINPUICH, road inclusive.
          In compliance with these instructions the 20th In
Infantry Brigade was ordered to assault the enemy's second
line, with the 22nd Infantry Brigade in support,

                                                    the/

the 91st Infantry Brigade being in Divisional Reserve.

The objectives assigned were as follows:-

1. The enemy's front line between point S.15.a.15.40 and the road at S.14.a.70.35.

2. The enemy's support line from S.15.a.15.10. to point in BAZENTIN-le-GRAND WOOD where CIRCUS TRENCH turns Northwards, thence due West to edge of WOOD.

3. The whole of BAZENTIN-le-GRAND WOOD.

This was the final objective allotted to the 20th Infantry Brigade.

From this line the 22nd Infantry Brigade was ordered to capture BAZENTIN-le-PETIT Village East of the MARTINPUICH Road, Road inclusive, and the CEMETERY, and to establish a line from S.15.a.20.95. through the CEMETERY to the Northern exit of BAZENTIN-le-PETIT Village, there establishing touch with the 21st Division.

The 22nd Infantry Brigade was also ordered, in the event of the 21st Division being delayed in BAZENTIN-le-PETIT WOOD, to capture and consolidate that portion of BAZENTIN-le-PETIT Village lying on the West of the MARTINPUICH Road.

Accordingly on the afternoon of the 13th, the 2nd Bn. Gordon Highlanders moved up to a position of readiness in the vicinity of the HAMMER HEAD of MAMETZ WOOD - point S.19.b.8.4.,-where they dug themselves in.
The 8th Bn. Devonshire Regt and the 2nd Border Regt deployed on their right during the evening, on the slopes North of CATERPILLAR VALLEY with their left resting on FLAT IRON COPSE and their right extending across MARLBOROUGH TRENCH. During the night the 2nd Bn. Rl. Irish Regiment and the 1st Bn. Rl. Warwickshire Regt, 22nd Infantry Brigade, also moved up to a position of readiness in the Hammer Head of MAMETZ WOOD. These operations were conducted with conspicuous skill and success.

A heavy bombardment of the enemy's second line was maintained throughout the day, all observation tending to prove that the wire was being cut most efficiently.

At daybreak on the 14th, under cover of this bombardment the assaulting companies of the 8th Bn. Devonshire Regiment and the 2nd Bn. Border Regiment moved up to within striking distance of the enemy's line.

At 3-20 a.m. intense artillery fire was developed and at 3-25 a.m. the barrage was lifted to BAZENTIN-le-PETIT and BAZENTIN-le-GRAND WOODS, and the two assaulting battalions attacked and captured the enemy's line almost at the moment of the lift.

Up to this point the losses had been very slight, the enemy's wire and trenches having been completely destroyed

by/

by our bombardment, and the assault having been delivered in the closest co-operation with the artillery.

The assaulting Companies moved straight on to the second line, which they entered simultaneously with the lift of the barrage at 3.35 a.m. Once again very little resistance was encountered. Many dead Germans were found, and the enemy appears to have been completely surprised both by the short period during which our intensive bombardment lasted, and by the rapidity with which the assaulting companies launched their attack.

There were a few dug-outs in both lines, one in particular, a long tunnel dug-out, containing many of the enemy. This was bombed at one end, a Lewis gun covering the further exit. Both lines were completely clear by 4 a.m. and the assaulting troops lay down until 4.25 a.m. when the barrage was lifted off BAZENTIN-le-GRAND WOOD, which in its turn was quickly cleared. Close touch and co-operation were continuously maintained with the 9th Brigade (3rd Division) on the right, and a considerable number of prisoners were captured in both lines of trenches and in the WOOD, among them being included a Colonel of the LEHR Regiment.

A line in front of the WOOD was then occupied and consolidated, with a support line in the WOOD itself. Machine guns were brought forward, and Pioneers and R.E. detachments came up to construct strong points and to establish Machine gun emplacements.

In the meanwhile the 2nd Bn. Rl. Warwickshire Regiment, (22nd Brigade) had passed through and had taken CIRCUS Trench with no opposition.

The 2nd Rl. Irish Regiment of the same Brigade then advanced to the attack of BAZENTIN-le-PETIT Village, one Company attacking the Village, one Company moving on the CEMETERY, and one Company forming a defensive flank along the East of BAZENTIN-le-PETIT WOOD, with the fourth Company in Battalion Reserve.

The assaulting Company entered the Village immediately the barrage lifted, a few casualties being caused by our own fire, and captured the Officer (Colonel) Commanding the garrison, and about 100 men, none of whom had emerged from the shelter of their dug-outs.

By 7.30 a.m. the 2nd Rl. Irish Regiment had captured the Village, by 8.15 the CEMETERY was taken, and a patrol with a Lewis gun was sent to seize the WINDMILL, the task being accomplished without difficulty.

Meanwhile, as there was some enfilade fire from BAZENTIN-le-PETIT WOOD, the company in Battalion Reserve was sent into the Southern end of the WOOD to clear up the situation. After locating the 110th Brigade - 21st Division - it returned to its own Battalion.

The Company forming the defensive flank then established connection with men of the Leicester Regiment (110th Brigade) who occupied the Northern edge of BAZENTIN-le-PETIT WOOD. Touch, however, was difficult to maintain as

the/

the troops in the WOOD were continually forced to withdraw from the Northern end by shell fire; they suffered severe casualties, inspite of which they always returned to the line, but their action necessarily made the situation on the flank of the 2nd Rl. Irish Regiment very uncertain, and at 9.45 a.m. the Commanding Officer reported that a counter-attack from the Northern edge of BAZENTIN-le-PETIT WOOD was threatening.

Meanwhile one Company of the 2nd Bn. Rl. Warwickshire Regiment moved from the Northern end of BAZENTIN-le-GRAND WOOD along the gully running to the East of BAZENTIN-le-GRAND Village. On reaching the cross-roads at the Northern end of the Village they found some dead Northumberland Fusiliers and some dead Germans. The enemy was discovered to be holding the orchards and ditches to the North and North-east of the Village, and was receiving re-inforcements from the direction of HIGH WOOD. A scout (Sergeant Pulteney) was sent to establish touch with the 1st Northumberland Fusiliers (3rd Division) and to inform them of the situation. While returning to his Company this N.C.O. located a German machine gun in a cellar; he entered the cellar, killed the only German there, and found four Machine guns.

A joint attack was then organised to clear the orchards and ditches. A stokes gun with the Northumberland Fusiliers did excellent work, and the Germans were driven out. A counter-attack was initiated at once from the direction of HIGH WOOD, but failed to materialize, as the Warwicks lined the SUNKEN ROAD running North from the WINDMILL, thereby commanding the enemy's line of advance.

In the meanwhile the Officer Commanding the 2nd Royal Irish Regiment received a written message from troops on his left asking for assistance. He accordingly despatched one company and some bombers to their aid, subsequently sending a platoon from the company forming the defensive flank along the East of BAZENTIN-le-PETIT WOOD. These troops were not seen again as a formed body for the rest of the day, and the situation in the WOOD remained obscure. The General Officer Commanding the 22nd Infantry Brigade then asked permission to send forward the 1st Bn. Royal Welsh Fusiliers to clear up the position and to render the left flank of the 2nd Rl. Irish Regiment secure. At this time, however, the 2nd Rl. Irish Regiment the 21st Division considered the situation well in hand.

Simultaneously with the counter-attack from HIGH WOOD an attack in force was developed from the North against the Northern edge of the Village and WOOD and against the WINDMILL. The line was penetrated and the WINDMILL captured, but the garrison at the 5 road junction - S.8.b. 57.85 - and of the road thence to the CEMETERY succeeded in holding out.

When the North-east of the Village was first occupied the 54th Field Company, R.E. and two companies 24th Bn. Manchester Regiment (Pioneers) were sent forward

to/

5.

to consolidate the position.
Their work was carried out under very great difficulties, as they were continually harassed by machine gun and rifle fire from BAZENTIN-le-PETIT WOOD, and at noon, when the enemy's counter-attack was temporarily successful, the 54th Field Company retired to the South end of the Village. The 24th Bn. Manchester Regiment completed the strong point at the CEMETERY and consolidated a "keep" in the centre of BAZENTIN-le-PETIT Village. During most of the day they were engaged in defending this position and suffered severe casualties.

While the enemy's counter-attack was in progress a crowd of men of several regiments, including the 2nd Bn. Royal Irish Regiment, came out of the WOOD and withdrew to the southern end of the Village where they were halted and reformed by Captain Lowe, Adjutant of the 2nd Bn. Royal Irish Regiment. This Officer then led an assault against a party of Germans who had penetrated between the WINDMILL and the CEMETERY and were advancing against the Village, from the East. This was completely successful and the whole of the Germans were destroyed. The party then extended along the Southern edge of BAZENTIN-le-PETIT WOOD through which they advanced in open order. They found a line along the northern face of the clearing S.8.central - composed of men from several units; through this they advanced and finally gained the northern face of the WOOD, where they found many dead men of the Leicester Regiment, but no troops in the shallow trench which had been commenced early in the day. This they occupied and held with a few men until relieved later by the 2nd Bn. Gordon Highlanders.

Simultaneously with this advance, a company of the 2nd Bn. Royal Warwickshire Regiment moved up from CIRCUS TRENCH through the Village and after severe fighting succeeded in bombing the enemy back. In their retirement the Germans came under fire from a Lewis Gun posted at the 5 cross roads-S.8.b.57.85.- and were exterminated.

At 1-0 p.m. a company of the 21st Bn. Manchester Regt. (91st Infantry Brigade) was sent up to support the 2nd Bn Royal Irish Regiment on the CEMETERY - WINDMILL line, and at about 2-0 p.m. a counter-attack was organised by the 1st Rl. Welsh Fusiliers on this line. By 3-0 p.m. the enemy was driven out and the line was firmly held for the rest of the day, the 21st Manchesters returning to their own battalion.

At 5-0 p.m. the 2nd Bn. Gordon Highlanders, 20th Infantry Brigade, who had been sent forward to clear up the general situation, both in the WOOD and the North of the Village, ascertained from their scouts that neither the North-east portion of BAZENTIN-le-PETIT WOOD nor the North-west portion of BAZENTIN-le-PETIT Village were occupied by our troops. These areas were cleared by that Battalion by 6-30 p.m. and 22 prisoners were taken. Touch was established with the Leicester Regiment on the left, but on the right a gap existed in the line as far as the CEMETERY. Shortly after 7-0 p.m. this gap was filled by two companies of the 20th Bn. Manchester Regiment,

and/

6.

and the Gordon Highlanders were relieved a little later.

During the night the line from the North-east corner of BAZENTIN-le-PETIT Village to the Northern point of BAZENTIN-le-GRAND Village was taken over by the 2nd Bn. Royal Warwickshire Regiment and the 1st Bn. Rl. Welsh Fusiliers.

On the night 15/16th the Brigade was relieved by the 98th Infantry Brigade, but at noon on the 16th the 20th Bn. Manchester Regiment re-occupied the line from the WINDMILL to the cross-roads North of BAZENTIN-le-GRAND Village, the line held by the Brigade being subsequently extended along the road running from HIGH WOOD to the North-west corner of BAZENTIN-le-GRAND Village.

In view of the possibility of a further advance in co-operation with the 2nd Indian Cavalry Division, the 91st Infantry Brigade had been ordered to establish itself East of MAMETZ WOOD during the morning of the 14th, and by 12 noon the Brigade was concentrated in FLAT IRON VALLEY.

At 3.20 p.m. orders were issued to this Brigade to seize and consolidate HIGH WOOD. The hour of assault was fixed at 6.15 p.m., after half an hour's artillery preparation. Some delay, however, took place, as the 91st Infantry Brigade expected to be in touch with a Brigade of the 33rd Division on its left. The 2nd Bn. "Queens" Regiment and 1st Bn. South Staffordshire Regiment, therefore, did not advance from FLAT IRON VALLEY until 6.45 p.m., 2 Regiments of the 2nd Indian Cavalry Division - 7th Dragoon Guards and 20th Deccan Horse - co-operating on their right flank.

Brigade Headquarters were established at the South-east corner of MAMETZ WOOD S.19.d. 7.8.

Little opposition was met with during the early stages of the advance; but as the two Battalions approached HIGH WOOD they were enfiladed by machine guns from SWITCH Trench on their left, and a counter-attack in force was launched from the West of HIGH WOOD. This was repulsed, but progress was considerably delayed, and it was not until 8.40 p.m. that the WOOD was entered.

During the advance 3 field guns, one machine gun, and 100 prisoners were captured.

In the meanwhile two Battalions of the 100th Infantry Brigade, 33rd Division, had been sent forward from MAMETZ WOOD at 7.45 p.m. to co-operate on the left of the 91st Infantry Brigade. Touch was established at 12.30 a.m. on the 15th, and the work of clearing the WOOD was carried on without intermission during the night.

The 1/3rd Durham Field Company with 100 men of the 22nd Bn. Manchester Regiment as a carrying party, were sent forward at about 10.0 p.m., and strong points, in which Machine guns were mounted, were consolidated at S.4.c.8.0. and S.4.d. 3.8. By the morning the whole of the WOOD South of a line running

East/

east and west through S.4.central was held; but in spite of every effort the sections told off to consolidate strong points at the west and north corners of the WOOD found it impossible to carry out their tasks and became involved in heavy fighting.

During the night the 21st Bn. Manchester Regiment was pushed up to the south of HIGH WOOD and held a line on the road running south to point S.16.a. 5.9. At 4 a.m. one company was sent forward to occupy the road running south-east from point S.4.c. 8.0 and touch was obtained on the right with the XIII Corps near LONGUEVAL. The other three companies of the battalion were withdrawn into Brigade Reserve. At about the same time the two cavalry regiments, which had been operating upon each flank, were also withdrawn.

During the day of the 15th several local attacks were made by the Brigade with the object of securing the whole of the WOOD; no success, however, was achieved, as the enemy held SWITCH TRENCH and the north-west corner of the WOOD in force, and were able to bring enfilade fire from machine guns to bear. The same cause prevented the 33rd Division from advancing on the left of the Brigade.

At 2.30 p.m. the enemy counter-attacked, and a heavy artillery barrage was directed on the southern portion of the WOOD. Our troops were forced for a time to give ground, but the Brigade Reserve - three companies, 21st Manchester Regiment, and two companies 22nd Manchester Regiment - were at once sent forward to the attack, and succeeded in re-occupying the original line.

At 4.45 p.m. a artillery barrage was developed on the enemy portion of the WOOD. This was closely followed by assaulting infantry, but once again machine gun fire from SWITCH TRENCH and cross roads at S.3.b. 8.2 made it impossible to advance, and the original line through the centre of the WOOD was re-occupied.

During the evening, the enemy made local attacks which were easily repulsed. The general situation, however, was unsatisfactory and confused. Shelling had been continuous; there had been constant fighting in thick undergrowth, detachments had lost their bearings, and had failed to maintain touch with their own units. Small bodies of other formations had also entered the WOOD, and organisation, whether for attack or defence, had become a matter of great difficulty.

By this time also it had become evident that until SWITCH TRENCH was clear of the enemy the effective occupation of HIGH WOOD was impossible, owing to the heavy enfilade fire, both by machine guns and artillery, which could be directed on it.

Losses were out of all proportion to results, and at 11.15 p.m. orders were issued to withdraw before dawn on the morning of the 16th, so as to enable the whole of the WOOD to be re-bombarded. The withdrawal was successfully carried out, and by 8 a.m. the Brigade was concentrated in the HALT VALLEY, after losing 41 officers and 1,176 other ranks.

No.

8.

No further operations were undertaken by the Division until the dawn of the 20th.

The situation in DELVILLE WOOD and the northern end of LONGUEVAL had, in the meantime, become very involved, and it was hoped to relieve hostile pressure by an attack on HIGH WOOD and the roads running south-west to LONGUEVAL from S.4.c. 9.0 and S.4.d. 2.8.

To the 33rd Division was allotted the attack on HIGH WOOD; the task of the 7th Division being to capture and consolidate the roads, and to obtain touch with the 5th Division at the junction of roads point S.10.d. 85.85, and at the junction of roads point S.11.c. 45.80.

The 20th Infantry Brigade was ordered to carry out this attack, the 2nd Bn. Gordon Highlanders being on the left, and the 8th Bn. Devonshire Regiment on the right. The 2nd Bn. R. Warwickshire Regiment was attached to the Brigade for this operation. The assaulting Battalions were deployed with four platoons each in extended order in the front line, followed by four platoons in similar formation at one hundred yards distance, one company of each Battalion was entrenched in support, and one company held as Battalion reserve.

The enemy maintained a heavy artillery barrage from the commencement of our bombardment, which, owing to the difficulty of observation our own artillery lacked its usual accuracy and caused some casualties to the assaulting Battalions. In spite of this, however, the line moved on and the first objective was occupied at zero hour - 3.35 a.m. - without opposition, apart from the heavy artillery fire. Up to this point, the enemy had no direct observation of the advance, the ground to the east being covered with thick crops, and the road itself being on the reverse side of the slope. Touch was at once established with the 5th Division and the line passed on to its second objective. This was at a distance of approximately 500 yards; the Brigade on the left, theoretically in touch with the 2nd Bn. Gordon Highlanders, had to advance through HIGH WOOD. Only ten minutes, however, was allotted before the barrage on the second objective was lifted, with the result that when the assaulting troops reached the road, some twenty minutes later, heavy machine gun and rifle fire was opened from strong points on the road and in the crops, and from SWITCH TRENCH, east of HIGH WOOD, on which no barrage was maintained. Our own artillery fire continued to be short, and the Brigade attacking HIGH WOOD found it impossible to advance. The assaulting Battalions were in consequence subjected to very severe machine gun fire from the WOOD on their left rear as soon as they attempted to dig themselves in.

For upwards of an hour the attempts to dig in on this line, some 25 yards west of the road, continued; on the left, however, the 2nd Bn. Gordon Highlanders suffered very heavy casualties; in the two leading platoons only one wounded officer and 5 men remained, and eventually the whole line crawled back in small groups to the first
objective,

objective, which was now being consolidated by the companies in support and reserve.

It was at first intended to re-bombard the second objective, and to attack again. A very careful reconnaissance of the position made it clear, however, that until SWITCH TRENCH was neutralised and HIGH WOOD captured, an attack by daylight was doomed to failure. Under these circumstances the easternmost road from the south corner of HIGH WOOD was consolidated and held.

The situation in HIGH WOOD on the left continued most confused throughout the day, but at 8 p.m. that night it was believed to be clear of the enemy.

At 9.30 p.m. the relief of the 20th Infantry Brigade by the 13th Infantry Brigade commenced. While this relief was in progress the enemy made a strong counter-attack on HIGH WOOD and placed a very heavy artillery barrage on the ground to the south and west. During this bombardment Lieut.-Colonel GORDON, Commanding the 2nd Bn. Gordon Highlanders, was killed. Apart from this very serious loss, the relief was smoothly carried out and casualties were few. The 22nd Infantry Brigade was relieved at the same time by the 100th Infantry Brigade and both Brigades were withdrawn to DERNANCOURT early the following morning.

ARTILLERY.

The wire-cutting in front of the enemy's second line between MAMETZ WOOD and BAZENTIN-le-PETIT WOOD, as also on the whole of the Divisional objective, was admirably carried out. No wire at all was left and the accuracy of the fire was most marked.

Immediately this line was captured, Horse and Field Artillery and Howitzers were pushed up with great boldness to FLAT IRON VALLEY, CATERPILLAR VALLEY, and to positions immediately South and South-west of MAMETZ WOOD. They remained in action throughout the period covered by this report, though continuously enfiladed by the enemy's heavy artillery, and under constant fire from Gas and Lachrymatory shells.

During the operations against HIGH WOOD and the roads connecting it with LONGUEVAL, no observation of fire was obtainable either by F.O.O's or, owing to weather conditions, by balloons or aeroplanes. When these positions were assaulted it was found, in consequence, that the wire had not been sufficiently cut and that artillery barrages, for the first time during these operations, did not work with perfect smoothness. In the attack on HIGH WOOD, also, the increased angle of elevation rendered necessary by the height of the trees made close co-operation with the Infantry impossible, enfilade fire not being obtainable.

Observation of fire on SWITCH TRENCH was equally impossible and the enemy was, in consequence, able with comparative ease constantly to re-inforce the troops holding the portion of SWITCH TRENCH running through HIGH WOOD itself. Every effort was made by F.O.O's to observe the result of fire, and it was owing to no fault of the Artillery personnel that, for the first time, their operations were not entirely successful.

R.E.

Somewhat heavy casualties were suffered both during the consolidation of BAZENTIN-le-PETIT Village and during the attack by the 91st Infantry Brigade on HIGH WOOD.

In each case reports were received from the assaulting Battalions that the positions had been won and that R.E. were required to establish strong points; but in both instances it would appear that the request for R.E. personnel was submitted before consolidation was sufficiently advanced to warrant their despatch. Under the circumstances both the R.E. and the Pioneer Battalion did admirable work, although suffering heavy casualties while holding positions against counter-attacks.

In the case of BAZENTIN-le-PETIT Village, the work of consolidation was much delayed, while in HIGH WOOD the R.E. were not able to carry out the task allotted to them, and became merely fighting men.

On the other hand the consolidation of BAZENTIN-le-GRAND WOOD proceeded with perfect smoothness, as the assaulting infantry had already definitely secured the position before the R.E. allotted for the task were sent up.

Medical/

MEDICAL SERVICES.

The evacuation of wounded presented no great difficulty except in the case of the withdrawal of the 91st Infantry Brigade from HIGH WOOD and of the 2nd Bn. Gordon Highlanders and the 8th Bn. Devonshire Regiment from the road running from the East point of HIGH WOOD to LONGUEVAL.

In both cases regimental stretcher-bearers and R.A.M.C. personnel rendered devoted service. The wounded were evacuated under very heavy shell fire and very great credit is due to the Officers and men concerned.

SUPPLY SERVICES.

Supply services continued excellent in every way. Even under the heaviest fire the supply of rations and ammunition was constantly maintained.

PRISONERS.

During the operations about 300 prisoners, including two Colonels, were captured by the Division.

BOOTY.

2 Heavy Howitzers.
4 Field Guns.
5 Machine Guns.
1 Trench Mortar.
3 Automatic Rifles.
besides many rifles and much ammunition were captured.

CASUALTIES.

The total casualties from July 14th to July 21st were:-

Officers			Other Ranks		
K.	W.	M.	K.	W.	M.
23	106	5.	298	2,164	817.

GENERAL.

It seems clear that the remarkable success of the attack on the enemy's second line was due almost entirely to the admirable co-operation between Artillery and Infantry. The assaulting Companies entered the enemy's front and support lines simultaneously with the lift of the barrage, and while it is possible that a few casualties may have occurred from our own artillery fire, it is at the same time true that practically no loss was incurred either from hostile machine gun or rifle fire.

Similarly the ease with which BAZENTIN-le-PETIT Village was at first occupied was due to the same causes, the assaulting infantry advancing to the attack immediately under the fire of our own artillery; while the subsequent heavy fighting in which the assaulting Battalions were involved was entirely due to the difficulty experienced by the troops attacking BAZENTIN-le-PETIT WOOD, owing to the fact that our own artillery could not maintain an effective barrage against counter-attacks. The same situation arose at HIGH WOOD during the day of the 15th, and in the attack on the road running from the East corner of HIGH WOOD to LONGUEVAL on the morning of the 20th, our own artillery being unable to prevent the massing of hostile infantry under cover of a heavy artillery barrage.

It would appear from these operations that when Artillery and Infantry can act in close co-operation, and when the result of artillery fire can be accurately observed, there is no very great difficulty in occupying and consolidating the enemy's line. If, however, observation of artillery fire cannot be obtained, and co-operation between the two arms is, in consequence, not perfect, it may still be possible to drive an infantry attack home to its objective, but it appears very doubtful whether the positions gained are capable of consolidation against observed hostile artillery fire covering the assault of hostile infantry.

Report on part taken by the 2nd BORDER Regt.
in the engagement by MAMETZ on the 1st July 1916.

On the night of the night of the 30th June/1st July 1916
The 2nd BORDER Regt. moved up from MORLAN=
COURT & took up a position in B2 Sector of
the Trenches. The move was completed at about
1.30 a.m. on the 1st July 1916.
The Battalion was formed up as follows.

1st LINE
{
Right: "A" Coy. under Lieut G.M.F. PRYNNE
occupying RESERVE TRENCH from 70St.
to 71St.

Left: "C" Coy. under Capt. L.A. NEWTON
occupying RESERVE TRENCH from
71st up to about 72St. in ALBERT St.
}

2nd LINE
{
Right: "B" Coy. under Lieut R.F. MILLARD
~~occupying~~ having 2 Platoons in ALBERT St. on
N.W. of 70 St. +
2 Platoons in WELLINGTON Redt.

Left: "D" Coy. ~~2 Platoons~~ Lieut P.N. FRASER.
having 2 Platoons in ALBERT St. from
junction of WEBB St. to the left.
2 Platoons in WELLINGTON Redt.
}

Battalion Hd Quarters
Hd Qr Bombers
Signallers   } WELLINGTON
2 Lewis Guns in Reserve   REDOUBT.
Bn AID Post

Whilst the Artillery Bombardment of the hostile line continued the Battalion was subjected to a heavy bombardement in retaliation from the enemy but as this was mostly directed at our front & support lines little damage was done.

At 7.27 am the Battalion advanced in 4 lines from our trenches in the following order:—

1st Line { Right: 2 Platoons of "A" Coy.
          Left: 2   "   of "C" Coy.

2nd Line { Right: 2 Platoons of "A" Coy.
           Left: 2 Platoons of "C" Coy.
           Three Lewis guns

3rd Line { Right: 2 Platoons of "B" Coy.
           Left: 2 Platoons of "D" Coy.
           Three Lewis guns

4th Line { Right: 2 Platoons of "B" Coy.
or Reserve { Left: 2 Platoons of "D" Coy.
           Two Lewis guns.

Just as our first line had cleared our front trench the head of the Subway from 71ST. toward DANUBE TRENCH was blown out. Less hour.

The Battalion now moved forward until it reached its first objective DANUBE SUPPORT TRENCH. when the left wheel was commenced.

Up till now the casualties were small in the 1st & 2nd finest were caused by a machine gun firing from our right in the direction of GAP. A. in hostile trench

3

& also from one on our left in DANUBE SUPPORT. The wheat was now gradually completed & the advance continued towards our objective APPLE ALLEY. which was reached by our 1st line at about 8.30 a.m. During this advance our line was broken up into a line of groups bombing & bayonetting the enemy, who when they found that their line had been entered formed a new front facing us in shell holes & communication trenches facing us thus checking our advance.

On reaching SHRINE ALLEY the Bn. was temporarily checked through coming under heavy indirect machine gun fire from FRICOURT & enfilade fire from MAMETZ, but on the 1st & 2nd line being reinforced by the 3rd line the advance was continued to HIDDEN LANE. Here the line was again temporarily held up by fire from a M.G. & hostile party in HIDDEN WOOD & another party at about the junction of KIEL SUPPORT & BOIS FRANCAIS SUPPORT. The latter were bombed out without very much difficulty by our party working along KIEL SUPPORT but the former had to be attacked across the open as well as down HIDDEN LANE. This was done by a party organized & led by Lieut. S.T.C. RUSSELL. The advance was now continued to APPLE ALLEY by parties being pushed forward by the 1st & 2nd Lines whilst the 3rd consolidated HIDDEN LANE.

At this time the right of the 4th line moved up

to HIDDEN WOOD so as to strengthen that flank as it was found that the DEVON REGt. had not kept up with the advance of the Bn + this flank was very exposed. The left of the 4th line was still in reserve in KIEL TRENCH close up to junction of HIDDEN LANE.

The Bn was now checked in HIDDEN LANE with posts forward in APPLE ALLEY at junction of it + PEAR TRENCH — ditto BOIS FRANCAIS SUPPORT + also BOIS FRANCAIS TRENCH.

At 2.30 p.m. the 20th MANCHESTER REGt advanced across our front + bombing parties of the BORDER REGt worked along APPLE ALLEY without any opposition. —

At about 5 P.M. APPLE ALLEY was occupied by A+C Companies of the Border Regt with a party of the 8th Devon Regt on the right.

B & D Company 2nd Border R. held HIDDEN WOOD as a support line.

Head Qrs were established in an old Coy Dugout in SUPPORT Trench at its junction with 75 S.

This position was maintained until 8 a.m. on the 3rd July when the Battalion changed its position to BOIS FRANCAIS SUPPORT which was held by B+D Coys with A+C Coys in BOIS FRANCAIS TRENCH.

Bn Hd Qrs remaining in the same position.

Here the Bn remained until the evening of the 3rd July when the Battalion moved down to POST 71.300 in reserve. —

The casualties in the attack were not as heavy as they might have owing, firstly to the splendid way the wire had been cut by T Battery R.H.A. & secondly to the fact that the advance was very close behind the artillery barrage the whole time. During the latter half of the attack the Bn was subjected to a heavy sprinkling of hostile shrapnel which in addition to rifle & machine gun fire & bombs caused the losses sustained. The whole Bn behaved with their usual steadiness & coolness under fire & all orders were strictly carried out. No mistake was made in the advance & the wheel was carried out without any gaps being left in the line, which is entirely due to the care taken by all officers in instructing their NCOs & men in every point regarding the operation & the interest taken by all ranks in it.

The Battalion captured 3 Machine Guns.
           2 Trench Mortars.
           1 Projector
           5 Canister throwers.

The casualties were: 3 officers killed, 7 officers wounded
         92 other ranks killed, 182 ditto wounded
           48 ditto missing.

7.7.16

E. Thorpe Lt Col
Comdg 2nd Border R.

To The Adjutant
2nd Border Regt.

Sir

On the 1st July, 1916, I was in command of A. Company, 2nd Border Regt. At 9.15 P.M. of the previous day, I moved the Company into position in RESERVE TRENCH between 70 trench & 71 trench. The order in which I posted the platoons from right to left was Nos 3, 1, 2, 4.

At 7.27 A.M. Nos 3 & 4 platoons moved forward forming part of the front line, with C. Company on the left & the 9th Devons on the right. About 100 yards in rear of them, I came up with Nos 1 & 2 platoons. The lines advanced in quick time, only losing, at the most, two or three men before reaching the enemy's front line. This was crossed with comparative ease, & a few of the enemy showed themselves first in the SUPPORT LINE. Some of

2.

these were killed or taken prisoners & a few fled down the communication trenches & disappeared. Between the FRONT & SUPPORT lines I passed Lieut O'BRIEN walking back wounded.

From this point the enemy appeared to be scattered all over the field, in small groups or singly, bombing or firing from shell holes or pieces of trench. This had the immediate effect of completely breaking our lines into small parties formed of 1st, 2nd & 3rd lines. These sections had great difficulty in keeping direction & soon I noticed the right of our line was going to the right slightly, while the left wheeled round so far as to be advancing at an angle towards our own lines. I immediately ran & warned an officer leading them, & we returned to find the line distinctly thin on the left. From here we advanced in short rushes, all companies & lines

3. by this time mixed up. I saw 2nd Lieut. LUCAS leading one section here. By the time I had advanced another 50 yds, I found myself with a party of about 20 men held up by a party of Germans to our left & front. We proceeded to advance down a trench towards them, as a bombing section & soon found ourselves in contact with them, & both parties started bombing. We advanced 20 or 30 yds, when bombs began to run short, & as there was no sign of anyone on our right flank or in support the position seemed to be rather serious. Then our shells which had been falling just in front, began to fall short, so I immediately lit some flares on the parapet. This only had the effect of apparently drawing the enemy's fire, which soon grew very intense. I then sent one man back to fetch more bombers & bombs. I also ordered

4. 2nd Lieut MARSH, who joined up with a few men, to man a shell hole to our left which could command a view of the trench from which the enemy were bombing us. I also got a rifle grenade into action from a shell hole on the right. This was soon answered by a small aerial torpedo gun which fired incessantly, & also a "Cannister" battery. Several casualties were caused by this fire, but the enemy although they continued to bomb, did not attempt to advance, & some minutes later a reserve of bombs came up & the trench was cleared & held by a bombing section. I then went round to the right to find connection, & came across a large number of men under 2nd Lieut Holland & 2nd Lieut RUSSELL, holding HIDDEN LANE

From here we could see the DEVONS on the further side of HIDDEN WOOD, but there were a few Germans

5.

apparently in the WOOD itself between our right & the DEVON'S left. 2nd Lieut ROSSELL volunteered to clear them out, & organised two bombing sections who worked down two trenches leading to the front & rear of the wood, & cleared the wood taking a few prisoners, & connecting up with the DEVONS.

This completed our new front line, & we set off to consolidate the trench from BOIS FRANCAIS TRENCH down HIDDEN LANE through HIDDEN WOOD, joining up with the 9th DEVONS.

I also sent forward three bombing sections into APPLE ALLEY one by BOIS FRANCAIS TRENCH, one by LUKE TRENCH & one by HIDDEN WOOD, who found the trench clear.

At 2.30 P.M. we saw the 22nd Brigade pushing past our front.

6.

They took the part of BOIS FRANCAIS TRENCH to our front & attempted to push on, but were held up, & made strong the old German FRONT LINE.

We then worked round & connected up with them, occupying APPLE ALLEY by A & C Companies, & also two Machine Guns which were shortly afterwards brought up. B & D Companies continued consolidating HIDDEN LANE for a SUPPORT LINE.

While this was being carried on, a hostile Machine Gun suddenly opened enfilade fire from the valley, causing several casualties.

This was dealt with by 2nd Lieut LAWLEY who took a bombing party & a Machine Gun, & drove the enemy's gun away causing several casualties.

In this position we remained all night, losing a few

7.

...en through the enemy's heavy gun fire, which fired incessantly on HIDDEN LANE.

This fire ceased in the morning & all day (July 2nd) we strengthened our lines & reorganized the Coys., & collected & dumped ammunition, bombs, etc.

The following morning we took over the lines BOIS FRANCAIS SUPPORT & BOIS FRANCAIS TRENCH by B & D Coys & A & C. Coys. respectively. In the evening the batallion was withdrawn to the CITADEL, in Divisional Reserve.

10.30. A.M.

July 5th/1916.

G.M. Pryme
Lieut
O.C. A Coy.
2nd Border Regt

Report of Part taken in recent fighting by "B" Coy 2nd Bn The Border Regt.

"B" Coy was detailed for the right of the 3rd and fourth line of the advance. The 3rd line consisted of 5 & 7 platoons. The 4th line of 6 & 8. The 3rd line took up position in Wellington redoubt as place of assembly and went over the top at 7:30 am on July 1st 1916. and were followed at 100yds interval by Nos 6 & 8 platoons.

It will be easier from this point to trace the advance of the two lines separately until both became merged in the firing line.

The 3rd line after leaving their trench discovered that A Coy, which Coy they were supporting was making rather slow progress and wheeling too far to the left flank. They did not appear to be in effective touch with the Devons on the right.

2.

When the enemy front line had been reached, 5 & 7 platoons came under considerable rifle and machine gun fire and before Shrine Alley was reached, numerous casualties had occurred, these including 2/Lt D.R. Robertson.

Prisoners had been taken and dugouts bombed in the support lines during passage.

To avoid difficulties that might have arisen a portion of No 5 platoon was moved up to the right of A Coy.

At Shrine the 3rd line became part of the 1st line.

At Hidden Lane B Coy's bombers and Lewis Gunners were of very great value and lost heavily.

4th line of advance. 6 & 8 platoons.
Went over the top from Wellington redoubt trench at 7.32 a.m. 1.7.16. Only about three casualties occurred before arrival at our own front line

3

very great difficulty was experienced in keeping touch with the Devons on our right.

Machine gun & rifle fire were encountered after passing our first line, and in a subsidiary trench behind German 1st line. The first batches of prisoners were taken. Behind German [line?] supporting the wheeling movement was started but was rather too accentuated, the right being left with only very few men, and any connection almost impossible with the Devons, who did not advance as quickly as the right wing of the Border Regt. Result was that Hidden Wood was still occupied by Germans and A & B Coys 2nd Borders were on left in Hidden Lane.

A small party of A Coy still was in front lead of into Hidden Wood and unfortunately was put out of action by a rifle grenade which fell in a shell hole they were occupying, only

only one man escaped being either killed or wounded.

The far man of the Borders on the right of B Coy with some borders found it impossible under the circumstances to enter Hidden Wood any further at this time and concentrated his attention on a party of the enemy about 20 strong on their right flank.

The enemy here attempted a small assault but were eventually put to flight. At this point the Devons came up and took over the position on our right allowing the remainder of the party of B Coy to join up with their company which was with Mr Millard who had been wounded but had not yet gone back. A small bombing post was left at Hidden Wood to hold the corner of the lane where some Germans had also made an attempt to return. This corner of Hidden Wood was a very

difficult position to hold with so few men for about half an hour. Eventually B Coy took up its station in Hidden Lane and consolidated its position.

Thomson 2/Lt
W.W. Hinton 2/Lt

N.B.
The above two officers have compiled this report, as I was not with the Coy at the time, & therefore would not do so myself.

B F Newdigate
Capt
O.C. B Coy
2nd Border Rgt

The Adjutant.
2 Border Regt.

I enclose report on the recent fighting.

E Holland. Lt.
O C C Coy

6/7/16

6/7/16.

Report on the part taken by "C" Company in the recent operations

---

For the attack which was to be launched on the morning of the 1st July the Company was put into position in RESERVE TRENCH between 71 STREET & ALBERT STREET, reaching this trench about 12.30 a m on the 1st July without casualties. The order of platoons from right to left was No 11 platoon under 2nd Lieut E L Holland, No 9 platoon under 2nd Lieut L Mash, No 12 platoon under Sgt Knox & No 10 platoon under 2nd Lieut Ewshaw. There were two Lewis gun teams with the Company. Captain A E Newton was in command of the Company, which was on the extreme left flank of the Division

At 6.30 a.m. began the intense bombardment of the enemies front trenches, which was to last an hour, & at 7.27 the two platoons on the right left RESERVE TRENCH & advanced over the open, followed at a hundred yards by the remaining 2 platoons, the Lewis gun teams advancing in the interval between the two waves.

The forward end of a shallow gallery which had been mined towards the German parapet from our front line at 71 STREET had been timed to be exploded at 7.30 a.m., & as 11 & 9 platoons reached our own front line this was blown, & the barrage lifted from the German front trench.

It is attributed to the Company's having advanced so near its first objective under cover of our own artillery fire, that up to this point not a single casualty had occurred.

Machine gun fire, however, now opened from the right & a number of small land mines were exploded causing the first of our men to fall, but the first & second German lines were crossed with hardly any other opposition, & the leading platoons wheeled to the left making the line of SHRINE ALLEY their new front.

No 10 platoon, on the left of the Company's second wave wheeled to the left at the first German trench & drove out some hostile bombers who were throwing their grenades from behind the right craters. The Lewis gun under L/Cpl Clarke greatly assisted in this act, but unfortunately the entire team, coming under machine gun & rifle fire was shot down. Sgt Knox also fell dead at the same spot, shot through the head. His platoon, No 12, following in rear of the other three, which owing to their wheeling were now in one line, came under the command of Sgt Gronow. All four platoons soon after became merged into one line.

The first serious show of resistance by the opposing infantry began as the Company attacked the two communication trenches, SHRINE ALLEY & KIEL LANE, & from these onwards to our final objective enemy riflemen & bombers, hiding in the innumerable large shell-holes, put up a good fight, breaking up our line to a certain extent, but not checking our advance as the occupied shell-holes were worked round, and their holders shot or bombed.

Captain Newton was well in the lead, encouraging a party of men to oust some Germans as above, & was in the act of shooting one of the latter when he was hit by a bullet in the left hand. The wound was a serious one, half the hand being blown away, & the command of the Company fell to 2nd Lt Holland.

The advance of the line on the left was slower than on the right, German bombers made stubborn stands in KIEL TRENCH, but our bombers drove them out & some 25 of the enemy were captured as they emerged from dug-outs. Other dug-outs were bombed.

At 8.45 am parties of our men reached our final objective, APPLE ALLEY, & smoke candles

flares were lighted there.
Bombing posts were established as follows

(i) At the Junction of JOHN TRENCH & APPLE ALLEY under Sgt Gronow. The remaining "C" Coy Lewis gun was placed here & did excellent work.

(ii) At the Junction of BOIS FRANCAIS SUPPORT & APPLE ALLEY, under 2nd Lieut Holland. It was attempted to block the BOIS FRANCAIS SUPPORT trench forward, but this trench had been so badly knocked about by shell fire ~~that~~ & had become so shallow that the men on this work were shot as they exposed themselves, & this post were employed in firing at the enemy who were holding the un-named trench joining BOIS FRANCAIS & BOIS FRANCAIS SUPPORT trenches about 40 yards to their front.

(iii) At the junction of HIDDEN LANE & BOIS FRANCAIS trenches, with a ~~bom~~ party of three bombers pushed up BOIS FRANCAIS trench (which was blocked) under 2nd Lieut Marsh. This post did very excellent work & was made a target ~~by for~~ by aerial torpedoes & canisters. It constantly repulsed enemy bombers who attempted its dislodgement.

In the mean-time the remainder of the battalion had reached HIDDEN LANE, which they were consolidating. HIDDEN WOOD had not been captured, but 2nd Lt Russell lead down a party of bombers who cleared the wood & a Lewis Gun was put into position to fire down the HIDDEN WOOD valley from HIDDEN LANE protecting the right of the trench. Touch with the battalion on our right seemed to be lost, & it was

43

decided to make HIDDEN LANE as strong as possible & to wait until our right was secure before holding APPLE ALLEY in strength.

At 2.30 pm the 22nd My Brigade attacked across our front, & while the Borde Left party advanced down LUKE TRENCH & along APPLE ALLEY, another party of 6 bombers & 10 men under 2nd Lt Holland proceeded down BOIS FRANCAIS TRENCH & along the unnamed trench mentioned above. There was no opposition but about 20 Germans surrendered. Trench was now garried with the 2.0th Manchester Regt at F10 c 4380. The unnamed trench was watched by 2nd Lt Holland's party & orders were issued for APPLE ALLEY to be garrisoned. Unfortunately the intended garrison was led astray, Sbeing informed by the 9th Devon Regt, which had news come up on our right, that they were holding APPLE ALLEY, it returned to HIDDEN LANE. However this error was soon after put right, APPLE ALLEY occupied & work was done to put it in a state of defense. With the exception of apparently only one heavy gun, which fired at our position at about one minutes interval till the next morning there was no molestation by the enemy.

The Company remained in APPLE ALLEY, from its junction with MARK TRENCH & BOIS FRANCAIS SUPPORT until 8.0 a.m on the morning of the 3/7/16 when it proceeded to BOIS FRANCAIS TRENCH & the same evening to the CITADEL.

I consider the bearing of the Company was at all times most praiseworthy. The casualties wire.

Killed 31.
Wounded 40
Missing 14.

Holland Lt.
OC "C" Coy.

6/7/16.

The Elephant   "Bodil" ky

(Attack Serven Trenches July 1 1916)

The Regiment advanced in four lines kept
the formation till it hit the (C2nd) DANUBE TRENCH
was reached. Here men began to fill up the
front line because within the enemy's entanglements
& mines especially on the left crude enos
hesitate. The regiment crossed DANUBE
TRENCH in a hurry & the wheeling movement
arose of the men pushed to far to the left &
was lost with others [?] from DANUBE
SUPPORT there was rifle & many bombs
were thrown. A machine gun in TIRPITZ
TRENCH & another thought caused several
casualties. The few in TIRPITZ TRENCH were
& I believe it was taken into a dug out by the
Junior. I was in the right [?] with Lea
Lewis Guns which fired repeatedly preventing

the German resistance on the front gathering strength. When we reached SHRINE ALLEY the right of the line turned half left under pressure from the 9th DEVONS. This caused the left of the line to become thicker than the right. A machine gun in HIDDEN WOOD & fire from MAMETZ kept the men from the former place which seemed to inspire a certain amount of fear. Attempts to approach the ravine by bombing up trenches failed as the German defenders were in strong positions amply supplied with bombs & ammunition. 2nd Lt HOLLAND was the first to reach APPLE ALLEY with a few men & he lit red flares. Men with me lit one near the junction of LUKE TRENCH & APPLE ALLEY. As the left was held up & there was no support from the right where the DEVONS did not reach HIDDEN WOOD we withdrew from the shallow trench, APPLE ALLEY & HIDDEN LANE. We then got some shelter from machine gun & rifle fire which came from BOIS FRANCAIS SUPPORT, MARK TRENCH right, HIDDEN WOOD in our rear. At once we proceeded to consolidate HIDDEN LANE & BOIS FRANCAIS SUPPORT under the orders of Lieut. MILLARD who though badly wounded in the arm continued his duties & gave his orders clearly & coolly. There was an attempt by the enemy to collect men along PEAR TRENCH & LUKE TRENCH but Lewis Gun fire drove them off. Interchange of sniping with HIDDEN WOOD was continuous, & as the right battalion was held up some of us pushed the wooded ravine in open order & dislodged the enemy. Some were killed, several were captured & the rest fled. We then organised the forward side of the ravine from a point 100 yards North of MARK TRENCH. During this movement we were subjected to heavy machine gun fire from the direction of MAMETZ. This operation rendered the move forward to APPLE ALLEY much easier, & it cleared the way for the advance of the right hand battalion.

At this point, after seeing that the 5 Lewis guns which had arrived with the first line were in good working order & well supplied with magazines, I returned to Batt'n H.Q. with messages from Lieut. BRYNNE. The men advanced all the time with splendid spirit & endeavoured to consolidate at once. Many tools had been dropped. The men were evidently very fatigued. The smoke barrage during the advance was of the greatest value as it hid us from hostile machine guns.

D.K. Russell 2nd Lt.
Lewis Gun Officer

6/7/16

20th Brigade.

7th Division.

2nd BATTALION

BORDER REGIMENT

AUGUST 1916

War Diary

2nd Battalion Border Regiment

From 1/8/1916 to 31/8/1916.

Army Form C. 2118.

WAR DIARY
INTELLIGENCE SUMMARY.   August 1916.
(Erase heading not required.)

Instructions regarding War Diaries and Intelligence Summaries are contained in F. S. Regs., Part II. and the Staff Manual respectively. Title pages will be prepared in manuscript.

Place	Date	Hour	Summary of Events and Information	Remarks and references to Appendices
BREILLY	1/8/16 to 11/8/16		The Battalion remained in rest billets.	
BREILLY	12/8/16		The Battalion marched to HANGEST and entrained for MERICOURT arriving about 5 p.m. The Battalion then marched to billets at BUIRE.	
BUIRE	13/8/16		The Battalion encamped in a field North of the Church, BUIRE.	
BUIRE	14/8/16 to 31/8/16		The Battalion remained encamped in reserve.	
BUIRE	25/8/16		The Battalion attended a ceremonial parade for the presentation of honours to Officers, NCOs & men of the French Army by the Army Commander. Drafts as under joined the Battalion during the month:- 15/8/16 :- 3 Other Ranks. 21/8/16 :- 11 Other Ranks. The men of these drafts had all served with the Battalion previously. Lieut. W.B. BUTLER and 2nd. Lieut. J.S. WILLOX joined the Battalion on 26/8/16. 38 Other Ranks were evacuated sick during the month. The strength of the Battalion on the last day of the month was 32 Officers 785 Other Ranks.	

_____ Lieut. Colonel.
Commanding 2nd Bn. The Border Regt.

20th Brigade.

7th Division.

WAR DIARY

2nd BATTALION

BORDER REGIMENT

SEPTEMBER 1916

WAR DIARY

2ND. BATTN. BORDER REGIMENT.

From:- 1st. September 1916.

To:- 30th. September 1916.

WAR DIARY

INTELLIGENCE SUMMARY

Army Form C. 2118

Place	Date	Hour	Summary of Events and Information	Remarks and references to Appendices
BUIRE	1/9/16		The Battalion remained encamped N. of the Church, BUIRE.	
"	2/9/16		" " " " " " "	
"	3/9/16		The Battalion was ready formed up to entrain our lorries at 7.15 p.m. but did not actually leave until about 8.30 p.m. On arrival at FRICOURT the Battalion left the lorries & made a temporary halt in a field while rations and bombs were issued, the latter having to be detonated.	
	4/9/16		Major G.E. BEATY-POWNALL was left in charge of the Battalion to bring it on to MONTAUBAN where it arrived just after the 9th Devon Regt at about 2 a.m. on 4th September. New Guides were picked up and the Battn proceeded to BERNAFAY WOOD to pick up tools. On completion of this the move was continued & in a very short time it was found that the Guides had unaltered so the forward move was continued without them. The Battn catching up the 9th DEVON REGT who had also apparently lost their Guides these occurrences considerably delayed the advance. The Battn was under fairly heavy shell fire during this movement. By about 5 AM the Battn was in position as follows:—	
			'A' Company (under CAPT. P.R. DOWDING). :— 2 Platoons in STOUT TRENCH.	
			" " " " " " :— SUPPORT TRENCH. N. of GINCHY AVENUE	
			'B' Company (under CAPT. R.F. NEWDIGATE) :— In SUPPORT TRENCH N. of GINCHY AVENUE.	
			'C' Company (under 2ND. LT. J.A. MALKIN) :— In GINCHY AVENUE.	
			'D' Company (under LIEUT. R.K. EHRENBORG) :— In a trench N. of YORK ALLEY (this was believed to be LONGUEVAL AVENUE.	
			Battalion Headquarters :— At the end of YORK ALLEY.	
			At 10 A.M. on an attack for support from O.C. 9th DEVON REGT A Company was ordered to support this Battn and 2 sections Maxims were ordered up to STOUT TRENCH July by the time this had been done a report was received that the Devons were being forced	

WAR DIARY or INTELLIGENCE SUMMARY

Army Form C. 2118

(PAGE 2)

Place	Date	Hour	Summary of Events and Information	Remarks and references to Appendices
	4/9/16		back by shell and machine gun fire. B. Company remained in position later owing to the Battalion being under heavy shell fire the front was extended a little way along ZZ.TRENCH. The Battn. was under very heavy shell fire all day but owing to the men employed to improve the existing trenches by deepening them the casualties were comparatively few, although very many men were buried. CAPT. R.F.NEWDIGATE and 2ND.LT. J.A.MALKIN were killed during the day and 2ND.LT. S.MARTINDALE missing - believed killed. Late on the evening of the 4th orders were received for 2 Companies to relieve the 12TH. KINGS LIVERPOOL REGT in the GUILLEMONT area. "B" Company under Lieut W.B.BUTLER and "D" Company under Lieut R.K.EHRENBORG moved to the new area at about 11 P.M. Commanded by Lieut-Colonel E.J. de S.THORPE "A" and "C" Companies under Lieut & Adjutant D.STRANGE went back to Reserve in MONTAUBAN REDOUBT where MAJOR G.E. BEATTY-POWNALL took command of they	
	5/9/16		At about 4 a.m. on 5th the 2 Companies completed their relief of the 12TH. KING'S LIVERPOOL REGT. their positions being as follows:- "D" Company in a trench N.W. of GUILLEMONT opposite GINCHY "B" " " " " in support in rear. Batt. Battalion Headquarters in a dug out by NEW TRENCH. On the left of the Battalion were the 2ND. GORDON HIGHLANDERS & on the right the ROYAL MUNSTER FUSILIERS	
	6/9/16		On the 6TH Sept the 2ND GORDON HIGHLANDERS and 9TH DEVONS REGT made two attempts to take GINCHY in front of the trenches held by the Battalion. Although they got into the village they were unable to hold it owing to hostile machine gun and shell fire & had to fall back. The Lewis guns of the Battalion endeavoured to assist the attack by	

1875 Wt. W593/826 1,000,000 4/15 J.B.C. & A. A.D.S.S./Forms/C. 2118.

WAR DIARY or INTELLIGENCE SUMMARY

Army Form C. 2118

(PAGE 3)

Place	Date	Hour	Summary of Events and Information	Remarks and references to Appendices
	8/9/16		lying how advanced positions & continued to do so until but out of action by being being one also being damaged.	
	9/9/16		On the morning of 9th Sep about 2am Bayd D Companies were relieved by 7th ROYAL IRISH RIFLES & moved back to MONTAUBAN where relief of the Battn was gradually completed at 11AM - after which the Battn re-assembled in Trones South of FRICOURT Casualties 3/9/16 to 11/9/16 :- CAPT R.F.NEWDIGATE and 2ND LT: J.A.MALKIN Killed 4/9/16. 2ND LT: S.MARTINDALE Wounded (Relieved killed) 4/9/16. 2ND LT: J.S.WILLOX. Shell Shock 4/9/16. Other Ranks :- KILLED :- 10 WOUNDED :- 52 MISSING :- 3 SHELL SHOCK 14. TOTAL :- 79.	
BUIRE	9/9/16		The Battalion marched to BUIRE starting at 1-30am and on arrival occupied North of the Church BUIRE	
AIRAINES	10/9/16 to 16/9/16		The Battalion marched to ALBERT starting at 4-45am* and entrained at 10-30am for AIRAINES arriving at about 4pm. The Battalion remained in no Billets battalion training being carried out.	
AIRAINES	17/9/16		The Battalion marched to LONGPRE and entrained at 10-45pm for BAILLEUL	
BAILLEUL	18/9/16		On arrival at BAILLEUL the Battalion marched to billets at NIEPPE and PONT DE NIEPPE arriving at about 12 noon.	
	19/9/16		(Reference Maps :- BELGIUM & FRANCE Sheet 28 S.W. 1/20,000 and FRANCE Sheet 36 NW (Edn 6) 1/5000) The Battalion proceeded to trenches (LE TOUQUET LEFT SUB-SECTOR) relieving 17th WELSH FUSILIERS the relief was completed by 12 noon and the Battn was distributed as follows :- FRONT LINE front (right) ESSEX CENTRAL FARM C4.a.65.00. to left U.28.a.2.7. RIGHT :- A Company CENTRE :- B Company LEFT :- C Company SUPPORT :- LANCASHIRE FARM :- D Company.	

Army Form C. 2118

WAR DIARY or INTELLIGENCE SUMMARY (PAGE 4.)

(Erase heading not required.)

Instructions regarding War Diaries and Intelligence Summaries are contained in F.S. Regs., Part II. and the Staff Manual respectively. Title Pages will be prepared in manuscript.

Place	Date	Hour	Summary of Events and Information	Remarks and references to Appendices
BATTN HEADQUARTERS in DESPIERRE FARM	19/9/16		The 17th KINGS OWN REGT. were on the left of the Battn. & 9th DEVONS REGT. on the right. There was little activity during the day. A patrol was sent out from left Company during the night - no movements of the enemy were heard. Enemy machine guns were active at night. Casualties:- Nil.	
	20/9/16		The situation remained normal. Patrols were sent out from 3 hour Line Corp during the night. Enemy wiring parties were encountered by patrol of Centre Coy. Enemy machine guns were very active from 7.15 p.m. to 7.45 p.m. Casualties:- NIL	
	21/9/16		There was little enemy artillery activity & a few small trench mortars were fired by the left Company during the morning. We retaliated with Stokes Mortars & rifle grenades. Patrols were sent out at night. The Vedette from Centre Coy located 3 enemy working parties which were fired on later by Lewis Guns & dispersed. Casualties:- Nil.- Our artillery shelled positions behind enemy line during the day. In the afternoon enemy fired rifle grenades at left & Centre Coy in retaliation for our Trench Mortar fire. Enemy machine guns were active at night. Patrol of left Company located enemy working party. Casualties: 3 wounded	
	22/9/16		There was little activity during the day & much work in repairing trenches in some Patrols went out but enemy were not seen or heard. Casualties:- 1 wounded	
	23/9/16			
	24/9/16		The enemy fired a few Trench Mortars at the Right Coy during the day. Our Stokes	

WAR DIARY or INTELLIGENCE SUMMARY

Army Form C. 2118

(PAGE 5)

Place	Date	Hour	Summary of Events and Information	Remarks and references to Appendices
	24/9/16		Battery retaliated & silenced him. Casualties :- 1 Killed 1 Wounded	
	25/9/16		Enemy snipers were active in early morning - we retaliated. The Battalion was relieved by 8TH DEVONS REGT and Companies after relief were located as follows :- B Company garrisoned the following Strong Posts :- LYS FARM, STATION REDOUBT, SEVEN TREES. D Company garrisoned PATERNOSTER ROW, RESERVE FARM, FORT PAUL, LANCASTER SUPPORT FARM. C Company (1 Platoon) garrisoned GUNNER FARM. A and C Companies and Battalion Headquarters in billets at LE BIZET in Brigade Reserve. The relief was completed by 12 NOON. Casualties :- 1 Killed	
	26/9/16 to 30/9/16		The Battalion remained in billets. Posts as above. Work was done - repairing and strengthening Strong Posts and trenches. Casualties :- 28th :- 2 Wounded. 29th :- 8 wounded. Drafts as under joined the Battn during the month :- 5/9/16 :- 180 Other Ranks. 30 of these men had served with the Battn previously, the remaining 150 were transferred from 2/5th Lanc. Fusrs. Place where trained :- WITLEY CAMP, SURREY. State of training :- Good. 9/9/16 :- 12 Other Ranks. These men had served with the Battn previously. 10/9/16 :- 17 Other Ranks transferred from 2nd 8th & 9th Battns K.O.Y.L.I. Place where trained :- RUGELEY, STAFFS. State of training :- Fairly Good. 11/9/16 :- 100 Other Ranks transferred from 2nd & Y 20th Battn MANCHESTER REGT. Place where	

Army Form C. 2118

WAR DIARY
or
INTELLIGENCE SUMMARY
(Erase heading not required.)

(PAGE 6)

Instructions regarding War Diaries and Intelligence Summaries are contained in F.S. Regs., Part II. and the Staff Manual respectively. Title Pages will be prepared in manuscript.

Place	Date	Hour	Summary of Events and Information	Remarks and references to Appendices
			Trained :- ALTCAR, LIVERPOOL. State of training :- Good.	
	16/9/16		:- 9 Other Ranks. Had all served with the Battn previously	
	23/9/16		:- 6 Other Ranks. " " " " " " "	
	25/9/16		:- 10 Other Ranks. " " " " " " "	
			2ND LIEUTS. E.W. GREEN and W. COWPER joined the Battn on 6/9/16	
			2ND. LIEUT. T. GRONOW joined the Battn on 8/9/16	
			2ND LIEUTS J. MOORE, J.G. CAMPBELL and J. HAYTON joined the Battn on 13/9/16	
			25 Other Ranks were evacuated sick during the month.	
			Total casualties during the month :- Killed 12; Wounded 67, Missing 3, Shell Shock 14.	
			Strength of Battalion on last day of the month :- 34 Officers 1051 Other Ranks	

Lieut. Farnell Major
Commanding 2nd Bn. The Border Regt.

1875 Wt. W593/826 1,000,000 4/15 J.B.C. & A. A.D.S.S./Forms/C. 2118.

Headquarters
20th Inf Bde

Herewith a short account of the part taken by this Battn in the recent operations.

D Strange Lt & adj
for Lt Col
Commdg 2nd Border Regt

11.9.16

I

Report on movements of the
2ⁿᵈ Bⁿ Border Regᵗ from the
3ʳᵈ to 8ᵗʰ Septʳ 1916.

On the 3ʳᵈ of Sept. 1916
The Bⁿ was ready formed up to entrain on
lorries at 7.15 p.m. at BUIRE but did not
actually leave till about 8.30 p.m. The lorries
proceeded to FRICOURT where the lorries were
left & the Bⁿ made a temporary halt in a
field whilst rations & bombs were issued
the latter having to be detonated.
Major BEATTY-POWNALL (2ⁿᵈ in command)
was left in charge of the Bⁿ to bring it on to
MONTAUBAN where it arrived just after the 9ᵗʰ
DEVON REGᵗ at about 2. a.m. on the 4ᵗʰ Sept.
Here guides were picked-up & the Bⁿ proceeded
to BERNAFAY WOOD to pick up tools. On completion of this the move was continued & in a
very short time it was found the guides had
disappeared so the forward move was continued
without them. The Bⁿ catching up the 9ᵗʰ DEVON
Regᵗ who had also apparently lost their guides
These occurrences considerably delayed the advance
The Bⁿ was under fairly heavy shell fire during
this movement. — By about 5 a.m. the
Battalion was in position as follows.
"A" Coy. 2 Platoons in STOUT TRENCH. Capt Dowding
    2   "   SUPPORT TRENCH. N of
                GINCHY AVENUE
"B" " in SUPPORT TRENCH, N of GINCHY AVENUE.
                Capt NENDIGATE.

II

"C" Coy. in GINCHY AVENUE. Lt MALKIN.
"D" " in a trench [crossed out] YORK ALLEY this was
believed to be LONGEVAL AVENUE. Lt EHRENBORG
Bn HdQrs at the end of YORK ALLEY.

At 10.15 a.m. on an appeal for support from the O.C. 9th DEVON REGT I ordered "A" Coy to support this Regt. they moved up to STOUT TR. 2 extra Platoons but by the time this had been done a report was received that the DEV were being forced back by shell & machine gun fire. So the company remained in position. – Later owing to the Battalion being under heavy shell fire the front was extended to a little way along ZZ. TRENCH.

The Bn was under heavy shell fire all day but owing to the men working hard to improve the existing trenches by deepening them the casualties were comparatively few, although very many men were buried. Three officers were killed during the day Capt NEWDIGATE, Lieut MALKIN & 2nd Lt MARTINDALE

Late on the evening of the 4th orders were received for 2 companies to relieve the 12th KING'S LIVERPOOL REGT in the GUILLEMONT AREA.

"B" Coy under Lt BUTLER
"D" " " Lt EHRENBORG
were moved to the new area at about 11 p.m.
I (Lt. Col. E Thorpe) went in command of them leaving [crossed out] Lt D. STRANGE to take the other two, "A" & "C" Coys back to Reserve in MON–

III

TAUBAN REDOUBT here Major BEATTY-POWNALL took command of them.

At about 4 a.m. on the 5th Septr. the two Cos. completed their relief of the 12th KING'S LIVERPOOL REGT. Their positions being as follows:-

"D" Co. in a trench N.W. of GUILLIMENT opposite GINCHY.

"B"   " in SUPPORT in rear.

& Bn. H Qrs in a dug-out just by NEW TRENCH. On the left of the BORDER REGT. were the 2nd GORDON HRS. & on the right the ROYAL MUNSTER FRS. — On the 6th Sept the 2nd GORDONS & 9th DEVONS made two attempts to take GINCHY in front of the trenches held by the 2nd BORDER REGT & although they got into the village they were unable to hold it owing to hostile machine gun & shell fire & they had to fall back. The Lewis guns of the 2nd BORDER REGT endeavoured to assist the attack by firing from advanced positions & continued to do so until put out of action by being buried, one also damaged.

On the morning of the 7th Septr. about 2 a.m. the two BORDER Companies were relieved by the 7th ROYAL IRISH RIFLES & moved back to MONTAUBAN where relief was reported completed at 4 a.m. & after which the Bn. reassembled in bivouac south of FRICOURT.

During these days the casualties were small as shown separately. This was mainly due to the men digging themselves well in & being fairly widely extended in their trenches —

10.9.16.

L. Thorpe Lt Col
Comdg 2nd Border R.

NARRATIVE of EVENTS in the recent OPERATIONS

September 24th.

On Saturday September 24th, the 20th Infantry Brigade Battle Station was established in CHAPPEL ALLEY at 4-15 p.m. at which hour the Brigadier General, Comdg: Brigade Major, and A.D.C. arrived

The Brigadier General went up to the front line and there met Colonels Tudor and Stansfeld and watched the wire cutting. There still remained a certain amount of wire in between the two lines of trenches, and as it was too late for Artillery to cut this, it was decided to send out parties of men with wire cutters during the night. This would take place under cover of Shrapnel Fire

No time as yet had been settled for the attack to begin but a message came from 7th Division at 7-15 p.m. that it was not likely that any decision would be come to on this matter until 2 hours before the attack was to take place.

The 7th Divisional Head Quarters moved up to NOYELLES CHATEAU at 10 p.m., and about this hour the 20th Infantry Brigade began to concentrate in the trenches, some of which had been specially prepared for them.

The night was wet and very dark and there was no wind to speak of.

September 25th

By 2-30 a.m. the whole Brigade had concentrated, and a report to this effect was sent to 7th Division

At 3-40 a.m. a message was received that the hour of attack would be 5-30 a.m. and that the actual assault would take place at 6-30 a.m. and orders were sent round to this effect.

The morning was drizzly and there was a slight wind from the South West.

The Brigadier-General went round and saw Commanding Officers of 2nd Bn Gordon Highlanders, and 8th Bn Devon. Regiment at 4-50 a.m. and found that everything was prepared for the attack. These two Battalions were the leading Battalions and it was arranged that they should issue to the assault at the same moment in five lines from their respective trenches. This was made possible by the placing of ladders & bridges in & across the trenches

A Report was received at 5-40 a.m. from the two leading Battalions that they were quite satisfied that all the wire on their front had been cut including that which had been cut by hand during the night.

At 5-30 a.m. the attack began, and messages were continually received from Colonel Tudor, Commanding 14th Brigade R.H.A. who was watching the progress of the attack from his observation station and who was in telephone communication with 20th Infy. Bde. Hd Qrs. These messages for the first 40 minutes were chiefly with reference to the effect of the smoke candles and concerning our own and enemy's artillery.

At 6-30 a.m. the Infantry left their trenches and advanced at a walk in line up to the enemy's trenches, and in 12 minutes were on the enemy parapet. In the meantime the remainder of the 20th Infy. Brigade was on the move and the 2nd Battalion BORDER REGIMENT and 6th Battalion GORDON HIGHLANDERS were already up in the front line trenches, and ready to advance in support of the two leading Battalions.

In 35 minutes from the hour of assault the first line of enemy trenches in front of 20th Infy. Brigade had been captured with rather heavy losses, including Colonel Grant and Major Carden of 8th Bn Devons: Regiment both killed and Colonel Stansfeld, 2nd Bn Gordon Highlanders, badly wounded.

Soon after 7 a.m. the Division reported that the 22nd Infy Brigade were held up by enemy in POPES NOSE Redoubt, and two sections of Bombers were ordered up from 2nd Bn. BORDER REGIMENT to try and bomb down towards this obstruction.

At 7-25 a.m. the front system of the enemy trenches opposite the 20th Infy Brigade had been captured, and both the 8th Bn DEVON: REGT: and 2nd Bn. GORDON HIGHLANDERS were steadily advancing in spite of their losses.

The 6th Bn Gordon Highlanders had shortly after 8. a.m. moved up past old German line and were re-inforcing the 2nd Battalion. This was also being done by the 2nd Bn BORDER REGT. who were supporting 8th Bn DEVON. REGT.

Shortly before 8. a.m. 7th Division reported that 22nd Infy Brigade was still held up, and that the artillery of the 20th Infy. Brigade was to be used for its own support as it was considered that if the success already obtained were to be further supported in this way, the result would be to automatically clear the right of the 22nd Infy Brigade. For this reason at 8-15am. Colonel JOHNSTONE Commanding 22nd Brigade R.F.A. and Colonel TUDOR were ordered to bring guns forward the former, one Battery, and the later, one section. Colonel TUDOR placed his section immediately in rear of the old German trenches, which gave effective support. The Battery of 22nd Brigade R.F.A. was placed just in rear of the old British line on South of VERMELLES - HULLUCH ROAD. and eventually one more Batty: of this Brigade was brought up to this same position and also another section of "T" Battery joined the first section sent up

At 8-5 am the Brigade Major was sent forward to report on the situation and reported at 8-20 am that 4 Battalions had gone forward and that the 9th Bn Devonshire Regt were just about to leave the first line of trenches.

The first prisoners, a party of 24 passed Brigade Headquarters at 8.26 am and at this hour a man from 8th Bn Devon Regt came and reported that his Battalion had reached "a big colliery"

At this hour No 1 Trench Mortar Battery under Lieutenant CARRIGAN, R.F.A. was ordered to advance to first German line of trenches, and then to act on his own initiative, bearing in mind the importance of getting as far forward as possible to deal with any houses which might hold up the advance.

Shortly before 9am. two Companies of the BEDFORDSHIRE REGT: of 21st Infy Bde were sent up to old British line, and a message was received from the Division at 9am. to say that 21st Infy Brigade would advance in support, as all the Troops of 20th Infy Bde were engaged.

At this hour also a man of 8th Bn DEVON REGT. came in and reported that his Battalion was at PUITS.13. and after it had been definitely ascertained from him that this was the case, it was reported to the Division. This was more or less confirmed by O.C 117th Battery who reported this Battalion near PUITS 13, and by a message written at 8.50am by Colonel THORPE O.C. 2nd Battalion BORDER REGT.

This man also reported that a batch of 150 prisoners was on its way down

The resistance of a party of the enemy about POPES NOSE still continued at 9.30 am and the Division were most anxious to break this down, on his own initiative and before a message reached him the Staff Captain seeing this resistance was affecting the advance, organised a party of 2nd Bn BORDER REGT under Captain Sutcliffe of that Regiment, who led his men out with great dash and assisted by Captain Ostle with half a Company, broke down the resistance and took the enemy in this place prisoners to the number of about 70. This set the example to the lines behind, which came on and carried the advance forward to join the remainder of the Brigade.

The cross roads at H.7.c.4.4 were reached at 8-45 am. by 6th Bn GORDON HIGHLANDERS who joined up with the 2nd Battalion and some of the 8th Bn: DEVON: REGT.

About 9 am a party of Germans estimated at 500 with a mounted officer at their head marched into CITE-ST-ELIE from a N.E. direction. The 2nd Bn GORDON HIGHLANDERS opened rifle and machine gun fire on them and broke column in half in the main street of the village. The attack had now come to a standstill for want of further backing, and the position was, that a forward line east of HULLUCH cross roads on the point G.7.c.5.5., 5.2 13.A.2.6. was held connecting up on the right with 1st Division but with the left in the air. Behind this the Gun Trench was held with 8 enemy guns in it which was being heavily shelled.

At 10-50 am General Watts, 21st Infy: Bde. came up and two of his Battalions were ordered to reinforce 20th Infy Bde. One Company at least of BEDFORD: REGT: had previously gone forward, but no forward movement from Gun Trench was possible as yet. O.C. 22nd Bde R.F.A. was ordered to shell HULLUCH and PUITS 13 and the Division were asked to turn heavy guns on to both these places later on, about 12-50 pm.

Some enemy were seen to be advancing from CITE.ST.LEONARD. on to CITE.ST. ELIE about 1 pm. and 22nd Brigade R.F.A were ordered to fire on them.

meanwhile messages had been received that 4th Corps were to attack HULLUCH, and 21st Infy Bde were ordered to co-operate. So far as can be ascertained nothing came of this attack and the enemy continued to hold HULLUCH and CITE ST. ELIE, and were presumably getting more troops into both places. Report came back to the effect, that the front houses in both these villages were strongly held by machine Guns, and in a few houses at least, there were field guns, besides a trench with strong wire in front.

At 2-15 p.m. the Brigadier Generals of 20th and 21st Infy Bde: went forward nearly up to Gun Trench to reconnoitre the position so as to be able to report the situation as it appeared to them to Divisional Headquarters.

An attack was ordered on CITE-ST-ELIE for 4-45 p.m. but the views of the two Brigadier Generals having been communicated to the Division this did not come off. It seemed that the greatest chance of success would be to attack HULLUCH in S.E. direction with 2 fresh Battalions as the outskirts of this place were reported to be held by 4th Corps.

At 4-30 p.m. the Division sent orders to consolidate positions gained. The positions of Units in 20th Infantry Brigade at 6-30 p.m. was as follows:-

2nd and 6th Bn GORDON HIGHLANDERS about H.7.c.4.4. with a mixture of 8th and 9th DEVON: REGT. These were ordered to dig in and make the cross roads a strong point with the aid of two 1½ inch mortars under Lieutenant CARRIGAN who had his Guns well forward.

The 2nd Battalion BORDER REGIMENT some 8th and 9th DEVON: REGT. and details 21st Infy Brigade in GUN TRENCH in touch on the right with 1st Division, and on left with 22nd Infy Brigade, and the whole were ordered to dig themselves in, and R.E. were ordered to put out wire on their front.

At 8-10 p.m. General Capper came up and talked over the situation with Brigadier General Comdg: 20th Infy Brigade and then went back to see Brigadier General Comdg 21st Infy Brigade who came up to Headquarters 20th Infy Brigade to settle how best to deal with the advanced position at the

HULLUCH Cross Roads. It was decided to hold these cross roads as an advanced post, connected up to the main line by an old German communication trench. About 500 yards of new line had to be dug, and Brigadier General Commanding 21st Infy Bde: ordered up the ROYAL SCOTS FUSILIERS to do this while the wiring was to be done by the 2nd HIGHLAND FIELD COY: R.E. Brigadier General Commanding 21st Infy Bde with his Brigade Major went up accompanied by Brigade Major 20th Infy Bde: to start the work off.

Shortly before midnight 25th-26th the enemy made a determined counter-attack on the advanced position near HULLUCH Cross Roads just before it had been put in a state of defence. This attack was pressed home in the endeavour to recapture the Field Guns in GUN TRENCH. The men in the forward positions gave way and fell back on GUN TRENCH and some even went back further than this but were rallied by officers of the 2nd Battalion BORDER REGT and Brigade Major and taken back to help the men in GUN TRENCH.

The enemy's foremost attackers actually reached this trench and were killed almost on the parapet whilst a good many others variously estimated at anything between 50 and 100 were killed in this attack, which was beaten off. Thus the advanced position at HULLUCH Cross Roads was lost, but all other ground gained by 20th Infy Bde: during the day was held and consolidated before daylight.

September 26th

About 1 am the Brigadier General was informed that the Quarries had been captured by the enemy and a little later that some Germans had penetrated into their old line. On this information being received the Staff Captain was ordered to take 8th Bn: CAMERON HIGHLANDERS (at request of 21st Infy Bde) to turn them out of these trenches, and 2 Coys: of ROYAL SCOTS FUSILIERS were sent to hold BRESLAU AVENUE in order to protect the left flank of the troops holding GUN TRENCH. It was eventually made known that the enemy had not penetrated to their old line but still held Quarries, and about 3 am. General CAPPER informed Brigadier General that he was organizing a counter attack on them by a fresh Battalion, so the 4th Bn CAMERON HIGHLANDERS were withdrawn to their former position.

The counter-attack on Quarries failed at 7am and none other was attempted till 5-30 pm. This was done by CARTERS DETACHMENT and 20th Infy Bde sent one section of Bombers to assist. These men bombed down one of the communication Trenches leading into the Quarries This attack was only partially successful.

General CAPPER was wounded during this attack.

During this day the Battalions of the 20th Infantry Brigade held on to all the positions they had captured and so far as was possible collected their men together. Their line was taken over by 21st Infantry Bde with the exception of the 2nd Bn BORDER REGT. who took the place of the Royal Scots Fusiliers in BRESLAU AVENUE.

The remaining Battalions 20th Infy Bde moved back to trenches in the old British line, East of CHAPPEL KEEP.

Headquarters 20th Infy: Bde: moved to Battle Station of 21st Infy Bde, just east of VERMELLES railway crossing on HULLUCH ROAD, and after being in support till 29th inst, went back to billets in BEUVRY.

Brigade Headquarters   (Sd) J F Trefusis Br: General
10th October 1915   Comdg: 20th Infantry Brigade

Operations Orders by
 Lieut Col C J de S Thorpe
  Cmdg 2nd Bn Border Regt

24th Sep: 1915.

1. The 20th Infantry Brigade will be formed up on the night of 24th-25th September on a front VERMELLES-HULLOCH ROAD - SAP.2. preparatory to an attack on 25th Sep: The 95th Field Coy R.E. and No.1 Trench Mortar Battery are attached to the Brigade.) On the right of the 20th Infy Brigade is the 1st Infy Brigade, 1st Division - on the left the 22nd Infy Brigade - 7th Division.

2. The Brigade will be distributed as follows:-
   <u>1st Line</u> 2nd Gordon Highlanders on the right (in four lines) HULLOCH ROAD to Sap.1.
   8th Devons on the left (in four lines) Sap.1. to Sap.2.
   <u>2nd Line</u> 2nd Bn Border Regt (in two lines)
   <u>3rd Line</u> 1/6th Gordon Highlanders
   <u>Brigade Reserve</u> 9th Bn Devons: Regt

3. 2nd Border Regt will occupy the following position
   <u>1st Line</u> OLD SUPPORT TRENCH from CHAPPEL ALLEY to FROG LANE as follows: From Right to left:-
      1 Machine Gun
      "B" Company
      "D" Company
      1 Machine Gun (on left of FOSSE WAY)
   <u>2nd Line</u> CURLEY CRESCENT from CHAPPEL ALLEY to 100 yards N. of FOSSE WAY. as follows. From Right to left:-
      1 Machine Gun
      "C" Company
      "A" Company
      Headquarter Dug-out
      Headquarter party } on N. side of
      1 Machine Gun   } CURLEY CRESCENT
   Company Orderlies will join Battalion Headquarters as soon as Coys: are in position.

4. The Battalion will move into the Trenches by CHAPPEL ALLEY and FOSSE WAY at X pm

5. Order of march:-
   1 Machine Gun   1 Machine Gun   'A' Company   } at 10
   'B' Company   1 Machine Gun   Headquarters   } minutes
   'D' Company   'C' Company   1 Machine Gun } Interval

6. Great care must be taken during the concentration that the presence of troops in large numbers is not observed by the enemy. Troops must remain under cover and only move about by order of an Officer. Even this should be avoided in open places not usually occupied by troops. Lights will not be used. Bayonets will not be fixed except at the last possible moment and they must not be allowed to shew above the parapet.

7. Great Coats will not be carried but will be stored, rolled in bundles of 20, in the last house in NOYELLES, E side of the main road (L.19.b.6.8.) at times to be notified later. Packs will be worn and the following will be carried:—
   Waterproof Sheet
   Cardigan or Extra Vest
   1 Pair Socks
   3 Sand Bags.

8. One days complete rations and the iron ration will be carried by all ranks.
The iron ration is not to be touched except by order of the OC Battalion. Water bottles are to be taken into the trenches filled and are not to be touched except by order of the OC Company.

9. Every man except Bombers will carry 200 rounds of S.A.A.
Advanced Reserve S.A.A. Store is situated at the corner of FOSSE WAY and 1st SUPPORT TRENCH.
Intermediate Reserve is situated in FOSSE WAY 100 yards W of CORLEY CRESCENT.
S.A.A. Carts will be concentrated at L.11.a. by x-45 p.m.
Bomb Store is situated at corner of FOSSE WAY and CORLEY CRESCENT.
Water is stored in FOSSE WAY at a point 100 yards W of CORLEY CRESCENT.
1st Line Transport and Tool Carts will be at LABOURSE.
Baggage will be concentrated at FOUQUEREUIL by 6 p.m. to night.
Machine Gun Limbers to join S.A.A. Carts at L.11.a. by 2 a.m. 25%.
Advanced Dressing Stations. Eastern end of STANSFELD RD. just W. of the Railway and S. of HULLOCH ALLEY. in G.8.b.
Each Coy. will have one Stretcher and 4 bearers with it.
Divisional Collecting Station. VERMELLES.
Brigade Head Quarters CHAPPEL KEEP
Battalion   —   In CORLEY CRESCENT in a Dug-out just S. of FOSSE WAY.

12. **Upkeep of Trenches.** - The nearest troops will at once retire any damage done to trenches with as little noise as possible.

Badges - Men carrying wire cutters will wear a piece of rifle rag on the sleeve of the jacket on right forearm.

Bomb Carriers will wear a piece of rifle rag on the right shoulder strap.

(Sd) R.H. Durmann Lieut
Adjutant 2nd Bn Border Regt

Operation Orders by
Lt Colonel E.J. de S. Thorpe
24th Sept 1915

Information
Enemy defences consist of 2 well defined lines of trenches
1st runs from FOSSE No 8 southwards to Loos
2nd 1500 yards to East running through HAISNES-CITE-ST-ELIE-HULLUCH. Both systems protected by wire.
Enemy troops holding this front is the 117th Re-constructed Division in following order from NORTH
11th Reserve Regt - 22nd Reserve Regt - 115th Reserve Regt.
Our troops are:-

1st Division (4th Corps) on right Eastwards
9th " (1st ") on left Southeast between HULLUCH and LOOS

Intention.
In conjunction with the French the British Force will make an attack on 25th Sep: 15
The task of the 7th Division is to clear the trenches in front, occupy HULLUCH - PUIT 13 - CITE ST ELIE - from here on to line PONT-A-VENDIN-MEURCHIN, seizing the canal crossings about that place.

Task of 20th Infy: Brigade
The 20th Infy Brigade will clear the trenches in front and occupy HULLUCH and BENEFONTAINE pushing on thence to PONT-A-VENDIN and seize canal crossings after the 1st German trenches have been captured the OC 2nd Gordons will make a supporting point at Cross Roads G.11.d.9.3. 8th Devons will do the same at Point BRESLAU AVENUE crosses HAINES ROAD.

Distribution
As stated in formation orders
1st line 2nd Gordons on right) To lead the
           8th Devons on left) assault

(CONTD)

Distribution (cont:)	2nd line :- 6th Gordons on right moving up into position at time of assault
	2nd Border Regt on left
	3rd line 9th Devons Regt
	(Time table will be issued later)
Artillery	On an obstruction being met and reported, the point will be bombarded by artillery for ½ hour, the last 5 minutes intensive. Thus officers will recognise when the bombardment is about to cease. In the case of small obstructions the bombardment will be for 10 minutes intensive, if this is not sufficient it will be repeated for another 10 minutes intensive, if asked for
Battalion Advance.	The 2nd Border Regt will support the 8th Devons, as the 8th Devons vacate each line in their assembly formation the Battalion will move forward line by line until the new fire trench is vacated.
Work.	The OC 'A' Co will detail 2 Platoons to dig a communication trench to connect the captured German trench with our fire trench - one Platoon each way. This party will be pushed up FOSSEWAY and the Platoon to dig back will move forward as soon as the first German trench is occupied by 8th Devons, and start their work. Each Coy will arrange to carry forward 1 bundle of 50 Sandbags
Ammunition	Sergt Loughman will be in charge of the forward Reserve Ammunition O.C. Coys: will please detail 1 L.Cpl: and 5 Ptes: to report to him at that point. When the Bn: moves Sgt Loughman will take forward 25 boxes to the German Fire trench
	Position of other Ammunition Units as notified.
Prisoners of War	A collecting station for Prisoners will be established west of MALINGARBE - VERMELLES ROAD in G-7-d.
Distinguishing Flags	7th Division - Red and Blue Diagonal
	1st Division - Red with white stripe
	9th Division - Red and Yellow Diagonal
Smoke Signals	Each Coy will be issued with 6 Smoke Candles - These are to denote the position of the leading Company
Vermorel Sprayers	The Battalion will have no Vermorel Sprayers, but should any be found they should be taken on. But O.C. Coys should arrange to take forward a refill. Men must be cautioned not to enter hostile Dug-outs unless they have been sprayed.
Brigade Ammn Column	14th H.A. Brigade Ammn Column L-1-d-2-4
R.E. Stores	Advanced Depôts :-
	Fallen tree North of VERMELLES
	HULLOCH ROAD G-11-C-4-1
	South of HAINES ROAD G-4-d-8-0.

Visual Signalling Station	Call up Battalion Hd Qrs for 2 minutes and then send message slowly, repeating it 3 times in case no reply can be sent, owing to enemy seeing it. Sergt Treatorex is in charge of the Battalion inter-communication and will make all necessary arrangements
Bn. Reserve Ammⁿ	The R.S. Major will be in charge of the Battalion Reserve Ammunition
Liaison's Offr:	2nd Lt R Rawlinson will report himself to O C 8th Devons. to keep up communications with 8th Devons and 2nd Border Rgt on arrival in trenches.
Medical	Dressing stations as notified.
Personnel of R.E. Corps:	Personnel of N° 186 and 188 Special Coys R.E. will wear red white and green brassards.
Water	Company Commanders will see that all ranks realize the importance of the water purifying tabloids and that they are carried. We must be on the lookout for poisoned water. Even boiling will not mitigate the effects of this.
Correspondence	No orders letters or maps, capable of giving the least information to the enemy, are to be taken into the trenches or field
Battalion HdQrs	When 8th Devons advance the Battalion Head Quarters 2nd Border Rgt will move to those vacated by 8th Devons.

(Sd) R M Burmann Lieut
Adjutant 2nd Bn Border Rgt

20th Brigade.

7th Division.

2nd BATTALION

BORDER REGIMENT

OUTOBER 1916

WAR DIARY.

2ND. BATTALION BORDER REGIMENT.

PERIOD:-

FROM:- 1ST. OCTOBER 1916.

TO:- 31ST. OCTOBER 1916.

WAR DIARY

INTELLIGENCE SUMMARY

(Erase heading not required.)

Army Form C. 2118.

Place	Date	Hour	Summary of Events and Information	Remarks and references to Appendices
LE BIZET.			Reference TRENCH MAPS:- FRANCE Sheet 36.N.W. 1/20,000 BELGIUM & FRANCE Sheet 28 S.W. 1/20000	
	1/10/16		The Battalion proceeded to trenches LE TOUQUET Left Sub-Sector, relieving 8th Bn Devons Regt. On arrival the Battalion was distributed as follows:- Firing Line:- U.28.a.2.1. (left) to C.4.a.65.00. (Right) RIGHT:- D.Company. CENTRE:- A.Company. LEFT:- B.Company. LANCASHIRE SUPPORT FARM:- C.Company. DESPIERRE FARM:- Battalion Headquarters. The 20th Bn Manchester Regt. were on the left of the Battalion and 9th Bn Devons Regt on right.	
	2/10/16		There was little activity on either side during the day. During the morning a few trench Mortars were fired by the Hun X Ray Companies. Our trench Mortars retaliated. A sniper was accounted for by the Centre Fire Curtain during the afternoon. Machine Gun and Sniping fire was normal during the night. Much work was done in repairing the Trenches. Casualties:- 1 Killed 2 Wounded.	
	3/10/16		Enemy trench Mortars were active between C and N.N. our barrage, being slightly damaged otherwise the enemy were very Quiet. Our trench Mortar Battery retaliated in the morning the shells being seen to fall into the Front Line doing considerable damage. Our Lewis Guns were very active during the night about 1800 rounds being fired.	
	4/10/16		Two enemy working parties were observed between L.am and 2.am, shewis east of the Houx Fire Companies. They were dispersed by Lewis Gun fire. Our heavy artillery was active between 10 am and 11 am and our trench Mortars between 3-30 and 4-30 pm in retaliation for enemy trench Mortar fire. A party of Germans were observed in View at a range of 900 yards one man being seen

WAR DIARY or INTELLIGENCE SUMMARY (PAGE 2)

Army Form C. 2118.

Place	Date	Hour	Summary of Events and Information	Remarks and references to Appendices
	4/10/16		sent for all. Listening Patrols went out at intervals from the three, the companies during the night. An enemy wiring party was located and engaged by Lewis Guns. May in rewiring & draining the trenches. The working was hindered by rain. The enemy fired a few shrapnel shells in the vicinity of LANCASHIRE SUPPORT FARM and RESERVE TRENCH wounding three. Enemy trench Mortars were active at intervals. An enemy working party was located at about 80m and was dispersed by Lewis Guns, casualties three. Enemy fire was K.O.B. who by our M.G. who by our Lewis Guns during the night, the Lewis Gun at Right fire Compart. effectually silenced enemy Machine Gun at point afterwards. V4.a.55. Casualties :- 4 wounded	
	5/10/16		Enemy trench Mortars were less active than usual during the day. Vickers went out from the Centre fire Compart. during the night to reconnoitre the TRIANGLE. They reached a divided trench believed to be N.side of the TRIANGLE. They were fired on but returned safely & over lines at 3am on 6th.	
	6/10/16		There was little enemy activity throughout the day. Our Machine Lewis Guns were active at intervals during the night. Patrols went out from each of the flank fire Cops at night. No enemy were seen or heard. Casualties :- 1 Killed 1 wounded	
PONT DE NIEPPE	7/10/16 8/10/16	11/10/16	The Battalion was relieved by 8th. Ru Devons Regt and proceeded to billets at PONT DE NIEPPE. The Battalion remained in billets in Brigade Reserve.	
	12/10/16		In accordance with instructions from Hd.quarters , 20th Infantry Brigade arrangements had been made for a raid on the enemy trenches to be carried out by the Battalion. The raiding party had been selected & the ground culminally patrolled at night. All arrangements were completed and the assault hour to take place at 7.30pm 13/10/16.	
			N.B.6.58 The raiding party (consisting of 2nd Lieut S.B.BENDLE (O.C. ------) 2nd Lieut J.B.WOOD (O.C. Assault) Lieut R.G.HENNESSY (O.C. Enterprise) & 35 Other Ranks) was assembled at their rendezvous.	Notice the

WAR DIARY or INTELLIGENCE SUMMARY (PAGE 3)

Army Form C. 2118.

Place	Date	Hour	Summary of Events and Information	Remarks and references to Appendices
			When the barrage commenced 2nd Lieut R.B.WOOD led the way to the triangular trench in front of the front of attack. Unfortunately No1 and 2 parties following in rear of him came under heavy Machine Gun fire from the right, losing both leaders (one to a few isolated axes) took up shelter low in the road. 2nd Lieut R.B.WOOD's party pushed on & finding they were enfiladed rapidly entered the German trench at the point of attack. Lieut WOOD assumed command of the right party & himself bombed down the German trench accounting for two Germans who were seen to fall. This officer went back to find the remainder of the raiders & during the return allotted having stayed his party retired. At 10 minutes after parti Zwen entered the German trench. A German who was waiting his way towards what appeared to be a fixed rifle was bombed. This party also retired bringing in some wounded. The fact that up more than 80 Germans entered the German trench was not probably owing to both leaders being wounded by Machine Gun fire early in the venture. Our Casualties were:- Other Ranks Officers 1 (2nd Lieut R.B.WOOD) 1 (2nd Lieut S.B.BENDLE) Killed — Wounded — 3 Missing (believed Killed) — 2 The Battalion proceeded to Trenches LE TOUQUET left Sub-Sector relieving 8th Bn. Devons Regiment The Battalion was distributed as follows:- Right Coy:- B Company Centre:- C Company Left:- D Company LANCASHIRE SUPPORT FARM:- A Company DESPIERRE FARM:- Battalion Headquarters.	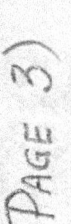
PONT DE NIEPPE	13/10/16			

WAR DIARY
or
INTELLIGENCE SUMMARY

Army Form C. 2118.

(PAGE 4)

Place	Date	Hour	Summary of Events and Information	Remarks and references to Appendices

The 20th Bn Manchester Regt were on the Left of the Battalion and 7th Bn Devon's Regt on the right.

14/10/16 — There was little activity during the day. Patrols from all 3 Fire Trenches went out during the night. Patrol from Centre Coy located enemy working party which was dispersed by Lewis Gun fire. The 2 bodies of the enemy in front of the Centre Coy wire were removed by the enemy at night.

15/10/16 — An enemy working party was located at O.H.8.b.6 at about 11.00pm & was dispersed by Lewis Gun fire. There was the usual subdued Machine Gun fire during the night. There was little activity on either side during the day. Patrols went out from all 3 Fire Trenches. No enemy were seen or heard. An enemy working party was located working on the wire during the night & was fired on by Lewis Guns. Casualties - 1 Wounded.

16/10/16 — One Trench Mortar fired about 40 rounds between 2 and 3 am doing considerable damage to enemy trench & destroying a suspected Machine Gun emplacement. Enemy Trench Mortars were very active on the front & on the Left of Fire Trench. Our trench was damaged & there were several Casualties. Our artillery retaliated. Casualties - 2 Killed 8 Wounded.

17/10/16 — There was little enemy trench Mortar fire during the morning. A patrol from the Centre Fire Coy located a small party of the enemy which were fired on.

18/10/16 — At about 8.30 am an enemy working party was observed repairing a gap in his trenches. It was dispersed by Lewis Gun fire. Enemy snipers were active during the morning. At 7 pm our Stokes Mortar Battery carried out a short bombardment of the enemy trenches. Monte BURNT OUT FARM. Considerable damage was done. The enemy made a feeble reply. Patrols went out but no enemy were seen or heard. Casualties - 2 Wounded.

19/10/16 — The Battalion was relieved in the Trenches by 8th Bn Devons Regiment. On relief

Army Form C. 2118.

WAR DIARY or INTELLIGENCE SUMMARY (PAGE 5)

(Erase heading not required.)

Place	Date	Hour	Summary of Events and Information	Remarks and references to Appendices
			On relief the Battalion was distributed as follows:-	
			C Company garrisoned the following Strong Points:- PATERNOSTER ROW - RESERVE FARM - FORT PAUL LANCASHIRE SUPPORT.	
			A " " " " " :- STATION REDOUBT - SEVEN TREES REDOUBT - LYS FARM.	
			Band D Companies to billets at LE BIZET	
			Battalion Headquarters to billets at LE BIZET.	
LE BIZET	20/10/16 to 24/10/16 25/10/16		The Battalion remained in billets & found Strong Posts in Brigade Support.	
			The Battalion proceeded to trenches LE TOUQUET Left Sub-Sector relieving 8th Bn Leinster Regt.	
			The Battalion was distributed as follows:-	
			Firing Line :- Right:- C Company Centre:- D Company Left:- A Company	
			LANCASHIRE SUPPORT FARM:- B Company	
			DESPIERRE FARM:- Battalion Headquarters	
	26/10/16		There was little activity throughout the day.	
			Enemy Trench Mortars were very active between 11 am & Noon but little damage was done.	
			Our Artillery & Trench Mortars executed a bombardment of enemy front line from 3.45 to 4.30 pm. Fired from the Centre Free Company & carried several enemy saillies between the parapet & the wire. The ground was subsequently swept by Lewis Gun fire.	
			Casualties 2 killed 11 wounded - by enemy Rifle Grenades in afternoon	
	27/10/16		During the morning the enemy sent over a few small shells near RESERVE FARM.	
			Our Artillery silenced a large enemy Trench Mortar which placed fire on Right free Coy at about 5.30 pm. Patrols went out but no enemy were seen or heard.	
	28/10/16		Enemy Trench Mortars were active between 10.30 and 11 am and 2-30 to 4 pm & 2.45 am. Our Artillery bombarded enemy's front line with good effect. Parties from Left Centre (?Centre?)	

WAR DIARY or INTELLIGENCE SUMMARY (PAGE 6)

Army Form C. 2118.

Place	Date	Hour	Summary of Events and Information	Remarks and references to Appendices
	29/10/16		encountered enemy working parties which were dispersed by Lewis Guns. One of the enemy was captured during the night. Casualties 3 killed 4 wounded	
	30/10/16		Enemy artillery was rather active during the morning between 3.45am enemy trench Mortars opened fire on Centre Sub Company doing considerable damage to our front line. Our Artillery & Heavy trench Mortars retaliated & effectually silenced their Mortars. Our Patrols went out from all Companies & reported all quiet Enemy Patrols Casualties 3 killed 11 wounded. There was little activity during the day.	
	31/10/16		Enemy working parties again were fired on at night located Two enemy Mortars were very active from 9.25 to 9.30pm on the front of the Right Sub Coy. There was little activity on either side during the day. The usual Patrols went out at night - nothing unusual was reported.	
			No Drafts joined the Battalion during the month. No Officers " " " " " 17 Other Ranks were evacuated sick during the month. 2 Officers & 20 Ranks The Strength of the Battalion on the last day of the month was :- 30 Officers	

Commanding 2nd Bn The Border Regt.

20th Brigade.

7th Division.

2nd BATTALION

BORDER REGIMENT

NOVEMBER 1916

WAR DIARY

2ND BATTN. BORDER REGIMENT

FROM :- 1ST. NOVEMBER 1916

TO :- 30TH. NOVEMBER 1916.

WAR DIARY or INTELLIGENCE SUMMARY

Army Form C. 2118.

Place	Date	Hour	Summary of Events and Information	Remarks and references to Appendices
	1/11/16		The Battalion was relieved in the trenches (LE TOUQUET Right Sub-Sector) by 10th Bn Cheshire Regt on relief proceeded to billets in the vicinity of STEENWERCK	
	2/11/16		The Battalion marched to billets at COURTE CROIX and ROUGE CROIX near FLETRE	
	3/11/16 to 8/11/16		The Battalion remained in billets. Training was carried on daily	
	9/11/16		The Battalion marched to billets at EBBLINGHEM	
	10/11/16		The Battalion marched to billets at TILQUES	
	11/11/16		The Battalion marched to billets at ZOUAFQUES	
	12/11/16 to 14/11/16		The Battalion remained in billets & continued its training	
	15/11/16		The Battalion marched to billets at ACQUIN	
	16/11/16		The Battalion marched to billets at AUDINCTHUN	
	17/11/16		The Battalion noted in billets	
	18/11/16		The Battalion marched to billets at FIEFS	
	19/11/16		The Battalion marched to billets at HERNICOURT and PIERREMONT	
	20/11/16		The Battalion marched to billets at NUNCQ and HAUTE COTE	
	21/11/16		The Battalion marched to billets at AUTHIEULE	
	22/11/16		The Battalion marched to billets at BERTRANCOURT	
	23/11/16		The Battalion marched to billets near MAILLY-MAILLET arriving about 4 pm	
			REFERENCE MAP FRANCE 57 D. N.E. 1/10,000	
	23/11/16		The Battalion proceeded to Support trenches (K.35.c.4.7. to K.35.c.2.2.) relieving 2nd Bn MANCHESTER REGT	
	24/11/16 to 27/11/16		The Battalion remained in Support line. Casualties :- 1 man wounded 25/11/16	

Army Form C. 2118.

WAR DIARY
INTELLIGENCE SUMMARY
(Erase heading not required.)

Place	Date	Hour	Summary of Events and Information	Remarks and references to Appendices
	27/1/16		The Battalion relieved 2ND GORDON HIGHLANDERS in the front line (K.35.a.30 to K.35.d.5.b.) at night, relief commencing at 4pm. Casualties:- 4 Killed 1 wounded	
	28/1/16		The enemy shelled various points on the line during the day. Our artillery retaliated. Owing to the condition of the ground patrolling was impossible. Casualties:- 1 wounded	
	29/1/16		Enemy artillery was quiet during the day until about 4pm when a heavy bombardment was opened on our front line. Our artillery retaliated strongly & about 6pm enemy fire slackened & died away. Enemy snipers were active during several casualties. Casualties:- Captain D. ELLIOT wounded. - 4 Killed 3 wounded	
	30/1/16		Enemy artillery was less active. Enemy snipers were again active, our snipers retaliating. Casualties:- 3 Killed 10 Wounded	
			2ND LIEUT S.J. LOCKYER joined the Battalion on 13/1/16. Drafts as under joined the Batt. during the month:- 6/1/16:- 3 O.Ranks; 11/1/16:- 10 O.Ranks; 11/1/16:- 6 O.Ranks; 26/1/16:- 5 O.Ranks. 9 other Ranks were evacuated sick during the month. The strength of the Battalion on the last day of the month was:- 30 Officers 823 O.Ranks.	

H.C.E. Trench
Lieut. Colonel.
Commanding 2nd Bn. The Border Regt.

20th Brigade.

7th Division.

2nd BATTALION

BORDER REGIMENT

DECEMBER 1916

WAR DIARY.

2ND. BATTALION BORDER REGIMENT.

PERIOD:-

FROM:- 1-12-1916.

To:- 31-12-1916.

WAR DIARY or INTELLIGENCE SUMMARY

Army Form C. 2118.

Place	Date	Hour	Summary of Events and Information	Remarks and references to Appendices
Trenches K35a.3.0. to K35.d.56.	1/12/16		Reference:- Trench Map REDAN 1/5000. Artillery on both sides was active during the day. Owing to the state of the ground there was little movement on the part of the enemy infantry and practically no rifle fire. The support line and Battalion Headquarters were shelled at intervals during the afternoon. The Battalion was relieved at night by 2nd Bn. Gordon Highlanders "A" C and "D" Companies, and Battalion Headquarters on relief proceeded to billets in Brigade Reserve at MAILLY-MAILLET. "B" Company on relief moved to their old position in the support line. The relief was completed at about 1.a.m. on 2/12/1916. Casualties 1/12/16: 2 wounded.	
MAILLY-MAILLET	2/12/16		The Battalion remained in billets. During the morning the village was shelled by an enemy high velocity gun but no casualties occurred in the Battalion. B Company was relieved in support trenches by 1 Company of 6th Bn Seaforth Regt at night and on relief joined the Battalion in billets at MAILLY-MAILLET. Casualties 2/12/16: 2 Wounded	
	3/12/16		The village was again shelled by the enemy about mid-day but no casualties occurred. The Battalion (less B Coy who remained in billets at MAILLY-MALLET) proceeded	

Army Form C. 2118

WAR DIARY
or
INTELLIGENCE SUMMARY
(Erase heading not required.)

(PAGE 2)

Place	Date	Hour	Summary of Events and Information	Remarks and references to Appendices
	3/12/16		to trenches (from line K35.a.3.0 to K35.d.5.6) at night relieving 2nd Gordon Highlanders. The relief was completed about 12 midnight & the Battalion was then disposed of as under:- Front Line:- Right:- "A" Company Left:- "D" Company Support Line:- "B" Company Reserve:- "C" Company. The 8th Bn. Devons Regiment were on the right of the Battalion & the Right Battalion of the 3rd Division on the left. Up to 11pm the situation was reported quiet by the Officer Commanding 2nd Gordon Highlanders. After 11pm the Front line and Support line was accidentally shelled by H.2 and 5.9 enemy guns. This was apparently in retaliation to a bombardment by our heavy guns. Work in strengthening the wire and improving bombing posts was carried out. Casualties:- Lieut R.W. CHETHAM-STRODE (employed at Bombing Officer 20th Infantry Brigade) Wounded.	
	4/12/16		1 man Died of Exposure at the Advanced Dressing Station. Enemy Artillery was active during the day between Points 56. 17 and 95. Enemy Snipers were very active firing from	

WAR DIARY
or
INTELLIGENCE SUMMARY.
(Erase heading not required.)

Army Form C. 2118.

(PAGE 3)

Hour, Date, Place	Summary of Events and Information	Remarks and references to Appendices
4/12/16	The trench running from Point 17 to 88. They were kept down by our snipers who accounted for at least four of the enemy in this neighbourhood during the day. Many of the enemy were seen during the day. Groups were seen moving back soon after daybreak to their support line. No new enemy work was observed - a party digging behind trench 17-88 ceased when fired at by our snipers. Aircraft on both sides was active. One of our aeroplanes was brought down on the right of the Battalion. Work in improving & strengthening of trenches was carried on. Barbed wire was laid in the front of each fire company at night. Casualties: Nil.	
5/12/16	Our artillery bombarded Point 88. The bombardment was accurate & had the effect of silencing enemy snipers. Enemy artillery retaliated particularly on front of Left Fire Company and Battalion Headquarters which	

WAR DIARY or INTELLIGENCE SUMMARY.

(PAGE 4)

Army Form C. 2118.

Hour, Date, Place	Summary of Events and Information	Remarks and references to Appendices
5/12/16	were shelled intermittently during the day. A few of the enemy were seen during the day but no new work was observed. Our snipers were again active. The Battalion were relieved by the 1st Bn South Staffordshire Regiment at night and on relief marched to billets at BERTRANCOURT. B Company were relieved in billets at MALLY-MAILLET by 1 Company of 8th Bn Devonshire Regiment and joined the Battalion in billets. Casualties:- Nil	
6/12/16 to 10/12/16 BERTRANCOURT	The Battalion remained in billets in Divisional Reserve. Working parties for work in repairing roads were furnished daily.	
11/12/16	The Battalion marched to BEAUMONT HAMEL in the morning relieving 2nd Bn Royal Warwickshire Regiment in the trenches. The relief was completed by 10PM. Aircraft on both sides was active during the morning. The enemy periodically shelled the defences during the day.	
12/12/16	The Battalion remained in BEAUMONT HAMEL defences in Brigade Support. Enemy artillery was again active	

WAR DIARY
or
INTELLIGENCE SUMMARY

(PAGE 5.)

Place	Date	Hour	Summary of Events and Information	Remarks and references to Appendices
	13/2/16		especially at night against the BEAUMONT-AUCHONVILLERS Road. Casualties :- 1 Wounded.	
			Owing to the exceedingly bad weather the Battalion relieved the 9th Battalion Devonshire Regiment in the front line (Q.5.6.9.7. to Q.6.C.4.5. alternately) in the early morning. The relief was completed by about 6 a.m. and the Battalion was then distributed as under :-	
			Front line :- RIGHT :- "A" Company, LEFT :- "B" Company	
			Support line :- "D" Company	
			Reserve line :- "C" Company.	
			The 2nd Battalion Gordon Highlanders were on the right of the Battalion and 21st Battalion Manchester Regiment on the left. Artillery on both sides was active during the day. Enemy Infantry was very quiet. Several small working parties were seen opposite Right Fire Company. Work in strengthening the Posts was carried on at night. Casualties :- 1 Killed	

WAR DIARY or INTELLIGENCE SUMMARY.

(PAGE 6.)

Hour, Date, Place	Summary of Events and Information	Remarks and references to Appendices
14/12/16	Our heavy artillery shelled various portions of the enemy line during the day, the enemy retaliating on support and reserve lines. Enemy infantry were very quiet, no sniping being done. Several enemy working parties were seen occasionally, but no new enemy work was observed. Patrols at night examined the line from Q.6.a.6.2. to Q.6.a.3.9. and the area between the lines. No enemy patrols were seen. Casualties:- Nil	
15/12/16	The Battalion was relieved by 9th Bn Devonshire Regt in the early morning and moved back to BEAUMONT HAMEL. Relief was completed by 6 am.	
16/12/16 to 19/12/16	The Battalion remained in BEAUMONT HAMEL Reserves in Brigade Support furnishing working & carrying parties daily. During this period the enemy periodically shelled the BEAUMONT- AUCHON VILLERS Road and surrounding areas. Casualties:- 17/12/16:- 1 Wounded. 19/12/16:- 1 Killed 1 Wounded	
20/12/16	The Battalion moved back to hutteb at MAILLY-MAILLET arriving at about 12 noon	

Army Form C. 2118.

WAR DIARY
or
INTELLIGENCE SUMMARY (PAGE 7)

Army Form C. 2118

Place	Date	Hour	Summary of Events and Information	Remarks and references to Appendices
20/12/16 to 31/12/16			The Battalion remained in billets in MAILLY - MAILLET. From 29th to 31st December patrols went out nightly to reconnoitre the ground enclosed in the area O.6.d.8.3, O.12.b.8.4, O.6.c.4.0. and O.6.c.5.3. for a special purpose. These patrols were much hampered by the very bad condition of the ground which was cut up by shell holes which the surface was so soft as to make it impossible to move without any sound. One patrol consisting of 2nd Lieut J. HAYTON and three NCOs which went out on the night of 30/12/16 encountered two of the enemy. 2nd Lieut HAYTON's revolver had slipped round his belt and he was unable to draw it. He therefore drew his pipe and pointed it at one of the enemy who put up his hands and was taken prisoner. The other was turned and fled and got away in the dark. Lieut. Colonel E.I. de S. THORPE rejoined the Battalion on 20th December 1916 and took over command from newly Lieut Colonel G.E. BEATY-POWNALL. Drafts as under joined the Battalion during the month:- 3/12/16.- 4 Other Ranks, 12/12/16.- 12/12/16.- 4 Other Ranks, 15/12/16.-	

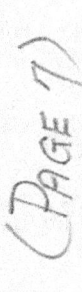

Army Form C. 2118.

WAR DIARY
or
INTELLIGENCE SUMMARY.
(Erase heading not required.)

(PAGE 8.)

Instructions regarding War Diaries and Intelligence Summaries are contained in F. S. Regs., Part II. and the Staff Manual respectively. Title pages will be prepared in manuscript.

Hour, Date, Place	Summary of Events and Information	Remarks and references to Appendices
3 Other Ranks 22/12/16 :- 1 Other Ranks	The men of these drafts had all served with the Battalion previously. Captain T. Wilson, 2nd Lieuts R.L. Beckh, S.Y. Croft, and H.B. Warren and 96 Other Ranks were evacuated sick during the month. The large amount of sickness in the Battalion was owing to the bad weather and the wet condition of the ground. The strength of the Battalion on the last day of the month was 26 Officers and 726 Other Ranks.	

Burn.
Lieut. Colonel.
Commanding 2nd Bn. The Border Regt.

7th DIVISION.
20th INF BDE.

2nd BORDER REGIEMNT.

JANUARY 1917.

War Diary

2nd Battalion Border Regiment

From:- 1st January 1917.
To:- 31st January 1917.

Vol 24

Army Form C. 2118

WAR DIARY
or
INTELLIGENCE SUMMARY
(Erase heading not required.)

Place	Date	Hour	Summary of Events and Information	Remarks and references to Appendices
MAILLY-MAILLET	4/1/17 to 6/1/17		Relieved REDAN - PENDANT COPSE - BEAUMONT HAMEL WOOD 1500 The Battalion remained in billets in Brigade Reserve training the attack which went out on the nights of 1st, 4th & 5th January to reconnoitre the ground enclosed in the area Q.6.d.8.3. Q.R.6.8.4. Q.6.c.4.0 & Q.6.c.5.3 with a view to an attack on LEAVE AVENUE and MUCK TRENCH. They were much hampered by the bad condition of the ground.	
	7/1/17		The Battalion moved from billets at MAILLY-MAILLET and occupied dugouts about Q.11.a.8.9. The move was commenced at 4 p.m. and completed by 7 p.m. Battalion Headquarters were established at Q.17.a.8.8.	
	8/1/17		The Battalion remained in its position. The day passed quietly except for the usual amount of artillery fire on both sides. Casualties:- Nil	
	9/1/17		The Battalion was ordered to attack LEAVE AVENUE and MUCK TRENCH on the morning of 10th January 1917 with a view to establishing a line running through Q.6.d.8.3 - Q.6.d.2.4 - Q.6.e.9.3 - Q.6.c.5.3. On the night of 9th January "A" "B" & "C" Companies moved to shelters in STATION ROAD, the move being completed by 8 p.m. By 11 p.m. on 9th January the Battalion had occupied its preliminary position & was disposed to go as follows:- "A" Company on Right in an assembly trench - Objective Point 24 in LEAVE AVENUE and to make a block some 50 yards E of junction of MUCK TRENCH and LEAVE AVENUE. "C" Company in Centre in BEAUCOURT TRENCH - Objective Point 93 in LEAVE AVENUE	

WAR DIARY or INTELLIGENCE SUMMARY

Army Form C. 2118

(PAGE 2)

Place	Date	Hour	Summary of Events and Information	Remarks and references to Appendices
	10/1/1917		B Company on left in BEAUCOURT TRENCH.- Objective Point 63 in LEAVE AVENUE and to make a block some 50 yards N in MUNICH TRENCH. Supporting troops of each Company in HARDWICK TRENCH. "D" Company was in Reserve. Each Company had to form a Strong Point at objectives and to find its own supporting troops. Zero Hour was 2 a.m. At Zero Hour on 10th January 1917 our field guns placed a barrage on NO MANS LAND & attacking troops had by this time formed up and commenced to move at 2-30 a.m. the attacking troops overran Enemy positions capturing 2 Machine Guns, 1 Automatic Rifle and 3 Officers and 142 Other Ranks prisoners. The captured positions were consolidated immediately. The going in NO MANS LAND was very bad and numbers of men were stuck in the mud and had to be dug out. Oblique lines were run out to the Strong Points immediately objectives were taken. Our casualties were slight and occurred chiefly owing to the fact that our troops followed up the barrage so closely suffering casualties from our own guns, but preventing the enemy getting out of his dug-outs in time with his machine guns. A few of the enemy attempted to approach Point 63 but were driven back by our bombers. Method of attack. Each Company to go straight for its objective in as close a formation	

As possible:-

Bombers ⎫
"Mopping Up" Party ⎬ 1st Line
Riflemen ⎭

Rifle Grenadiers ⎫
Lewis Carriers ⎬ 2nd Line
S.A.A. Carriers ⎭
Wire Carriers

There were no extended lines.
The Battalion remained in the captured trenches which were heavily shelled by the enemy throughout the day.
The Battalion was relieved by 1st Batt. Royal Welsh Fusiliers at night and proceeded to billets at MAILLY-MAILLET.
Total casualties for 10/11/17 were:-
OFFICERS:- Killed:- Captain S.F. JOHNSON.
Wounded:- Lieut R.K. EHRENBORG., 2nd Lieut C.F.E. INGLEDOW.
OTHER RANKS:- Killed 6.
Wounded 44
Missing 2.

The following Officers, Warrant Officers, NCO's and men were awarded decorations for gallantry displayed in the action:-
MILITARY CROSS:- 2nd Lieut U. HAYTON, 2nd Lieut H.D. LEES, 2nd Lieut S.J. LOCKYER, No 1800 Coy Sgt Major J. STREETER,

WAR DIARY or INTELLIGENCE SUMMARY

Army Form C. 2118 (PAGE 4)

Place	Date	Hour	Summary of Events and Information	Remarks and references to Appendices
MAILLY-MAILLET	10/1/17		DISTINGUISHED CONDUCT MEDAL:- N° 21053 Lance Corporal F. COX.	
			MILITARY MEDAL. 23371 Sergt A. TURNER. 21487 Pte F. GRIMSHAW, 22013 C.S.M. F. THOMAS. 9802 Sergt G. HEPPEL.	
	11/1/17 to 14/1/17		The Battalion remained in Billets	
	15/1/17		The Battalion moved into Brigade Support, relieving 10 Batt. Royal Welsh Fusiliers. The relief was completed by 5pm and the Battalion was then disposed as follows. Battalion Headquarters and A and C Companies in the dugouts at O.17.a.3.8. B and D Companies in BURN WORK in BEAUMONT HAMEL. The Battalion remained in position in Brigade Support. Enemy artillery was active against BEAUMONT HAMEL and surrounding area. Casualties:- NIL	
	16/1/17 & 17/1/17			
	18/1/17		The Battalion relieved 4th Bn. Duke's (Princess Beaumont) in the front line. The relief was commenced at 4:30pm and by 7pm the Battalion was in position as follows:- Front Line:- RIGHT:- "D" Company. LEFT "C" Company. Support:- "B" Company. Battalion Headquarters at WALKER QUARRY. Reserve :- "A" Company in dugouts in WAGON ROAD. Enemy artillery was active during the early part of the night. Patrols from the 6th Seaforth Regiment who had been left behind for this purpose went out during the night. The enemy were reported to be holding FRANKFORT, SALFORD and DOUBLE TRENCHES. The 2nd Batt. Gordon Highlanders were on the Right of the Battalion and the 1st Battalion Royal Scots on the left. Touch was kept with these Battalions by day and night Casualties :- 2 Other Ranks Wounded.	

WAR DIARY or INTELLIGENCE SUMMARY

(Page 5)

Army Form C. 2118

Place	Date	Hour	Summary of Events and Information	Remarks and references to Appendices
	19/11/17		Enemy artillery was active during the morning against WAGON ROAD and surrounding area. Our heavy artillery retaliated. Enemy infantry were very quiet during the day and up to several of our units gone forward. Patrols went out from each Coy Company at night. The patrol from the Right Fire Company under the command of 2nd Lieut T.GRONOW discovered that FRANKFORT TRENCH (reported as occupied by the enemy) was not occupied. The night passed quietly. Casualties :- 2nd Lieut D.A.GILLESPIE wounded.	
	20/11/17		Enemy artillery was active during the early morning against BEAUMONT HAMEL. A skilled reconnaissance was carried out in broad daylight by 2nd Lieut T.GRONOW and No.9565 Sgt C.GARWOOD. This officer and N.C.O. went out and examined FRANKFORT TRENCH and found it to be unoccupied. After examining the dugouts they went still further forward and located the true German line. They were heavily shelled when returning to our lines. No. 6183 Private J.THOMPSON went out in broad daylight and examined WAGON ROAD. He located the German positions and brought back first useful information. No.18349 Private W.ROONEY went out in broad daylight and examined SALFORD TRENCH which he found was unoccupied by the enemy. He went some 50 yards further forward when shrapnel fire was opened on him and he returned to Coy. Bn. The Battalion was relieved at dusk by 2nd Batty K.O.Y.L.I. The relief was completed at 10.30pm the Battalion proceeded to billets was MAILLY-MAILLET. Casualties: 1 Wounded.	
	21/11/17		The Battalion marched to billets at BERTRANCOURT arriving about 12 noon.	
	22/11/17		The Battalion remained in billets at BERTRANCOURT.	
	23/11/17		The Battalion marched to billets at BEAUVAL starting at 6-10am & arriving about 1pm.	

WAR DIARY or INTELLIGENCE SUMMARY

(PAGE 6)

Army Form C. 2118.

Place	Date	Hour	Summary of Events and Information	Remarks and references to Appendices
BEAUVAL	24/1/17 25/1/17		The Battalion remained in billets. Refitting and reclothing was carried out. The reorganisation of Companies was carried out. Bombing, Rifle Grenade and Lewis Gun sections were selected during the day & Companies were allotted training areas near billets.	
	26/1/17		The Battalion commenced its training. During the morning Bombing, Rifle Grenade, Lewis Gun, Vickers, Lewis Gun Training and instruction in Bombing, Rifle Grenade, Lewis Gun, Musketry, Bayonet fighting was carried out.	
	27/1/17		The afternoon was devoted to sport.	
	28/1/17		The Battalion continued its training.	
	29/1/17		The Battalion continued its training.	
	30/1/17		The Corps Commander visited Companies at training during the morning. The Army Commander visited Companies at training in the afternoon. He saw and personally congratulated all the Officers who took part in the attack on 19/11/17 and the daylight reconnaissance on 20/11/17 at 9AM and arriving about 2PM. The Battalion marched to billets at PERNOIS. Starting 10/11/17. Notification was received that the Corps Commander awards the Military Medal to 18347 Private W.J. ROONEY and No 6183 Private J. THOMPSON for gallantry in the field on 20/11/17.	
	31/1/17		2nd Lieut H.D. LEES was wounded on 31/1/17 whilst carrying out a reconnaissance of the trenches.	
			Drafts as under joined the Battalion during the month:- 1/1/17 :- 10 Other Ranks. 10/1/17 :- 65 Other Ranks. 21/1/17 :- 99 Other Ranks. 23/1/17 :- 18 Other Ranks. 24/1/17 :- 20 Other Ranks. 28/1/17 :- 10 Other Ranks.	

WAR DIARY
or
INTELLIGENCE SUMMARY

(Erase heading not required.)

Army Form C. 2118.

Place	Date	Hour	Summary of Events and Information	Remarks and references to Appendices
			The following Officers joined the Battalion during the month. 1/11/17 Captain C.E. GRAHAM. 2/11/17 Captain S.F. JOHNSON. 3/11/17 2nd Lieut. F.W. KEENAN. 5/11/17 2nd Lieut. J.J. DEDMAN. 13/11/17 Major S.H. WORRALL & Captain E.R. CHETHAM-STRODE. 23/11/17 2nd Lieut. A. HARPER. 28/11/17 2nd Lieut. J. HARDING & 2nd Lieut. R. ABRAM. 29 Other Ranks were evacuated Sick during the month. The strength of the Battalion on the last day of the month was 26 Officers & 814 Other Ranks.	

West Tunnell Major.
Commanding 2nd The Border Regt.

7th Division
20th Inf Bde

2nd Border Regiment.

February 1917

WAR DIARY.

2ND. BATTALION BORDER REGIMENT.

FROM:- 1ST. FEBRUARY, 1917.

TO:- 28TH FEBRUARY, 1917.

Army Form C.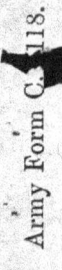

WAR DIARY

INTELLIGENCE SUMMARY.

(Erase heading not required.)

Instructions regarding War Diaries and Intelligence Summaries are contained in F. S. Regs., Part II. and the Staff Manual respectively. Title pages will be prepared in manuscript.

Place	Date	Hour	Summary of Events and Information	Remarks and references to Appendices
PERNOIS	1/2/17		The Battalion continued its training. During the morning Company Drill, Platoon and Section training and instruction in Bombing, Rifle Grenade, Lewis Gun, Musketry, Bayonet fighting was carried out. The afternoon was devoted to sport	
	2/2/17		The Battalion continued its training	
	3/2/17		The Battalion continued its training	
	4/2/17		The Battalion continued its training	
	5/2/17		The Battalion continued its training	
	6/2/17		The Battalion continued its training	
	7/2/17		The Battalion continued its training. Notification was received that the Commander in Chief awards the following decorations:-	
			MILITARY CROSS :- 2nd Lieut. T. GRONOW.	
			DISTINGUISHED CONDUCT MEDAL:- No 9565 Sergeant C. GARWOOD	
			for gallantry in the field on 20/1/1917.	
	8/2/17		The Battalion continued its training. A practice attack on a Strong Point which was carried out by the Bombing and Lewis Gun Sections of the Brigade. During the attack the undersigned Officer and NCO were accidentally wounded by the premature bursting of a rifle grenade:-	
			2nd Lieut W.B.START. No 6095 L/Cpl. J.CLARK.	

Army Form C. 2118.

PAGE 2

WAR DIARY
INTELLIGENCE SUMMARY.
(Erase heading not required.)

Place	Date	Hour	Summary of Events and Information	Remarks and references to Appendices
PERNOIS.	9/2/17		The Battalion took part in a Brigade Exercise.	
	10/2/17		The Battalion continued its training	
	11/2/17		The Battalion continued its training	
	12/2/17		The Battalion Continued its training	
	13/2/17		" " " "	
	14/2/17		" " " "	
	15/2/17		" " " "	
	16/2/17		The Battalion marched to billets at BEAUVAL starting at about 10am and arriving at 2pm.	
BEAUVAL	17/2/17		The Battalion attended a Devrcer Parade for the inspection of the Division by General NIVELLE, Commander-in-Chief French Army in the morning.	
	18/2/17		The Battalion marched to billets at BUS, starting at 9am & arriving at about 2pm.	
BUS.	19/2/17		The Battalion marched to billets at BERTRANCOURT starting at 11am and arriving about 12 noon.	
BERTRAN-COURT.	20/2/17		Working Parties for repairing roads were furnished by the Battalion.	
	21/2/17		The Battalion came under the Command of 90.B. 7ot Infantry Brigade. Working parties were furnished by the Battalion during the day.	
	22/2/17		The Battalion marched to billets in Brigade Reserve at MAILLY - MAILLET, starting at 11.15am & arriving about 12 noon.	

WAR DIARY
or
INTELLIGENCE SUMMARY.

Army Form C. 2118.

PAGE 3

Place	Date	Hour	Summary of Events and Information	Remarks and references to Appendices
MAILLY-MAILLET	23/2/17 24/2/17		The Battalion remained in billets in Brigade Reserve.	

REFERENCE MAPS:- SERRE 1/10,000. HEBUTERNE 1/10,000.

Orders were received that the 91st Infantry Brigade was moving into the line and that the Battalion would remain in Brigade Reserve at MAILLY-MAILLET.

At 11.15 a.m. orders were received from 91st Infantry Brigade as follows:-

"1. Meeg is reason to believe that the enemy has retired from his line of posts in rear of TEN TREE ALLEY and partly evacuated the village of SERRE."

"2. At 5 a.m. on 25th February 1917 OC 21st Manchester Regt will push forward strong patrols supported by 2 Companies (remainder in Reserve) with the following objectives:-

"(1) JOHN ALLEY - MAXIM TRENCH."

"(2) Line from K.30.c.2.5. - POM POM ALLEY."

"(3) Line K.30.c.6.8. - L.25.a.0.1. - L.25.a.7.5."

"3. At the same hour OC 1st South Staffs Regt will carry out a similar advance on a 2 Company front from the line of TEN TREE ALLEY with objectives as under:-

"1. Line from Northern Corner of PENDANT COPSE - along track running N.W."
"Through L.25.c.0.3 to junction MAXIM TRENCH - WAGON ROAD."

"2. PENDANT TRENCH."

"3. PENDANT ALLEY EAST."

"4. WING TRENCH - ie. a line from L.25.b.5.2. - L.25.a.7.5."

Army Form C. 2118.

PAGE 4

WAR DIARY
or
INTELLIGENCE SUMMARY.
(Erase heading not required.)

Place	Date	Hour	Summary of Events and Information	Remarks and references to Appendices
			"move his Battalion at short notice up the WAGON ROAD in support of 1st South Staffs Regt."	
			"(b) OC. 2nd Border Regt. will similarly be prepared to move by the"	
SERRE ROAD in support of 21st Manchester Regt.			× × ×	
			Orders were at once issued for the Battalion to pack up and to stack all kit and to "Stand to" from 4.30am 25th inst.	
	25/2/17	5.45am	2nd Lieut B. Cumpston was sent to Head Quarters 21st Manchester Regt. at MOUSE POST (K.35.c.8.8)	
			During the day the orders for the attack were changed four times — finally at 3.45am the Battalion left billets at MAILLY-MAILLET and moved up to dug-outs in the neighbourhood of K.35.c.3.1. in support of the Royal Welsh Fusiliers in WING TRENCH.	
			Orders were received and preparations made for an advance on PUISIEUX with the object of establishing a line through SOAP ALLEY and pushing strong patrols forward to take up a line of posts on the Northern and Eastern edge of PUISIEUX.	(2nd Border R. returned from front line about 9p.m. 22nd Feb 1917)
	26/2/17	1.15am	verbal orders were received that the attack was cancelled.	
			Two strong patrols were sent to be pushed forward — one by the Royal Welsh Fusiliers during the night, one by 2nd Border Regiment on the left.	
			Objective:— Junction of SOAP ALLEY and BATH LANE — Junction SOAP ALLEY and SUNSET TRENCH.	

Army Form C. 2118.
PAGE 5.

WAR DIARY
or
INTELLIGENCE SUMMARY.

Place	Date	Hour	Summary of Events and Information	Remarks and references to Appendices
	26/2/17		SUNSET TRENCH to the BEAUCOURT - PUISIEUX Road. Standing line between Royal Welsh Fusiliers and 2nd Border Regiment - SERRE - PUISIEUX Road inclusive to 2nd Border Regiment. D Company was detailed for this duty. The patrols advanced to WING TRENCH where they came up in line on the left of the Royal Welsh Fusiliers at 6am. The patrols advanced and reached KAISER LANE. Here it was found that the ridge on the left front was swept with machine guns. OC D Company (Capt McKenly-Bonall) decided that to advance without artillery support would mean sustaining heavy losses. He therefore gave the order to withdraw after being in action for an hour and a half. D Company then withdrew to WING TRENCH. At 12 noon information was received that the 2nd Division on the right had occupied GUDGEON TRENCH. The Royal Welsh Fusiliers were ordered to send up on our Company to occupy SUNSET TRENCH South of the SERRE Road and gain touch with the troops on the right. The Brigade on the Right were reported to be advancing on ORCHARD ALLEY. The Brigade on the Left were reported to be advancing on BOX WOOD. At 1 pm orders were sent out by Brigade that the Royal Welsh Fusiliers were to advance and occupy SUNSET TRENCH as far North as the SERRE Road, then extend Northwards & occupy SOAP ALLEY. Touch was to be gained with the 19th Division on	F.M.

Army Form C 2118.
PAGE 6.

Place	Date	Hour	Summary of Events and Information	Remarks and references to Appendices
	26/2/17		Left in FORK TERRACE and 12th Division on Right at 1.15@33 and Border Regt were ordered to move to WING TRENCH and support or exploitation. The 1st Royal Welsh Fusiliers moved forward at 3.45 p.m. At 5.52 p.m. a message was received from O/C Sup Brigade that the Battalion was not to be involved without reference to Brigade. No. Orders accordingly were made. However that 1 Company was to be at the disposal of O.C 1st Royal Welsh Fusiliers. "C" Company was detailed for this duty. At 6.15 p.m. information was received that the troops on our Right in WING TRENCH had been withdrawn. The nick nearest trops were at L.26.c. central. It was now reported that the troops in GUDGEON TRENCH had their left flank at L.21.c.0.7. The occupation by them of ORCHARD ALLEY was not confirmed. At 7.36 p.m. the left Company Royal Welsh Fusiliers were reported in KAISER LANE and orders were received that O.C 2nd Border Regt was to keep in touch with the Royal Welsh Fusiliers on his own initiative with the object of establishing a strong bridge in KAISER LANE astride the SERRE ROAD. "C" Company was ordered up to do this. In the meanwhile however the Royal Welsh Fusiliers had achieved its objective & was in occupation of KAISER and SOAP Trenches. O.C. Royal Welsh Fus. sent "C" Company back and consequently no further action was taken by O.C 2nd Border Regt. Patrols of the Royal Welsh Fusiliers were pushed on towards PUISIEUX. 10.50 pm. The following dispositions were then made for the night :-	

WAR DIARY
or
INTELLIGENCE SUMMARY

Army Form C. 2118.

PAGE 1.

Place	Date	Hour	Summary of Events and Information	Remarks and references to Appendices

26/9/17

(1) 1 Platoon of 1 Platoon on the SERRE ROAD immediately above R.M.12r.6. No 5 "Platoon "B"Coy under 2nd Lieut RUTHERFORD was detailed for this duty.

1 Platoon of 1 Platoon near the BRICKFIELDS at J.3.a. No 6 "Platoon "B"Coy under 2nd Lieut DEETMAN was detailed for this duty.

These Platoons were employed in posts already seen and consolidated these posts.

(2) 2 Companies occupied & consolidated
    (a) RHINE TRENCH   ("A" Company)
    (b) WING TRENCH   ("D" Company)

These were employed on the same manner as the Platoons in (1)

(3) This left a striking force of 6 Platoons — "C" Company had already been placed at the disposal of O.C. Royal Welch Fusiliers. Captain B.E. Graham was sent forward to Head Quarters 1st Royal Welch Fusiliers to understand their dispositions and to act as liaison to O.C. 1st Royal Welch Fusrs. At 11.30am orders were received that at 6am 27/9/17 2nd Bn. Royal Berks Regt. would push along patrols through PUISIEUX and establish posts at Northern and Eastern road exits and Van Torch with neighbouring troops.

The duty of organising these forces was entrusted to Captain B.E. Graham. The following were the orders issued by him :—

No 1 Patrol will endeavour to obtain touch with the troops on the left and move up ROSSIGNOL TRENCH. If this patrol gets in touch they will report to Company Hd.Qrs. If they fail to get touch they will form a block just outside the village.

No 2 Patrol will form a block in KNIFE TRENCH just outside the village (L.14.c.3.1.) They will

WAR DIARY
or
INTELLIGENCE SUMMARY.
(Erase heading not required.)

Army Form C. 2118.

PAGE 8.

Place	Date	Hour	Summary of Events and Information	Remarks and references to Appendices
	26/2/17		will watch FORK and KNIFE trenches.	
			No 3 Patrol will block the PUISIEUX - BUCQUOY Road at L.14.a.8.6.	
			No 4 Patrol will block the cross roads at L.14.d.3.9.	
			No 5 Patrol will block the road leading Eastward at L.15.a.5.5.	
			No 6 Patrol will endeavour to gain touch with the troops on the Right and with this object will move up GUDGEON TRENCH.	
			If unable to obtain touch they will leave a post (about 10 men) in GUDGEON TRENCH on the right flank of the Royal Welch Fusrs. the remainder of the Patrol will block the road leading Eastward at L.21.a.5.5. If used upon unable to move forward they will only extend the line eastward in GUDGEON TRENCH.	
			Should similar Patrols be sent further Eastwards.	
			If touch is obtained the Patrol will fill up the Gap between the Right flank of Royal Welch Fusrs and the left of the flank turned on our Right, the remainder of the Patrol to block the road as already indicated.	
			Report to be sent to Captain R. Graham at 1st Royal Welsh Fusrs Head Quarters.	
			The following were detailed for the above	
			No 1 Patrol	No 8 Platoon "B" Company under 2nd Lieut E.R.L. BISHOP	
			No 2 "	No 13 " "D" " " " T.GRONOW	
			No 3 "	No 12 " "C" " " " D.D.LOW	
			No 4 "	No 2 " "A" " " " R. ABRAM	
			No 5 "	No 3 " "A" " " " R.J.CUNNINGHAM	
			No 6 "	No 4 " "A" " " " J. MOORE	
	27/2/17		By 10-12 a.m. it was reported that the four Patrols concentrated in CITY VILLAGE trenches, had sent through the village had. and Lieut T.GRONOW took charge of the Patrols	

Army Form C. 2118.

PAGE 9.

WAR DIARY
or
INTELLIGENCE SUMMARY.
(Erase heading not required.)

Place	Date	Hour	Summary of Events and Information	Remarks and references to Appendices
	27/2/17		and took up a defensive position as follows:— From the junction of KNIFE and VILLAGE Trenches along VILLAGE TRENCH to CITY TRENCH. Along CITY TRENCH to a point L.20.b.2.6. The N.W. Corner of the village was then cleared of the enemy who were little resistance. Lewis Gun and rifle fire was brought to bear on the S.W. corner which was still in the hands of a few snipers and a machine Gun mainly concentrated in the Church. No 4 Patrol under 2nd Lieut R.ABRAM was the first to reach the village at L.20.c.6.9. They advanced up the Road running Northward and were always considerably (?) assisted by machine Gun fire at the corner L.20.a.60.05. Shortly afterwards this Patrol was joined by No 2 who entered the village in the dark under cover of gun and rifle fire along the road running Eastward from point L.19.d.55.65. No 2 Patrol under 2nd Lieut T.GIBNOW advanced up the road running N.E. of L.20.a.80.05 they then turned Northward into VILLAGE TRENCH and their advance was covered by a few men of No 4 Patrol led by No 10624 Sergt H. HURNDALL who stood up on a ledge of an old ruin and turned the machine gun (this NCO was subsequently Killed). The enemy now retired and enabled the Lewis Guns of No 4 Patrol to inflict some casualties on them as they retired up the main road running Northward through the village. Nos 2 and 4 Patrols now found hands & commenced to work their way to the Northern	

WAR DIARY
or
INTELLIGENCE SUMMARY
(Erase heading not required.)

Army Form C. 2118.
PAGE 10.

Place	Date	Hour	Summary of Events and Information	Remarks and references to Appendices
	27/2/17		Northern edge of the village. They advanced up VILLAGE TRENCH to the road running roughly East & West through Point L.20.a.55.60. The enemy were placed far from the Square at L.20.a.45.30. & the houses on the Eastern side of the BUCQUOY ROAD. No 4 Patrol now reached at L.20.a.55.60. & covered the advance of No 2 Patrol along the road from L.20.a.90. to L.14.c.10.35. Thence No 2 Patrol brought heavy Gun fire to bear on the enemy who retired into the NE corner of the village whereupon No 4 Patrol advanced up the village VILLAGE TRENCH to its junction with CITY TRENCH where consolidation was commenced, while 2nd Lieut T.GRODON took forward a few men from Y & a small Patrol and drove the enemy out of the NE Corner of the Village. We then retired up FORK TRENCH Y to Mock was made in KNIFE TRENCH. Nos 3 & 5 Patrols which had become separated thereupon when the Patrol leaders were wounded were now reorganised by 2nd Lieut T.GRODON who the Patrol and Sent forward to join No 4 Patrol in CITY TRENCH. Two Patrols was now under the leadership of N0 82 65 Serjt. R.IVES. No 1 Patrol which had been sent up on the left to gain touch with the troops on our Left flank were unable to regain anybody although they went 300 yards up BOSSIGNOL TRENCH. No 6 Patrol on the Right went some 400 yards East along GUDGEON TRENCH but were unable to find the succour body. They came across however a few isolated groups of the 62nd Division who had lost connection with the succour body At 10.17 a.m. a message was received that touch was to be gained by the left Royal Welsh Fusrs while the 2nd Border Regt continued reconnaissance of the village	

Army Form C. 2118.
PAGE 11.

WAR DIARY
or
INTELLIGENCE SUMMARY.
(Erase heading not required.)

Place	Date	Hour	Summary of Events and Information	Remarks and references to Appendices
	27/2/19		village. Therefore No 6 Patrol was ordered to advance on the Eastern portion of the village & clear the Church and outskirts of the snipers who were causing inconvenience to our troops in GUDGEON TRENCH. They attempted to advance along the MIRAUMONT - PUISIEUX Road but were unable to do so owing to machine gun and rifle fire which was opened on them from the Church & surrounding neighbourhood. They therefore came back along GUDGEON TRENCH, lined up VILLAGE TRENCH and advanced along ORCHARD ALLEY. No 1 Patrol was ordered to advance up SUNSET TRENCH to N.E Corner of PUISIEUX. Meanwhile 2nd Brigade had received information that the Church was strongly held by a large force with machine guns. Orders were received that no attempt was to be made to dislodge the enemy as heavy guns were going to be turned on to the Church. 2nd Lieut J. MOORE, O.C. No 6 Patrol, was therefore ordered not to advance on the Church. The Patrols in CITY TRENCH were ordered to extend their line Eastwards towards BM 103.8 on the PUISIEUX - ACHIET LE PETIT Road. "J" Coy me Company was ordered up to occupy VILLAGE TRENCH. "J" Company was detailed for this duty under the Command of Capt T.T. BEATY-POWNALL. On the night of 27th/28th February the Companies in reserve were relieved by Companies of 2/1st H.A.C. (Infantry) - The Companies in the front line dry and Royal Warwicks Regt. Relief was complete at 5.45 a.m 28th February and the Battalion marched to billets at MAILLY - MAILLET. Total Casualties sustained by the Battalion were :- OFFICERS :- 2 WOUNDED - 2nd Lieuts D.D. LOW and R.J. CUNNINGHAM.	
	28/2/19			

WAR DIARY
or
INTELLIGENCE SUMMARY.

Army Form C. 2118.
PAGE 12.

Place	Date	Hour	Summary of Events and Information	Remarks and references to Appendices
	28/2/17		OTHER RANKS:- KILLED:- 12	
			WOUNDED:- 28	
			NOT ACCOUNTED FOR:- 1	
			The following Officers Joined the Battalion during the month	
			6/2/1917:- 2nd Lieuts G.S. RUTHERFORD, J.B.R. EDWARDS,	
			2nd Lieuts D.B. DEMPSTER & R. ADAMSON - 3rd K.O.S.B.	
			10/2/1917:- Lieut R. MAXWELL, 2nd Lieuts E.R.L. BISHOP, E.J.H. METTAM - 3rd K.O.S.B.	
			10/2/1917:- 2nd Lieut R.J. CUNNINGHAM.	
			15/2/1917:- 2nd Lieut D.T. HOLMES - 2nd K.O.S.B. 2nd Lieut J.B. DUNLOP - 13th H.L.I - 21/2/17.	
			21/2/1917:- 2nd Lieut D.D. LOW	
			23/2/1917:- 2nd Lieut C.B. BARR.	
			The following Officers Joined the Battalion during the month:-	
			4/2/17:- 12 Other Ranks. 10/2/17:- 10 Other Ranks. 21/2/17:- 6 Other Ranks	
			16/2/17:- 9 Other Ranks	
			The supply of these Drafts had Greyerally served with the Battalion	
			57 Other Ranks were evacuated Sick during the month	
			The strength of the Battalion on the last day of the month was:-	
			35 Officers 820 Other Ranks	

Commanding 2nd Lt. The Border Regt.

7th Division
20th Inf Bde

2nd Border Regiment.

March 1917.

War Diary

2nd Battalion Border Regiment

Period

From :- 1st March 1917

To :- 31st March 1917

Army Form C. 2118.

WAR DIARY
OR
INTELLIGENCE SUMMARY.
(Erase heading not required.)

Instructions regarding War Diaries and Intelligence Summaries are contained in F.S. Regs., Part II. and the Staff Manual respectively. Title pages will be prepared in manuscript.

Place	Date	Hour	Summary of Events and Information	Remarks and references to Appendices
MAILLY MAILLET	1/3/17		The Battalion remained in billets.	
	2/3/17		The Battalion remained in billets	
	3/3/17		The Battalion remained in billets	
	4/3/17		The Battalion remained in billets	
	5/3/17		The Battalion marched from billets at MAILLY MAILLET to billets at BERTRANCOURT commencing at 6.30am and arriving at about 7.30am	
BERTRANCOURT	6/3/17		Working parties were furnished by the Battalion for work on roads.	
	7/3/17		" " " " " " " " " "	
	8/3/17		" " " " " " " " " "	
	9/3/17		" " " " " " " " " "	
	10/3/17		" " " " " " " " " "	
	11/3/17		" " " " " " " " " "	
	12/3/17		" " " " " " " " " "	
	13/3/17		The Battalion marched from billets at BERTRANCOURT to BOLTON CAMP (near MAILLY MAILLET) commencing at 4pm and arriving at 5.30am	
	14/3/17		The Battalion marched back to billets at BERTRANCOURT starting at 1.30pm and arriving about 3pm	
	15/3/17		The Battalion marched from billets at BERTRANCOURT to billets in MAILLY MAILLET WOOD starting at 2.30pm & arriving about 4pm	
	16/3/17		Working parties were furnished by the Battalion for work on roads.	
	17/3/17		" " " " " " " " " "	
			Notification was received that the Commander in Chief awards the bar to the Military Cross to 2ND LIEUT. T. GRONOW.	

WAR DIARY
INTELLIGENCE SUMMARY.
(Erase heading not required.)

Army Form C.2118.
PAGE 2.

Place	Date	Hour	Summary of Events and Information	Remarks and references to Appendices
	18/3/17		The Battalion remained in billets.	
	19/3/17		The Battalion marched to PUISIEUX starting at 10am arriving about 12 noon.	
	20/3/17		The Battalion remained at PUISIEUX	
	21/3/17		The Battalion marched to COURCELLES starting at 1am. It joined the Battalion moved into the line in front of ST. LEGER relieving 8th Bn Queens Regiment "A" Company was on the Right, "B" Company in the Centre, and "C" Company on the Left. The Right of the line was on ST LEGER Wood and the left was at T.21.a.2.1. The 7th Bn Queens Regt were on the Right of the Battalion and a Battalion of the London Regt was on the left. From an aeroplane report it was thought that CROISILLES was unoccupied by the enemy and two Officer Patrols were sent out on the night of 21st/22nd to verify this. One patrol under 2nd Lieut. J.J. DEDMAN advanced on CROISILLES from the SE. This was held up by machine gun fire 500 yards from the village. The other under 2nd Lieut W.G. GRAHAME entered the village from the SW and found the House surrounding Y the village strongly held. On 22nd a Lewis Gun of B Company was knocked out by shell fire. During the day the situation remained unchanged. On the night of 22nd/23rd Posts were pushed forward and CROISILLES was again reconnoitred.	
	22/3/17			

Army Form C. 2118.
PAGE 3

WAR DIARY
or
INTELLIGENCE SUMMARY.
(Erase heading not required.)

Place	Date	Hour	Summary of Events and Information	Remarks and references to Appendices
	22/3/17		reconnoitred. As it was not certain whether the Troops on the left were going to advance to the ST. LEGER – BOIRY Road it was decided to send up D Company from SAILLY to establish two posts on the West of CROISILLES so that in the event of the Troops on the left not moving forward D Company would have automatically come into support. The Posts were successfully pushed forward as required and on 23rd the line was held as follows.	

RIGHT :– A Company. Strong Posts at :–
(1) T.29.c.6.6. (2) T.29.c.5.9. (3) T.29.a.5.0.

RIGHT CENTRE :– B Company. Strong Posts at :–
(1) T.29.a.1.3. (2) T.29.a.2.9. (3) T.28.d.6.9. (4) T.28.b.7.2.
(5) T.28.b.4.6. (6) T.28.b.1.6. (7) T.28.a.8.7.

LEFT CENTRE :– D Company. Strong Posts at :–
(1) T.22.b.8.1. (2) T.22.b.3.1. (3) T.22.b.3.8. (4) T.22.a.2.1.
(5) T.22.a.3.0.

The road between Nos 4 & 5 Posts was consolidated and manned.

LEFT :– C Company. Strong Posts at :–
(1) T.22.c.5.3. (2) T.21.d.7.8. (3) T.21.d.3.8. (4) T.21.d.1.5.
(6) T.28.a.5.9. (5) T.28.a.8.7.

A patrol was sent up the ST. LEGER – BOIRY Road to a point 1000 yards beyond the cross roads in T.21.a. but could not get into touch with the Battalion on the left. On the

Army Form C. 2118.

PAGE 4.

WAR DIARY
or
INTELLIGENCE SUMMARY.
(Erase heading not required.)

Place	Date	Hour	Summary of Events and Information	Remarks and references to Appendices
	23/3/17		On the morning of 23rd it was reported that the Germans on the left had occupied the Cross roads in T21.a. A daylight patrol was therefore sent out and found that the Cross roads were not occupied.	
			All four Companies were consequently moved up to the front line. Two patrols were sent out towards CROISILLES under 2ND.LIEUT. E.J. PEACOCK during the night. Both these patrols reached the outskirts of the village but found it held in some strength by the enemy.	
			On the morning of 23rd a patrol of T22.U.S.2. under 2ND LIEUT. T. GRONOW and 2ND.LIEUT. supported by a Pat. in T22.U.S.2. The party swung round a bend in the road with orders to these Stragglers were immediately fired on by the Lewis Guns of the Bosch. Several casualties were inflicted on the enemy.	
			On the night of 23rd/24th the Bosch were again pushed a little nearer CROISILLES the nearest being within 500 yards of the village on the road in T.23.a.	
	24/3/17		On the night of 24th the Battalion was relieved by 2nd Bn Manchester Regt. Before relief however two Officers patrols were sent out to reconnoitre CROISSILLES which had again been reported evacuated.	
			These Patrols under 2nd Lieut A. PEPPER and 2nd Lieut J. DEDMAN advanced towards CROISILLES on either side of the road through T.23.S. + T.23.c. They reached the wire & started cutting it. The enemy had a sentry just a short way inside the wire. The Bosch was not alarmed until two of the enemy walking along the outside of the wire came up against our wire-cutting party, by endeavour was made to capture these two men but as they refused to put up their hands they were	

Army Form C. 2118.

WAR DIARY
INTELLIGENCE SUMMARY.
(Erase heading not required.)

PAGE 5

Place	Date	Hour	Summary of Events and Information	Remarks and references to Appendices
	24/3/17		They were shot. Men gave the alarm, the sentry fired the also automatic effort consequently our patrols retired.	
COURCELLES	25/3/17		The Battalion billeted at COURCELLES	
	26/3/17		The Battalion remained in billets at COURCELLES	
	27/3/17		" " " " " " "	
	28/3/17		" " " " " " "	
	29/3/17		The Battalion moved at 9.30am to ERVILLERS where it stood to in reserve to succeed to ST LEGER in support of an attack by Col Infantry Brigade on CROISILLES. During the afternoon "A" Company was sent up to support 7th Bn Wiltshire Regt. The remainder of the Battalion relieved the 8th Bn Devons Regt in front of ECOUST Front line:- Left:- B Company Right:- C Company D Company was in support. Battalion Headquarters were in NORY. A Patrol under 2nd Lieut. J HARDING was sent out on the night of 29th/30th to reconnoitre ECOUST which was reported to have been evacuated. This Patrol reported that not only was the village held but also posts out in front of the village were held by the enemy. On the 30th the village was again reported to have been evacuated. D Company was therefore ordered to send strong patrols into ECOUST. The village was still found to be held and D Company's patrols returned having suffered a few casualties. "A" Company joined the Battalion & went into reserve at the Abbey, MORY. On the	

Army Form C. 2118.

PAGE 6

WAR DIARY
or
INTELLIGENCE SUMMARY.
(Erase heading not required.)

Place	Date	Hour	Summary of Events and Information	Remarks and references to Appendices
	29/3/17		On the night of 29th/30th "B" Company was relieved by 2nd Royal Warwicks Regt and went into reserve at the Abbey N9FY. "A" and "D" Companies relieved 2 Companies of 2nd Gordon Highlanders on the right of "C" Company. Patrols were again sent out to reconnoitre ECOUST but the village was found to be held as on the night before. The posts held by the Battalion were as follows:- Right front Company:- (1) C8.d.21. (2) C7.d.6.2. (3) C7.d.9.2. (4) B2.d.8.7. Centre Company:- (1) C7.b.4.3. (2) C7.c.0.3. (3) C7.a.2.3 (4) B12.a.8.9. Left front Company:- (1) B12.b.9.9 (2) B6.d.central (3) B6.a.9.5 (4) B.6.c.1.7. Reserve Company at the Abbey B22.a.8.7. ECOUST was again reported by aeroplane to be evacuated. Daylight patrols were therefore ordered to be sent out. "B" Company under Lieut. T Maxwell and detailed for this duty. "B" Company advanced across the plateau of B23.a. and B17.c. they came in full view of the enemy & were heavily shelled suffering several casualties.	
	30/3/17		During the night 30/31st "B" Company attacked an enemy post at C No.55 under an artillery barrage and took it. They were temporarily checked by a rifle bombing post at C7.a.65.45. This check enabled the enemy in the string post to withdraw. The occupants of the bombing post were however killed. Simultaneous attack had been planned on an enemy post at C8.c.01. "D" Company was detailed for this duty. This Company had first to be relieved by	A Company

WAR DIARY
INTELLIGENCE SUMMARY
(Erase heading not required.)

Army Form C. 2118.
PAGE 1

Place	Date	Hour	Summary of Events and Information	Remarks and references to Appendices
	30/3/19		A Company at 2/1st HAC. and were late in starting because the relief were not be conducted in time. The consequence of this was that "D" Company was set get was engaged to reach the Post when the Barrage lifted & where they ad on were it they were was up by warding over for form the Post. When however the Post at M.a.55 was captured the occupants of the Post at O.7.c.9.7. retired. Two Posts were established at C.1.6.1.7 & C1.a.3.2. The Battalion was then relieved by the 2/6 & 4 AC & proceeded to Villets au Brulliers. Casualties from 2/3/19 to 3/3/19 were as follows:- OFFICERS :- Killed:- Capt T.T. BEATY-POWNALL (24/3/19) 2nd Lieut. A. HARPER, 2nd Lieut W. DEDMAN 3/3/19. Wounded :- 2nd Lieut. T. GRONOW MC (21/3/19) OTHER RANKS :- Killed:- $10 Wounded 35 Missing 15 north. The following Officers joined the Battalion during the month. 1/3/19 :- 2nd Lieuts W.G. GRAHAME and W. INKPEN 2/3/19 :- 2nd Lieut M. SEYMOUR - ISAACS. Drafts as under joined the Battalion during the month:- 5/3/19 :- 1 O. Rank 12/3/19 :- 1 O. Rank 14/3/19 :- 3 O. Ranks 26/3/19 :- 1 O. Rank. The was of these drafts were fully trained most of the men having previously served in the Battalion. 43 Other Ranks were evacuated sick during the month. The strength of the Battalion on the last day of the month was :- 33 Officers 729 Other Ranks.	

Commanding 2nd Bn The Border Regt

Recd

Administrative Orders for forthcoming
Operations by
Major G. E. Beaty Pownall
Commdg 2nd Border Regt
25th March 1917.

1. Dress and Equipment
   (a) The following fighting dress will be worn
   by all ranks except specialists:-
   (I) Rifle and equipment, less pack
   (II) 120 rounds S.A.A.
   (III) Haversack on the back, containing rations
   as in 3.
   (IV) Leather Jerkin
   (V) Waterproof sheet with jersey rolled inside,
   fixed on back of waistbelt by supporting
   straps of the pack.
   (VI) Two Mills Grenades, one in each bottom
   pocket of the jacket.
   (VII) Two Aeroplane flares, one in each top
   pocket of the jacket.
   (VIII) Box Respirator.
   (IV) 2 Sandbags carried by every NCO and
   man under the flap of the haversack.

   Greatcoats will be rolled in bundles
   and Packs will be filled with spare kit
   and personal property. They will be
   packed in store in the Billets at present
   occupied by each battalion under battalion
   arrangements. Packs will be clearly
   marked with the number name and

Packs of the men. Small arms of
Lewis pistols must not be left in the
pockets of the greatcoats to avoid loss should
it become necessary to leave the coats.

(b) Fighting dress for assaults will be:—
  (i) Arms, clothing and equipment, less pack.
  (ii) 50 rounds S.A.A.
  (iii) Haversack on back, as in (a) (iii).
  (iv) Leather jerkin.
  (v) Waterproof sheet as in (a) (v).
  Assailants moving:—
  Bombers, Signallers, Machine gunners, Lewis gunners, Scouts, Stokes mortar teams, Runners, Carrying parties.
  Bombers will be equipped in addition to the arms shown in (b) as follows:—

	MILLS	RIFLE GRENADES
NCO	6	2
2 Bayonet men	6	2
2 Leading Bombers	6	
2 Reserve Bombers	6	2
2 Rifle Bombers	2	6
Rations and water		

2. (a) Every man will carry an iron ration.
It must be impressed upon all ranks that the iron ration is NOT to be eaten, except by order of a Commanding Officer.
(b) Every man will carry the full day's ration with them in addition to the iron ration.

3. Supply of SAA, Bombs etc.
The Brigade Store is at the SUCRERIE COURCELLES and there are Bath Stores at ST. LEGER and MORY.
The Bath Stores may be drawn on to equip the recruiting troops and intends to replace will be sent to Brigade H.Q.rs. by wire.
Barbed wire and screw pickets have been collected at the ABBAYE MORY and may be drawn direct by units requiring them.

4. Casualties.
(i) The following instructions with regard to the reporting of casualties are issued.
The primary detailed casualty return will be rendered up to and including 12 NOON on the day before the receipt, after which a system of ESTIMATED CASUALTY RETURNS will come into force.
All wires will commence TOTAL ESTIMATED CASUALTIES aaa
(ii) Offrs: casualties, when required, should be reported as soon as possible after they occur, giving initials and names of Officers in BLOCK LETTERS, and the date of the casualty.
(iii) As soon as possible after the conclusion of active operations an ACCURATE return of casualties will be rendered.

ACCURACY is essential in this return.
(4) These returns are to be rendered punctually during forthcoming operations.
They will be rendered daily to reach Battn HQrs at 11 am and 6 pm.
5. The following will be left behind in Billets at COURCELLES
> Captain E.W. GREEN.
> Lieut R MAXWELL.
> Coy Sgt Major A Coy.
> Coy Sgt Major C Coy.

1 Sgt, 1 Cpl, 1 Lance Cpl per Coy
3 Ptes per Platoon.
33% of the Lewis Gunners per Coy.
6. Officers Kits, Coy and Mess Baggage will be stacked in present billets under Coy arrangements.
Capt E.W. GREEN will be in command of the above party, and will be responsible that guards are kept over the kits, and the billets kept clean.
O.C. Coys will render nominal rolls in duplicate of the men to be left behind by 10.30 pm.

R.S Dennessy
Lieut,
Adjt 2nd Border Regt.

Ref/

Operation Orders by
Major G.E. Beddy. Pownall
Commdg 2nd Border Regt
25th March 1917.

1. The 20th Infy Brigade will attack ECOUST LONGATTE on the 26th instant.
The 7th Australian Infy Brigade on our right will be co-operating by attacking simultaneously LEONICOURT and placing a heavy artillery barrage on NOREUIL.

2. Zero hour will be notified later.

3. The attack will be carried out by the 8th Devon Regt and 2nd Gordon Hdrs. The 2nd Border Regt will be in reserve. The 9th Devon Regt and guns of 20th M.G. Coy on the line will co-operate from their present position by seizing every opportunity of dealing with hostile machine guns and any parties of the enemy which may be observed.

4 (a) The attack will be made from a Southerly direction. The 2nd Gordon Hdrs on the right and 8th Devon Regt on the left.

(b) The centre of the 2nd Gordon Hdrs will follow the line of the road running from C.4.b.2.0. - C.8.a.3.7 - C.8.b.6.8 - and thence to C.2.d.5.6 - C.3.c.0.9.
The centre of 8th Devon Regt will follow the line of the road running from C.13.b.7.2 - C.7.d.8.2 - C.2.c.3.2 - C.2.a.8.2 - Railway crossing C.2.b.5.9.
The 2nd Gordon Hdrs will direct.

(c) The 2nd Gordon Hdrs will be responsible for the LONGATTE - NOREUIL road up to point C.9.b.4.1.
The 8th Devon Regt will form a defensive flank on his left by establishing posts to join up with the posts of the 9th Devon Regt.

(d) The attack will be made by strong patrols moving forward under the barrage & backed up by supports.

5 (a) At Zero minus one hour the attacking battalions will be formed up on the line held by the permanent posts and the 2nd Border Regt will be in position in the SUNKEN ROAD. B.17.c.6.9 to B.23.a.7.6.

5(b) When ECOUST - LONGATTE is captured, the village will be cleared of enemy and a line of posts established covering the village on the Eastern and Northern sides from C.3.c.4.0. thence to the Railway U.26.d. and thence along the Railway to U.25.b.4.3.

The 9th Devon Regt will push forward its posts to conform to the above line.

As soon as the village has been cleared of the enemy troops will be kept out of it.

6. Each man of the attacking troops will carry two flares and will be prepared to light them on demand from the Contact Aeroplane made either by dropping its white lights or by sounding its Klaxon Horn.

7. Advanced Brigade Hdqrs will be established in the Sunken Rd about B.15.d.9.5 from Zero minus one hour.

8. Orders for the move to the Assembly position will be issued later.

R.E. Hennessy Lieut
Adjt 2nd Border Regt

SECRET

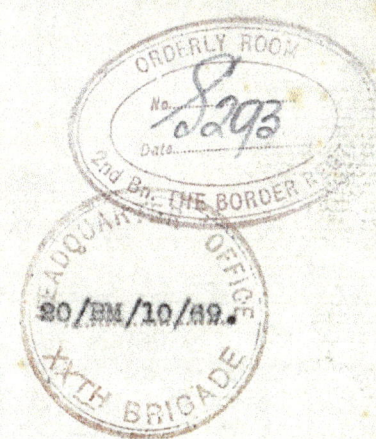

Officer Commanding,
    9th Devon Regt.
    2nd Border Regt.
    2nd Gordon Highlanders.

    The attached report on the Advance of Left Post of Left Subsector by Company of 8th DEVON REGIMENT in connection with operations carried out by 91st INFANTRY BRIGADE on 28th instant, is forwarded as it may be of interest to you.

                                                   Captain.
                                       Brigade Major.
29th March, 1917.   20th Infantry Brigade.

REPORT ON ADVANCE BY "A" COMPANY, 8th DEVON REGIMENT
on 28th March, 1917.

At 5'50 a.m. No 2 Platoon (32 strength) under 2nd Lieut Littlewood moved out in a N.E. direction from T.30.c.2.9. towards T.30.b.2.8. - which is the position of the new Post to be established.

2nd Lieut Littlewood's orders were to establish two new Posts i.e. No 2 Post at T.30.b.2.8. and No 3 Post at T.24.d.1.4.

The platoon moved out in four lines of sections in file, preceded by a screen of scouts - 30 paces between sections.

```
    ↑ °  °  °  °              Scouts.

           °                  O.C.No 2 Platoon.

      |  |  |  |              Sections.
      B  LG R  R
```

About 100 yards in rear moved one section of No 4 Platoon to form a connection Post between the new positions and the Support Post at T.30.c.2.9.

The advance was along the spur from 95 to 90 contour on the high ground, but on reaching about T.30.a.8.8. the platoon came under very heavy M.G. and rifle fire from the Railway Embankment on the left front and also direct front.

Judging it impossible to reach the WINDMILL T.24.d.1.4. the O.C. Platoon gave orders to double to the nearest cover which was found on the road where the 80 contour bends across it.

At the road was a bank about 4 to 5 feet high where the men at once dug themselves in.

A small party was left behind on the high ground about the 85 contour 100 yards N.W. to cover the left flank of the new Post.

8 casualties were incurred during the advance, including all the 5 scouts and the Platoon Sergeant killed.
N.B. This does not include 7 casualties in the section of No 4 Platoon in rear as connecting point.

At about 8 a.m. about a dozen of the enemy were seen advancing from the embankment towards No 2 Post; these were allowed to reach about 100 yards from the Post when rapid rifle fire was opened on them, killing as least four and wounding others. This checked enemy's advance and forced them to retire back to the embankment. They did not attempt any further counter attack but kept up continual sniping all day on any kind of movement in the Post.

O.C. No 2 Platoon sent back two reports, one about 6'30 a.m. and the other about 5'30 p.m. by runners both of which arrived safely, in spite of the complete absence of cover on the way back.

The enemy's position......

The enemy's position at the embankment was very strong and had great command to its front; it swept the whole spur and valley as well as T.30.a and b. with M.G. fire. About 25 heads were counted on the embankment; only one M.G. was spotted in left corner behind a sniper plate or some such protection.

At about 8 p.m. a Strong Point was established about 80 yards West of the Post, enough room for 10 men.

Enemy's M.G. appears to be at T.24.d.7.4.

Total casualties were:-

    No 2 Platoon:- 5 killed 3 wounded) Total 15.
    No 4 Platoon:- 4 killed 3 wounded)

The relief was carried out successfully at about 11'30 p.m.

All ranks behaved splendidly and held on to a very nasty position.

Army Form C. 2118.

WAR DIARY
INTELLIGENCE SUMMARY.
(Erase heading not required.)

PAGE 2

Instructions regarding War Diaries and Intelligence Summaries are contained in F. S. Regs., Part II. and the Staff Manual respectively. Title pages will be prepared in manuscript.

Place	Date	Hour	Summary of Events and Information	Remarks and references to Appendices
ERVILLERS	4/4/17		The Battalion was relieved at night by 2/5th West Yorks Regt. The relief was completed by 12 midnight, and the Battalion proceeded to billets at ERVILLERS	
	5/4/17		The Battalion marched to camp at ABLAINZEVILLE starting at 2pm and arriving at about 5pm.	
ABLAINZEVILLE	6/4/17		The Battalion commenced its training	
	7/4/17		" " " " " continued	
	8/4/17		" " " " " "	
	9/4/17		" " " " " "	
	10/4/17		" " " " " "	
	11/4/17		" " " " " "	
COURCELLES	12/4/17		The Battalion marched to billets at COURCELLES, starting at 1.55pm and arriving at 2.30pm	
			The Battalion marched back to camp at ABLAINZEVILLE, starting at 9.50pm and arriving at 10.30pm.	
ABLAINZEVILLE	13/4/17		The Battalion continued its training	
	14/4/17		" " " " " "	
	15/4/17		" " " " " "	
	16/4/17		" " " " " "	
	17/4/17		" " " " " "	
	18/4/17		" " " " " "	
	19/4/17		The Battalion relieved 22nd Bn. Manchester Regt. in the Subject Sector. Battalion Headquarters Y & B Coy's moved at 10am. C & D Coy's moved	
	20/4/17			
	21/4/17			

WAR DIARY
INTELLIGENCE SUMMARY.
(Erase heading not required.)

Army Form C. 2118.
PAGE 3.

Place	Date	Hour	Summary of Events and Information	Remarks and references to Appendices
	21/4/17	2.30 pm.	Arrived the Battalion was distributed as follows :- C & D Companies in dug-outs - Cellars in ECOUST ST MEIN A & B " Battalions Headquarters in shelter on Sunken Road B29.d.8.9. Casualties :- 1 Wounded	
	22/4/17 to 25/4/17		The Battalion remained in positions in Sector. During this period ECOUST ST MEIN was intermittently shelled by the enemy. Our casualties were:- 22/4/17 :- 1 Killed. 23/4/17, 2 Wounded. 24/4/17, 2 Wounded	
	26/4/17		The Battalion relieved the 5th Lu Pusvin Regiment in the front line at night. The relief was completed at about midnight. and the Battalion was then in position as follows :- Right. D Company in Posts at U.28.c.14, U.29.a.25, U.27.a.95, U.27.e.35%, U.27.a.74. Company Headquarters C.30.a.56. Right Centre. B Company in Posts at U.27.a.35, U.26.b.9.3, U.21.c.41, U.21.c.14. Company H. Qrs. U.26.5.70.05. Left Centre. A Company in Posts at V.26.c.65.15, U.26.c.70.05, C.3a.65.05 Left. C Company in Posts at U.26.d.61, U.26.d.25.55, U.26.d.88, U.26.6.20.65, U.26.9.2 - U.26.e.19. Company H. Qrs. U.26.c.08.	
	26/4/17		Enemy artillery was active during the night. Enemy artillery was rather the railway embankment and some of our forward posts were shelled with Tear Shells. No enemy movement was observed.	

WAR DIARY
of
INTELLIGENCE SUMMARY.
(Erase heading not required.)

Army Form C. 2118.

Place	Date	Hour	Summary of Events and Information	Remarks and references to Appendices
	27/4/17		Patrols went out from Right Centre, Right and Left Companys during the night. Several enemy posts were located but none of the enemy were encountered. Casualties :- 2 wounded.	
	28/4/17		The enemy shelled us opposite the railway embankment & Cottage trenches intermittently during the day. Several of the enemy were observed on the Right of BULLECOURT. An enemy working party were seen at U.29.B.2.3 at 11=30pm & dispersed by Lewis Gun fire. During the night the enemy used searchlights freely. Patrols went out from Right, Right Centre & Left Companys during the night but could not be ascertained in what strength the enemy are holding the line. Casualties :- 6 killed 6 wounded	
	29/4/17		Enemy artillery was again active throughout the day. Saw enemy trench mortar shells fell near posts of Rights Company. Patrols from Right, Right Centre & Left Companys went out at night. The Battalion was relieved in the line by 10 Royal Bn Manchester Regt. The relief was completed by about 2am and the Battalion marched to camp at ABLAINZEVILLE. Casualties :- 1 wounded	
ABLAINZEVILLE	30/4/17		The Battalion remained at billets.	

Army Form C. 2118.

WAR DIARY
or
INTELLIGENCE SUMMARY.
(Erase heading not required.)

PAGE

Place	Date	Hour	Summary of Events and Information	Remarks and references to Appendices
			The following Officers Joined the Battalion during the month.— 5/4/17:- 2nd Lieut J.A. Stephens 6/4/17 " J.S. Greenwood 13/4/17:- Lieuts. G.R. Hamilton, G. Neil, 2nd Lieuts. W. Carr, S.T. Stevens, R. Royston, V. Coulthurst. 24/4/17 Captain H.L. Chatterly, 2nd Lieut. J.R. Bartlett & A.J. Barnes. as aughter Joined the Battalion during the month:— 2/4/17 8 O.Ranks. 5/4/17 9 O.Ranks. 5/4/17 5 O.Ranks. 14/4/17 5 O.Ranks. 21/4/17 5 1 Roy.Ks. 25/4/17 1 O.Rank. 5 1 Offr. 1 Roy.K. 5 1 Offr. 1 Roy.K evacuated Sick during the month. The strength of the Battalion on the last day of the month was All Officers 686 Other Ranks.	

S. Duke... Lieut Colonel
Commanding 2nd Bn The Border Regt.

Chammine Camp Cyprus
Major G.E. Beaky Parnell
Comdg. 2nd Battalion .... Regt.

1st April 1917

The Battn. will move out Camp for the Northward operations on the morning of the 2nd inst.
Order of march:-
    Headquarters
    "C" Company
    "A"   "
    "B"   "
    "D"   "

Head of the column to be at the fork roads B.13.d.2.2. at 5.30am.
Fighting Order, General will be worn.

Officers Kits Company and Mess Baggage and Packs will be parked in the Batt. Pack Store by 11 pm.

The following details will be left behind:-
    C.Q.M.S. "A" Company
    "   "   "B"   "
    C.S.M.   "A"   "
    C.S.M.   "C"   "

Servants as detailed by the R.S.M. and the following:-

    A Coy.   7424   Cpl. Boyle
    B   2912   L/C. Farrell
    D   2494   L/C. Staley
    D   2002   Pte. Harris
    D   275   "   Kelly
    D   "   Turner
    D   "   Keane

These details will report to Batt. Ed Green at the Batt. Pack Store at 10pm.

R.G. Hennessy Lieut
Adjutant 2nd Battn. ..... Regt.

Operation Orders by
Major G.C. Bewley Personett,
Commanding 2nd Border Regt.

4th April 1917

The Battn. will be relieved tonight by the 7/8th W. Yorks Regt. Relieving troops are leaving Mory at 7.30 p.m.

Immediately on relief, all bombs will be checked at present Company H.Qrs. and handed over to the incoming troops. Receipt will be obtained.

The following will remain on the line after relief for 24 hours.

Captain E.W. Cowen
2nd Lieut. D.S. Rutherford
2nd Lieut. C.C. Graham
2nd Lieut. W.F. Latham
and 2 Lewis Gunners per Company.

On Completion of relief, Coys. will proceed direct to ERVILLERS.

Relief complete will be reported by the code word BOX.

Lewis Gun Centers and Company Commanders' Horses will meet the Battn. at MORY ABBEY.

Special Lookout will be kept against Counter-attack.

C.O. Coy. will report arrival of the Coys. or billet at ERVILLERS to Battn. Hqrs. in writing.

50 yards interval will be maintained between platoons throughout the march back.

R.S. Kennedy Lieut.
Adjutant 2nd Border Regt.

Operation Order by
Major G.E. Beaty Pownall.
Comdg. 2nd Border Regt.
5th April 1917

The Batt. will move to ABLAINZEVILLE to-day 5th inst.
Order of march:-
    Headquarters
    C Company
    D "
    A "
    B "

Head of the column to be at the Cross at 2 pm.

Officers Kit, Company and Mess Baggage will be stacked
at Company Stores by 1. a.m.

Reserve Amn. will be loaded on limbers on the main
road below Headquarters at 1.30 pm.

Dress Marching Order. S.D. Caps to be worn.

Usual certificates to be rendered.

                                    P.G. Hennessy Capt.
                                    Adjutant 2nd Bn Border Regt.

Operation Order by
Lieut Col E. Ivo B. Thorpe DSO
Commdg 2nd B. Border Regt
11th April 1917

The Batt will move to COURCELLES today.
Order of march:-
     "A" Company
     "B"   "
     "C"   "
     "D"   "
     Headquarters

Head of the column to be at the Cross HEBUTERNE at 1-55 pm.

200 yards interval between Coys will be maintained throughout the march.

Dress: Full marching order. Greatcoat to be carried in the pack.

R. G. Hennessy Lieut.
Adjutant 2nd Border Regt

Battalion Orders by
Lieut Col E Ives G Thorpe DSC
Commdg 2nd Bn Border Regt
12th April 1917

The Battn will move to the billets examined yesterday 11th inst, at ABLAINZEVELLE today 12th inst.

Order of march.
  Battn Headquarters.
  B Company.
  Remainder of A.C. & D Coys under
   Capt E.R. Thirlaw Stroke.

Head of the column to be at the road junction A.15.d.3.6. at 9.50am.

Working Parties. The working parties detailed for today will hold good with the exception of the party of 1 Sgt & 25 men reporting to Lieut Stroud O/C. and 1 NCO & 25 men on Sundries reporting to the Town Major, and will be to work fully equipped returning the Battn at ABLAINZEVELLE.

Officers Kits, Coy & Mess Baggage and Blankets tied in bundles of 10, will be stacked at Coy HQrs by 7.30am

Lewis Guns will be loaded on Lewis Gun limbers at Company HQrs at 7.15am.

A Echelon Transport will follow the Battn. B Echelon Transport will follow the Brigade.

Gas inspection of B Company today is cancelled.

       R. S. Hennessy Lieut
      Adjutant. 2nd Border Regt.

Operation Orders by
Lieut Col E La T Thorpe DSO
Comndg 2nd Bn Border Regt

20th April 1917

The Batt. will relieve the 2nd Manchester Regt in the
Support Line tomorrow 21st inst.
The Batt. will move in two parties.

(1)   Headquarters
      A Company
      B   "

Head of the column to be at F.23.d.9.0. at 11 am

(2)   D Company
      C   "

Head of the column to be at F.23.d.9.0. at 2.30 pm

Dress:- Full Marching Order.

Route:- ACHIET LE GRAND - BIHUCOURT - road junction G.11.d.6.3. -
SAPIGNIES - Cross roads H.15.c.3.6. - FAVREUIL - BEUGNATRE -
to Cross roads B.24.d.9.9.

100 yards interval between Coys will be maintained.

Blanket rolls in bundles of 10 will be stacked at the
Quartermaster's Shed by 9 am.
Officers Kit Coy mess Baggage will be stacked at the
Quartermasters Store - in case of the first party by 9.30 am.
and the second party by 2 pm.

One cooker will follow the first platoon of each Coy
in the case of the 1st party.
One cooker will follow the first platoon of the 2nd party.
OC 1st party will arrange to halt at a suitable place
to have dinner. This will be a halt of 1 hour.
OC 2nd party will arrange to halt at a suitable place
to have tea. This will be a halt of 1 hour.

R.G. Hennessy Lieut
Actg Adjt 2nd Bn Border Regt

Operation Order by
Lieut Col E. J. L. Gilbert DSO
Commdg 2nd Border Regt
26th April 1917

The Battn will relieve the 8th Devon Regt in the line today 26th inst.

D Coy will relieve C Coy 8th Devons on the Right
B "   "   D "   "   "   "   Right Centre
A "   "   A "   "   "   "   Left Centre
C "   "   B "   "   "   "   Left

C and D Coys will be clear of ECOUST by 10.15 p.m.
A and B Coys will leave their present positions, A Coy leading at 9.45 p.m.

100 yards interval between platoons will be maintained.
All other arrangements for relief will be made between Coy Commanders concerned.

Rations will be issued before moving from present positions.

Water bottles will be filled and O.C. Coys will be held responsible that they are not used before moving off. All ranks must be warned that the supply of water is difficult and can only be brought up at night.

There will be no fires.

The Aid Post will be at C.3.a.9.0.

R. G. Jameson Lieut
Adjutant 2nd Border Regt.

Operation Orders by
Lieut Col. H. de L. Thorpe DSO
Cmndg 2nd Bn Border Regt.
28th April 1917

1. The Batt. will be relieved in the line on the night 28-29th April by the 22nd Manchester Regt.

2. On relief Bat. will proceed to bivouac at H 30 d. and wouldly on PERY and BRUILLERS.

3. Order of relief. The relieving Batt. will send up one two parties –
   (1) "C" Coy 22nd Manchester Regt. the relief for "C" Coy 2nd Border Regt.
       "B" Coy 22nd Manchester Regt. the relief for "B" Coy 2nd Border Regt.
       "A" Coy 22nd Manchester Regt. (less 1 Platoon) the relief for "A" Coy 2nd Border Regt. (less 1 Platoon).
   (2) "D" Coy 22nd Manchester Regt. the relief for "D" Coy 2nd Border Regt.
       1 Platoon of "A" Coy 22nd Manchester Regt. the relief for 1 Platoon "A" Coy 2nd Border Regt.
   Contact Guides for No 1 party will meet the 22nd Manchester Regt at the Cross of cross roads in B.17.d. at 8.30 p.m.
   Contact Guides for No 2 party will meet the 22nd Manchester Regt at C.7.a.7.5. at 9. o'clock.

4. The Coys of the 22nd Manchester Regt will arrive detailed as follows:-

   C Coy   A Coy
   No 3. Post   No 3. Post
    - 2. Post   - 4. Post
    - 1. Post   - 1. Post
    - 4. Post   - 2. Post
    - 5. Post   Coy H Qrs

   A Coy   D Coy
   No 1. Post   No 3. Post
    - 2. Post   - 5. Post
                     - 1. Post
                     - 2. Post
                     - 4. Post
                    Coy H Qrs

5. Post Guides will meet the 22nd Manchester Regt at Company HQrs.
   The 1 Guide per Company mentioned in para 3 will report at Batt HQrs before dawn 29th inst.

R.G. Hennessy Lieut
Adjt 2nd Bn Border Regt.

Lieut Col & Hon E Thesiger DSO
Commdg 2nd Border Regt
28th April 1917

Para 2 of Operation Orders as cancelled.

1. The Battn. will proceed to the Camps and billets in ABLAINZEVELLE previously occupied when the Battn. was in that area.

2. Coys will form up near the crater at the cross roads in B.6.b. and will march as a Coy to ABLAINZEVELLE.

3. Officers per Coy from the Officers at the Transport will meet each Coy at the crater in B.6.b. and will guide them by the best route to ABLAINZEVELLE.

4. A halt will be made in the neighbourhood of ERSIRIERS at a spot to be chosen by the Quartermaster and to be known by the Officers guides mentioned above. At this point will be a cooker and cocoa or coffee will be ready.
    Packs may be stacked at a place where the cocoa is served and left in the charge of 1 man per Company if so desired by O.C. Coys.
    Coys who leave any packs at this point will report that they have done so at the same time as reporting arrival in billets.
    The Transport Officer will arrange transport for the packs on the day after next.

5. Coy Officers horses will meet them on the MORY-ECOUST road.

6. Lewis Gun limbers will meet the Coys on the MORY-ECOUST road between MORY and the crater at the Cross roads.

R.G. Hennessy Lieut
Adjutant 2 Border Regt

2nd Bn. Border Regiment

List of Officers and Warrant Officers – April 1917

Rank & Name		Remarks
Major Peaty Pownall	G.E.	Second in Command
Captain Mortall	S.H.	Appointed 2nd in Command, 8th Devons Regt.
Captain Graham		2/5th N. Staffs Regt.
Chatfield		Joined 20/4/17 (Commanding B Coy)
Chetham-Strode	E.R.	(Commanding C Coy)
2/Lt (T.Capt.) Green		(Commanding A Coy)
Lieut Harding		Attached General Staff
Hennessey		
Hamilton		Joined 15/4/17 — ADJUTANT
Neil		15/4/17 — MUSKETRY OFFICER
2/Lt Grange		Attached General Staff
2nd Lieut Kelley		Bombing Officer, 20th Inf. Bde.
Cunningham		TRANSPORT OFFICER
Cape		Joined 15/4/17
Symeston		INTELLIGENCE OFFICER
Keenan		To England for appoint as Probationer in Indian Army
Moore		(Commanding D Coy)
Campbell		BOMBING OFFICER
Low		Returned from hospital 16/4/17
Hockyer		SIGNALLING OFFICER
Abram		
Harding		
Carr		Sick
Grahame		
Rutherford		To England 15/4/17
Edwards		16/4/17
Grahame		
Gibbon		
Centock		
Seymour-Isaacs		
Steen		Joined 16/4/17
Bayntu		
Bartlett		20/4/17
Longthwaite		15/4/17
Stephen		7/4/17
Greenwood		15/4/17
Capt & QM Mitchell		QUARTERMASTER

ATTACHED

Lt Col Thorpe	E. de S.	(2nd Bedfords Regt.) — COMMANDING OFFICER
Capt Maxwell		(2nd K.O.S.B.)
Lieut Lancaster		(3rd ")
Holmes		(2nd ")
Adamson		(3rd ")
Matteson		
Bayne		(M.G. Corps)
Captain Allen		(R.A.M. Corps) — MEDICAL OFFICER

WARRANT OFFICERS.

No.	Rank & Name		Remarks
7892	A/S.M. Claley	G.H.	REGTL. SERGT. MAJOR.
7890	C.S.M. Stader	J.	COY. SGT. MAJOR A COY.
6403	... Fletcher	J.	" " " B "
6391A/	... Lord	A.	" " " C "
8174	... Ronald	J.	" " " D "

7th DIVISION.
20th INF BDE.

2nd BORDER REGIMENT.

MAY, 1917.

WAR DIARY or INTELLIGENCE SUMMARY

Army Form C. 2118.

Reference Maps: FRANCE 57.B S.W. and ECOUST ST. MEIN FRANCE 57c N.W.

MAY 1917

2nd York & Lancs Regt. Vol 28

Place	Date	Hour	Summary of Events and Information	Remarks and references to Appendices
ABLAINZEVILLE	1/5/17		The Battalion continued its training	
	2/5/17		" " " "	
	3/5/17		The Battalion moved to the vicinity of ERVILLERS at 9am. on a frontage of readiness in support to Corps Reserve in attack on BULLECOURT. The Battn moved at 5pm to Camp at A.30.d. Here it remained for the night.	
GOMIECOURT	4/5/17		At 4am. The Battalion moved to tent shelters just south of MORY, or about B.3P.a. 57 where it remained for the night.	
MORY.	5/5/17		At about 4.0pm. the Battalion left the Camp at B.3P.a. 5.7 & mat over the from Support Line. Distribution as follows:- A & "B" Coys in dugouts and cellars in ECOUST ST MEIN C & D "Batn Hedqrs in Shelters in SUNKEN ROAD B.24.E.8.9. The Battalion remained in Support. And the day passed quietly.	
	6/5/17		The Battalion relieved the 2nd Gordon Highlanders in the front line, commencing about midnight 7th – 8th May, and was distributed as follows:- All Companies in the front line. A Company on the right. D Company right centre. C Company left centre. B Company on the left. The line was run U.28.a.99 – U.28.a.35.55 – U.28.a.30.35. – U.28.a.25.35 – U.28.a.22. Battalion Headquarters were in a Culvert in the Railway Embankment at U.28.C. 85.20.	
	7/5/17		The night of 7th – 8th May was spent in digging a french and consolidation. The Enemy kept up continuous shelling throughout the night	

31.L Sheet

Army Form C. 2118.

WAR DIARY
or
INTELLIGENCE SUMMARY.
(Erase heading not required.)

Place	Date	Hour	Summary of Events and Information	Remarks and references to Appendices
	8/5/1917		Enemy shelling was continuous and was especially vigorous from 9pm to 10/pm. Casualties 6 OR killed 25 OR wounded. During the night 8⁵/9ᵗʰ a post was established at U 27 a 65.35 by 1 platoon of "B" Company under Lieut. G. NEIL. Rations were brought up by pack horses as far as Battn Headquarters.	
	9/5/17		Heavy shelling all day commenced again especially vigorous in the evening from about 7pm onwards. During this bombardment a shell landed in Battn Headquarters wounding Major G.E. BEATY-POWNALL and killing 3 other ranks. Lieut. B.L. CUMPSTON was also mortally wounded by this shell. Casualties for day:- Officers: 1 killed 4 wounded. O.R.: 8 killed. 25 wounded. 2 shell shock. The post at U.27.a. 85.35 was very heavily shelled during the day. Two Lewis Guns being blown in and the majority of the garrison of the post were knocked out. During the night of 9ᵗʰ/10ᵗʰ May this post was relieved by a platoon of "C" Company. Rations were again brought up to Battn Headquarters on pack horses.	
	10/5/1917		The station party came under heavy shell fire and several horses were lost. Enemy shelled our front line intermittently although not so heavy as the two proceeding days. Casualties were 5 OR killed 18 OR wounded 1 officer and 6 OR shell shock.	

WAR DIARY
INTELLIGENCE SUMMARY.
(Erase heading not required.)

Army Form C. 2118.

Place	Date	Hour	Summary of Events and Information	Remarks and references to Appendices
	11/5/17		On the night of 10th/11th May the Battalion was relieved by the 1st South Staffordshire Regt and 2nd Queens Regt and proceeded to Camps at 7.30 d.	
	12/5/17		The Battalion remained in Camp at A.30.d. The time was spent in generally cleaning up and re-organising.	
	13/5/17			
	14/5/17	11.0.a.m.	The Battalion proceeded to th old Camp at ABLAINZEVELLE arriving at 11.0.a.m.	
	15/5/17	At 5am	a "Special" Company consisted of 3 Officers and 100 OR (Capt J.F. MOORE in command) left the Camp to proceed to BULLECOURT to assist the 2nd Infantry Brigade on the capture of a strong point in that village, known as "The Red Patch". This party arrived at ECOUST ST MEIN and there awaited orders. Meanwhile the party was used for carrying water etc for the 5th S. Division. Meanwhile, news having been received that the enemy was heavily counter attacking in the vicinity of BULLECOURT, the remainder of the Battalion formed up the 2 Companies (No.1 and 2) East Cock at 11am and took up a position on the Defence Line near the Sunken Road at B.24 & B.9. Very heavy shell fire right.	
	16/5/17		Nos 1 and 2 Coys left the Sunken road at 5.30am arriving in Camp at ABLAINZEVELLE at 6am. The Special Company not being required for action arrived in Camp at 9.15am	

Army Form C. 2118.

WAR DIARY
or
INTELLIGENCE SUMMARY.
(Erase heading not required.)

Instructions regarding War Diaries and Intelligence Summaries are contained in F.S. Regs., Part II. and the Staff Manual respectively. Title pages will be prepared in manuscript.

Place	Date	Hour	Summary of Events and Information	Remarks and references to Appendices
ACHIET LE GRAND	17/5/1917		The Battalion continued its training	
	18/5/1917		" " continued	
	19/5/1917		" " "	
	20/5/1917		" " "	
	21/5/1917		" " "	
	22/5/1917		" " "	
	23/5/1917		" " "	
	24/5/1917		" " "	
	25/5/1917		" " "	
	26/5/1917		" " The Army Commander attended Church Parade	
	27/5/1917	at 11.0am		
			The Battalion continued its training	
	28/5/1917		" " "	
	29/5/1917		" " " and at 5.30pm attended a Gas and Smoke	
	30/5/1917		Demonstration held at F.26.C.08 on the BUCQUOY - ESSARTS Road	
	31/5/1917		The Battalion continued its training.	

Major G.E. BEATY-POWNALL rejoined the Battalion on 19.5.1917.
2/Lieut G. HASLAM joined the Battalion on 20.5.1917.

A5834 Wt.W4973/M687 750,000 8/16 D.D. & L. Ltd. Forms/C2118/13.

Army Form C. 2118.

WAR DIARY
or
INTELLIGENCE SUMMARY.
(Erase heading not required.)

Place	Date	Hour	Summary of Events and Information	Remarks and references to Appendices
			The following drafts joined the Battalion during the month.	
			18 OR 6.5.17 6 OR 7.5.17 10 OR 17.5.17 72 OR 20.5.17	
			5 OR 23.5.17 40 OR 31.5.17 8 OR 20.5.17	
			36 other ranks were evacuated sick during the month	
			The total strength of the Battalion on the last day of the month was:-	
			30 Officers 693 other ranks.	

M Clitter- Itod Capt
for Major

7th DIVISION.

20th INF BDE.

2nd BORDER REGIMENT.

JUNE 1917.

Army Form C. 2118.

WAR DIARY
or
INTELLIGENCE SUMMARY.
(Erase heading not required.)

2nd Border Regt

Reference Maps
France 51.b SW and ECOUST
57.c NW   ST. NEM

WK 29

Place	Date	Hour	Summary of Events and Information	Remarks and references to Appendices
ACHIET LE GRAND	1/6/17		The Battalion continued its training	
	2/6/17		" " " " "	
	3/6/17		" " " " "	
	4/6/17		" " " " "	
	5/6/17		" " " " "	
	6/6/17		" " " " "	
	7/6/17		" " " " "	
	8/6/17		" " " " "	
	9/6/17		" " " " "	
	10/6/17		" " " " "	
	11/6/17		" " " " "	
	12/6/17		" " " " "	
	13/6/17		The Battalion moved to camp in the vicinity of B.27.C. near MORY starting at 2.15pm and arriving about 4pm.	
	14/6/17		The Battalion relieved the 7th London Regt. in Right Support, leaving camp at 9.30pm. Regt was Relieved about 1am on 15th	
	15/6/17		The Battalion was disposed as follows. Batn. Hdqrs in ECOUST. A Coy in Railway Embankment in C.4 & 9.5. B Coy in Shelters in Sunken Road. C.4.a	

32.L
1 sheet

WAR DIARY
or
INTELLIGENCE SUMMARY

Army Form C. 2118.

(2)

Place	Date	Hour	Summary of Events and Information	Remarks and references to Appendices
	15/6/17 to 17/6/17		Coms "D" Coy to shelters in LONGATTE - MOREUIL Road. The Battalion remained in shelters in Subsect. During this period ECOUST ST MEIN was intermittently shelled by the enemy. Our casualties were:-	
	18/6/17		2 Killed. 5 wounded (while on working party) The Battalion relieved the 9th Devon Regt in the front line this evening. Conclusion about 12 midnight. The frontage held was from U.23.c.8.1. (right) to U.22.c.9.5 (left). Right Front Coy "D" Coy, Centre Front Coy "C" Coy, Left Front Coy "B" Coy. A Coy in Support in U.29.c. Batt'n Hdqrs LONDON	
	19/6/17		Dugouts in Railway Embankment in U.28.d.2.1. This day passed quietly. Barn and Barn TRENCH (U.38.6.1.9.) was shelled with whiz-bangs between Barn and Barn. Casualties:- 3 wounded	
	20/6/17		Enemy Artillery fairly active. BULLECOURT PK - TANK AV - RAILWAY TRENCH & LONDON TRENCH receiving direct hits in the evening. A H.V. Gun shelled various roads in the Sector during the afternoon. Casualties 1 wounded	
	21/6/17		Enemy Artillery generally quiet during day. During the night LONDON TRENCH was shelled at intervals. Casualties 3 wounded	
	22/6/17		Enemy Artillery active throughout the day. The Battalion was relieved by 9th Devon Regt and proceeded to Support line, relief being complete at 12.30am. The Battalion "A" and "D" Coys to shelters architect as follows Batt'n Hdqrs in ECOUST, "A" and "D" Coys to shelters in LONGATTE - MOREUIL	

A.5834. Wt. W4973/M687. 730,000. 8/16. D. D. & L. Ltd. Forms/C.2118/13.

Army Form C. 2118.

WAR DIARY or INTELLIGENCE SUMMARY.

(Erase heading not required.)

Place	Date	Hour	Summary of Events and Information	Remarks and references to Appendices
	23-24 2nd		B Coy to shelter in sunken road C.H.Q. Railway Embankment C.14.a.95. C Coy to shelter in	
			The Battalion remained in Support during this tour. ESCORT and full Garrison Picket Railway Embankment were recommenced. Relief of "B" Battery of art. Salibis and Prisoners P. Mesa patrol consisting of Serjeant F. MAHONEY and Serjt R. LYNE went out	
			on night 24/25. and 25/26. Enemy Post were located at U.22.c.2.u. and U.22.d.3.9.	
			Out post of the enemy were encountered.	
	27/4/17		The Battn was relieved on Right Sub-sect by 2/Royal Warwickshire Regt and proceeded to camp in the vicinity of B.28.a.R.4. Relief was completed about 1.30 am	
MORY	28/6/17		The Battalion remained in Camp refitting and reorganizing	
	27/6/17		The Battalion Commenced training	
	28/6/17		The Battalion continued training	
	29/6/17		" " " "	
	30/6/17		" " " "	
			The following Officers joined the Battalion during the month	
	3/6/17		Lieutenant L. Argles	
	15/6/17		Lieutent L. Mahony	

WAR DIARY
or
INTELLIGENCE SUMMARY.

Army Form C. 2118.

Place	Date	Hour	Summary of Events and Information	Remarks and references to Appendices
	23/6/17		2nd Lieut Geo. B Shepherd joined	
			2nd Lieut H.C. Hislop "	
	29/6/17		2nd Lieut H.S. Haynes "	
			2nd Lieut W.S. Warren "	
			Grays Re-union joined the Battalion during the month:	
	1/6/17	3/6/17	9/6/17 9/6/17 7 OR 9/6/17 3 OR 18/6/17 5 OR 22/6/17	
	29 OR were evacuated sick during the month			
	Total strength of Batt. on last day of month: 35 Officers 658 Ranks			

[signature]
Lieut Colonel
Commanding 2nd Bn. The Border Regt.

7th DIVISION.
20th INF BDE.

2nd BORDER REGIMENT.

JULY 1917.

WAR DIARY
or
INTELLIGENCE SUMMARY.

Army Form C. 2118.

(Erase heading not required.)

G Burdon Rh
Reference Maps
France 51E SW) and ECOUST ST MEIN
57c NW. } 51c 30

Place	Date	Hour	Summary of Events and Information	Remarks and references to Appendices
MORY	1/7/17		The Battalion remained in camp in the vicinity of B.28.a.8.4. and continued its training.	
	2/7/17		" " " " " " "	
	3/7/17		" " " " " " "	
	4/7/17		" " " " " " "	
	5/7/17		" " " " " " "	
	6/7/17		The Battalion relieved the 2nd Battn ROYAL WARWICKSHIRE REGT in the Front Line (Right Subsector), relief being complete about 12.30am on 7th. The Battalion was distributed as follows:- Right Front Company - D Company, Left Front Company - B Company. Frontage = U.23.c.5.1 (right) to U.23.c.98.25 (left) 'A' Company in Support in U.29.c. 'C' Company and Battn Headquarters at U.28.d.2.1.	
	7/7/17		The day passed quietly. At 1.50pm and 8.30pm TANK AVENUE and LONDON TRENCH were shelled with TMs and 5.9s.	
	8/7/17		Very quiet.	
	9/7/17		Hostile artillery very active throughout the day. The Left Company's sector received Harasser attention and considerable damage was done to the front line trenches	
	10/7/17		Hostile artillery again active TANK AVENUE and LONDON TRENCH being damaged in several places. The Battalion was relieved at night by the 9th (S) Bn DEVONSHIRE REGT relief being completed at about 1.0am on 11th.	
	11/7/17		The distribution was as follows:-	

A5834 Wt W4973 M687 750,000 8/16 D. D. & L. Ltd. Forms/C.2118/13.

Army Form C. 2118.

WAR DIARY
or
INTELLIGENCE SUMMARY.
(Erase heading not required.)

Page 2.

Instructions regarding War Diaries and Intelligence Summaries are contained in F. S. Regs., Part II. and the Staff Manual respectively. Title pages will be prepared in manuscript.

Place	Date	Hour	Summary of Events and Information	Remarks and references to Appendices
	11/7/17 to 13/7/17		C Company and B Company to Shelters on LONGATTE - NOREUIL Road. A Company in Railway Embankment in C.4.b.9.5. D Company to Sentier Road in C.4.a + c. Batn Hdqrs in ECOUST.	
	13/7/17		The Battalion remained in Support. Hostile artillery was active in ECOUST and on the Embankment in C9a. C3d and C4c. On night 13th/14th July the Battalion relieved the 9th Bn DEVONSHIRE REGT on the front Line. Relief being complete about 1 am on 14th. Distribution in Front Line - 'C' Coy right, A Coy left Subsect- B Company Reserve Company. D Company	
	14/7/17		During the day Hostile artillery was fairly active on LONDON TRENCH TANK AV TOWER TRENCH. Horseshoe in U.32.b. JOYRIDE and Railway Embankment. Only slight damage was done to our trenches	
	15/7/17 16/7/17		Fairly Quiet. Hostile Artillery active against BULLECOURT AVENUE. RAILWAY TRENCH TANK AVENUE and FOX TROT. The front Line Posts about U.33.c.5.2 and U.33.c.3.4. were shelled between 4 pm and 6 pm. Trench Mortars were also active against U.22.a.8.4. during the afternoon.	
	17/7/17		From 11 am to 11.30 am HORSESHOE TRENCH was shelled with 77 mm. About 4 pm the 6 post at U.22.d.0.2 was heavily shelled and considerable damage done to	

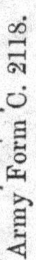

Army Form C. 2118.

Page 3.

WAR DIARY
or
INTELLIGENCE SUMMARY.
(Erase heading not required.)

Instructions regarding War Diaries and Intelligence Summaries are contained in F. S. Regs., Part II. and the Staff Manual respectively. Title pages will be prepared in manuscript.

Place	Date	Hour	Summary of Events and Information	Remarks and references to Appendices
	18/7/17		First LONDON TRENCH and JOY RIDE were also shelled.	
	19/7/17		TANK AVENUE LONDON TRENCH and Fox TROT were intermittently shelled throughout the day but no damage was done. During the night the Battalion was relieved by the 2nd Bn H.A.C. and proceeded to the camp at B.28.a.8.v. Relief was completed about 11am	
	20/7/17		The day was spent in generally cleaning up and reorganising	
	21/7/17		Training was commenced	
	22/7/17		The Battalion continued its training	
	23/7/17		"	
	24/7/17		"	
	25/7/17		"	
	26/7/17		"	
	27/7/17		"	
	28/7/17		"	
	29/7/17		"	
	30/7/17		At night the Battalion relieved the 2nd Bn HAC in Right Sub-sect. relief being completed about 12.30am on 31st. The Batt. was distributed as follows:-	

Army Form C. 2118.

WAR DIARY
INTELLIGENCE SUMMARY.
(Erase heading not required.)

Instructions regarding War Diaries and Intelligence Summaries are contained in F. S. Regs., Part II. and the Staff Manual respectively. Title pages will be prepared in manuscript.

Place	Date	Hour	Summary of Events and Information	Remarks and references to Appendices
	31/7/17		'C' Coy at Railway Embankment C.H.2.9.5. A Coy in Sunken Road C.H.4.C. B & D Coys on LONGATTE - NOREUIL Road. Battn HQrs in ECOUST. During the day ECOUST was intermittently shelled with 4.2" and H.E. At 10pm Battn HQrs moved to the banks under the Church ECOUST. Lieut R.K. EHRENBORG and 2nd Lieut H. RUNDLE-HARNESS joined the Battn on 22nd inst. Drafts as under joined during the month. 6 O.R. on 16.7.17. 30 O.R. on 22/7/17. 27 O.R on 28.7.17. 23 O.R. were evacuated Sick during the month. Casualties.	

	Killed	Wounded	Missing	Total
Officers	—	1	—	1
Other Ranks	6	16	1	23

Berk-Trimmell
Lieut. Colonel.
Commanding 2nd Bn The Border Regt.

7th DIVISION.
20th INF BDE.

2nd BORDER REGIMENT.

AUGUST 1917.

WAR DIARY
INTELLIGENCE SUMMARY

2nd Border Regt.

Ref Maps: France 51B. SW.} /ECOUST
57C NW.}
Belgium & France Sheet 33 1/40000

Month and year: AUGUST 1917

Army Form C. 2118.

Place	Date	Hour	Summary of Events and Information	Remarks and references to Appendices
	1/8/17		The Battn remained in Support. During the time hostile artillery was active in the vicinity of C.4.C. and C.3.d. ECOUST received a certain amount of attention from 4.2's	
	2/8/17			
	3/8/17		On night 3/4.8.Aug the Battn relieved the 1/Bn DEVON Regt in the front line, relief being complete about 1am. The Battn was distributed as follows. Right front = D Company. Left Front = B Company. Frontage = U.23.C.P.1 (exclu.) to U.22.C.98.75 (Left) "C" Company in Support in U.29.C. A Company in Support in Battn Hdqrs at U.28.d.2.1	
	4/8/17			
	5/8/17		The day passed quietly with the exception of intermittent shelling of C.3 and C.4. Very quiet until about 10pm when RAILWAY TRENCH at U.28.C.9.3 was shelled for an hour. Slight damage done to the trench. From 8.30am to 9am hostile TM's fired about 20 rounds in the vicinity of BUNNY HUG LANE and U.29.a.8.7. BULLECOURT was intermittently shelled throughout the day with 5.9's 4.2's & 77mm. Heavy artillery at RIENCOURT used	
	6/8/17		QUEANT	
	7/8/17		Fairly quiet on front during the morning. From 2.30pm to 4.30pm the enemy bombarded LONDON TRENCH FOXTROT and TANK AVENUE with 5.9's 4.2's and 77mm. From 9.30pm to 10.15pm LONDON TRENCH was bombarded with heavy TM's. About 300 rounds were fired. The valley in C.4 and C.3 was also shelled during the night	

Army Form C. 2118.

WAR DIARY
or
INTELLIGENCE SUMMARY.
(Erase heading not required.)

Instructions regarding War Diaries and Intelligence Summaries are contained in F. S. Regs., Part II. and the Staff Manual respectively. Title pages will be prepared in manuscript.

Place	Date	Hour	Summary of Events and Information	Remarks and references to Appendices
	8/8/17		Quiet during the day. At night the Battalion was relieved by the 2/6th Bn. W. YORKSHIRE Regt and proceeded to the Camp at B28.a.6.4. Relief was	
	9/8/17		completed about 1.30am. The Batn remained in Camp re-fitting.	
	10/8/17		At 6.45am the Battalion marched by march route to billets at BELLHCOURT arrived at 12 noon	
	11/8/17		The Battn remained in billets and commenced training	
	12/8/17		The Battn continued its training	
	13/8/17		" "	
	14/8/17		" "	
	15/8/17		" "	
	16/8/17		" "	
	17/8/17		" "	
	18/8/17		" "	
	19/8/17		" "	
	20/8/17		" "	
	21/8/17		" "	
	22/8/17		" "	
	23/8/17		" "	
	24/8/17		" "	
	25/8/17		Training was suspended for the day on account of the Divisional Horse Show was held at HENDECOURT X.17.b.8.7. (Ref. Map. 51C)	

Army Form C.2118.

WAR DIARY
or
INTELLIGENCE SUMMARY.

(Erase heading not required.)

Reference Maps
Onghorne 5A
France + Belgium 27

Place	Date	Hour	Summary of Events and Information	Remarks and references to Appendices
	26/8/17		The Battalion continued training.	
	27/8/17		" " " "	
	28/8/17		" " " "	
	29/8/17		At 6.05am the Battalion less A Company marched to SAULTY and entrained for the North. Heavy snowy at about 10.30am. The Battalion arrived at PROVEN at about 7.30am and detrained and at 9am proceeded by march route to Camp near WYPE GOED FARM.	
	30/8/17		A Company arrived in Camp at 13 midnight	
	31/8/17		The Battalion remained in Camp re-outfitting.	
			The following Officers joined during month:- Lieut Col. O'Brien DSO on 5/8/17 2nd Lieuts C. Dand and J. Harrison on 23/8/17. Major G. Ramsbottom (Manchesters) on 28/8/17	
			Casualties:- 1 Officer Killed. 4 OR wounded.	
			OR's:- 19 OR on 3/8/17 57 on 5/8/17 108 on 9/8/17 36 on 11/8/17 9 on 14/8/17 11 on 18/8/17 22 on 30/8/17 48 on 24/8/17 15 on 27/8/17	
			26 OR were evacuated sick during the month.	

[signature]
Commanding 2nd Bn The Border Regt

7th DIVISION.
20th INF BDE.

2nd BORDER REGIMENT.

SEPTEMBER 1917.

2 Border Regt
Army Form C 2118

Ref Maps
Belgium & France Sheets 27 and 28
Hazebrouck 5A

35.L
3 sheet

WAR DIARY or INTELLIGENCE SUMMARY

SEPTEMBER 1917

Place	Date	Hour	Summary of Events and Information	Remarks and references to Appendices
LINDE GOED FARM	1/9/17	2.0 p.m.	The Battalion marched to billets in the STEENVOORDE Area arriving about 7.30 p.m.	
	2/9/17		The Battalion marched to billets in OUDEZEELE at 3.0 p.m. arriving about 5 p.m.	
		At about 5.30 p.m.	2 Corps Conveying Officers Warrant Officers NCOs men & the 1st Batt. Border Regt. arrived. This is the first time in history that the 2 Battalions have met and the Rugby from the 1st Batt. detained at	
	3/9/17	9.30 p.m.	2 Battalions, after having contests in football and tug of war. The Battalion continued the march and arrived in billets at HONDEGHEM at 2.0 p.m.	
	4/9/17			
	5/9/17			
	6/9/17			
	7/9/17			
	8/9/17		The Batt. remained in billets and carried out training daily	
	9/9/17			
	10/9/17			
	11/9/17			
	12/9/17			
	13/9/17			

WAR DIARY
or
INTELLIGENCE SUMMARY.
(Erase heading not required.)

Army Form C. 2118.

Place	Date	Hour	Summary of Events and Information	Remarks and references to Appendices
	14/9/17		The Battalion moved to camp at V.3.C.6.6 near HONDEGHEM	
	15/9/17		The Battalion remained in camp	
	16/9/17		At 2pm the Battalion marched to billets at ARQUES arriving about 7.30pm	
	17/9/17		The Battalion marched to LONGUENESSE to join the Brigade for training	
	18/9/17			
	19/9/17			
	20/9/17		The Batn. Remained in Billets. Quiet carried out training under Bde arrangements	
	21/9/17			
	22/9/17			
	23/9/17			
	24/9/17		The Battalion attacked an attack scheme under Divisional arrangements.	
	25/9/17			
	26/9/17		Training was continued under Battn arrangements	
	27/9/17			
	28/9/17		The Batn marched to billets at COULOMBY and HARLETTES arriving about 2.30pm. Battn. Hdrs. A B & D Coys were billeted in COULOMBY and C Coy in HARLETTES.	
	29/9/17		The Battn. marched to ARQUES at 11am. and entrained at 9pm	
	30/9/17		The Battn. detrained at AISELL at 4.0am. and marched to camp near RENINGHELST arriving at 6.0am	

Army Form C. 2118.

WAR DIARY
or
INTELLIGENCE SUMMARY.
(Erase heading not required.)

Place	Date	Hour	Summary of Events and Information	Remarks and references to Appendices
			The following Officers joined during the month:–	
			2nd Lieut. Eric Little and 2nd Lieut. E. Sargent on 5.9.17. Capt. A. Wright on 8.9.17.	
			& Lieut. J.G. Russell M.C. and 2nd Lieut. W.A. Stewart on 17.9.17	
			Casts:– 6 OR on 5th 4 OR on 17th 4 OR on 20th 4 OR on 22nd	
			9 OR on 23rd 4 OR on 26th	
			87 O.R. were evacuated Sick during the month	

W.H. Trevall Lieut-Colonel
Commandg 2nd Bn Border Regiment

7th DIVISION.
20th INF BDE.

2nd BORDER REGIMENT.

OCTOBER 1917.

Army Form C. 2118.

2nd B. Devon Regiment.
Reference Maps
Sheet 27 and 28.

WAR DIARY
INTELLIGENCE SUMMARY.

OCTOBER 1917.

(Erase heading not required.)

Place	Date	Hour	Summary of Events and Information	Remarks and references to Appendices
	1/10/17	about 7.30pm	The Battalion marched from camp near REMINGHELST to camp near DICKEBUSCH during	
	2/10/17		The Battalion marched to dugouts on western side of ZILLEBEKE LAKE.	
	3/10/17		The Battalion billeted at ZILLEBEKE LAKE till 10.30pm when it moved up to assemble for the attack. The role of the Battalion was to leap-frog the 2nd Devon R17 on the RED LINE and to take the Blue Line from J12a 35.95 to J6c 2.6 and to dig in for Second Objective. the RED and BLUE Lines covered by Front Barrage A and B were the attacking Companies, C Coy Mappers us and D Coy in Reserve. The role was laid out in two Wave namely C to the objective and at the same time B went immediately behind the mound, the second Wave was reported in position on the tape.	
	4/10/17		By 3am the whole Battalion was reported in position on the tape. The enemy, who seems to have had his suspicions aroused, rained shells on to the area behind the Mound. Heavy fire died to close up behind the 2nd Devon R17 which was formed up 200' in front. The Mound was directly on the line of advance, and the ground on the far side was little better than a bog on the far side of which was barbed wire - the moon was that the troops got much disarranged before the start of the attack. At zero hour, the Battn moved forward onto the 3rd GORDONS and 2nd MANCHESTERS on the flanks. The indications were that having secured normal formation the Battn attacked the 2nd Objective about 100 yards the Mound. The Mound	

WAR DIARY
INTELLIGENCE SUMMARY

(2)

Army Form C. 2118.

Place	Date	Hour	Summary of Events and Information	Remarks and references to Appendices
			The Batns however were completely mixed up and the whole line consisting of Gordons Devons Manchesters and Borders went forward to the first objective as it was impossible to try and withdraw troops from the advancing lines. Mopping up was undertaken categorically and the Sobs left by mopping up easily fired up. On arrival at the 1st objective the Officers withdrew men of the Batns about 100 yds. in rear and reorganised them into platoons. As soon as reorganised the line moved forward close to the barrage. The layout was so accurate over the level to well defined that the men got up to it quite comfortably and the difficulty was not in keeping them up to it, but in keeping them back from getting into it.	
		At 9.40am.	the final objective was reported taken and consolidation in progress. About 40 men under 2nd Lieut LITTLE had had to move to the left to get into touch with 2nd Gordons on the left. About 80 men under 2nd Lieut ABRATS had kept in touch with 'B' Coy on the left. A portion of 'B' Coy had gotten to the right of 'A' Company. A Sub advanced between this part of 'B' Company and the 22nd Manchester on the right. 'C' Coy under 2nd Lieut ARGLES and 2nd Lieut HISLOP had filled this Gap and a further Gap appeared between 2nd Lieut ARGLES Company and 2nd Lieut ABRATS Company. This was filled by 6 Makers of 'D' Company under 2nd Lieut T. HARDING. The frontage held by the Battalion at this time was the entire frontage allotted to the Brigade with the exception of 100 X on the right which was held by the 22nd Manchester Regt. The line extended from	

WAR DIARY or INTELLIGENCE SUMMARY

Army Form C. 2118.

Place	Date	Hour	Summary of Events and Information	Remarks and references to Appendices
		T.5.b.25.30 to T.6.c.35.10	Consolidation in depth now seemed somewhat difficult owing to the extensive frontal. The first step taken was for certain Officers to get over to certain portions of the line and to reorganise within their power. The line was practically held in four sectors (1) 2nd Lieut LITTLE on the left from T.5.b.25.30 on the left slope of the valley to T.5.b.25.05. (2) 2nd Lieut ABRAMS in touch with him on the left and extending to T.5.a.10.90. (Some men of D Coy on the right of 2nd Lieut ABRAMS Company were apparently absorbed into it). (3) There was a gap between 2nd Lieut ABRAMS right and (4) 2nd Lieut ARGLES left at T.5.d.95.20. Some men of D Company had also been absorbed into 2nd Lieut ARGLES Company which held the BLUE LINE down to T.6.c.35.10. East of these Officers collected men of various Companies together returning to the sector organisation. Thus 2nd Lieut ABRAMS collected the men of 2/22nd Manchester Regt and sent out a post on his extreme right in order to get nearer into touch with 2nd Lieut ARGLES and to get the men nearer their own Regt. Next to them he had a part of D Company, then A Company and then B Company on the left. Touch was obtained between the Companies but the gap between A Coy and "C" Coy still remained although each had sent out posts in the neighbourhood. About 40 men of "D" Company were in the trenches in the neighbourhood of JAY COTTAGE.	

WAR DIARY or INTELLIGENCE SUMMARY

Army Form C. 2118.

Place	Date	Hour	Summary of Events and Information	Remarks and references to Appendices
	5/10/17		During the night of 4/5th Oct. the reorganisation continued and continued exchange was effected. A Coy all together and C Coy all together. A Coy extended slightly to the right and "C" Coy slightly to the left in order to get nearer rifle touch but in the morning of the 5th there was still an appreciable Gap. During the day some Officers came up from the Transport and were sent up to the Coys. Captain D.B. DEMPSTER was ordered to collect men of "B" Coy from the various Coy H.Q, and to fill the Gap between "A" & "C" Coys by this means the enemy had got two Artillery & T.M. Posts lines and Sniping were also active. Communication with "C" Coy by day was almost impossible. During the night 5th/6th in front of "B" Coy was established between "C" and "A" Coy and touch was gained along the whole line. Reinforcements was much hindered by the heavy S.O.S barrages which had to be put down each when caused a Stand Still of necessary supply by the enemy. During the night the Australian Brigade on the left have been ordered to relieve the 2nd Gordon Hlrs and the Northern of the Cross roads J5a 10 95. But in the morning of the 6th act it was found that the Coys of that Relieved had not been relieved nor had perfect LITTLES Watson which were also North of the Cross roads at J5d 10 95. A Liason Officer was sent to the H.Q. of the Australian Battn with a request that the 2 remaining Coys of the 2nd Gordon Hlrs and Lieut LITTLES Watson Section be relieved by them. This however they were unable to do, so they had not	

Army Form C. 2118.

WAR DIARY
or
INTELLIGENCE SUMMARY.
(Erase heading not required.)

Place	Date	Hour	Summary of Events and Information	Remarks and references to Appendices
			sufficient men.	
			In the meantime the front held by the Battalion had been divided into 4 subsectors. On the left the sector held by 2«Lieut LITTLE was known as "L" subsector next on his right from T.5.d.4.1. to T.5.d.7.8. A subsector held by 2«Lieut ASRAM with A Company. In the centre from T.5.d.7.8 to T.6.c.2.4. B subsector held by a small party of B Company under 2«Lieut HARRISON and Z subsector of D Company under 2«Lieut PAINTER. On the right from T.6.c.2.4. to T.6.c.4.0. "C" subsector held by Captain D.B.DEMPSTER who had now been sent to "C" Company. The D Company were in outpost in the trenches in vicinity of JAY COTTAGE. The intention was to relieve 2«Lieut PAINTER's party by 2«Lieut LITTLE's platoon as soon as the latter was relieved by the Australians. The platoon of D Company to relieved was to take up a position South of JAY TRENCH and East of the road joining JAY and JUDGE COTTAGE. By the evening it he 6th it had become clear that the two Companies of the Gordons and 2«Lieut LITTLE were not going to be relieved by the Australians. Further a message from 2«P Brigade showed that the relief of the two Companies of the Gordon Hldrs was inadvisable, as they were to become covering party Battalion. It was therefore decided that they must be relieved by 2«Lieut HARRISON's party and the remainder of D Company. The two 2«Coys of Gordon Highlanders was rather indefinite, as when arrangements were made for their relief it was found that they had been so reduced in numbers that the relief was effected by 2«Lieut HARRISON with 12 men. Much was gained with the Australian	

WAR DIARY or INTELLIGENCE SUMMARY

Army Form C. 2118.

Place	Date	Hour	Summary of Events and Information	Remarks and references to Appendices
			Battalion on the left and it was noted that by extending Lieut LITTLE's sector to the left and asking the Australians to expend slightly to the right the line could be properly consolidated. It was found however that the Coy of the Australian Battalion which was on the left of Lieut HARRISON consisted only of 1 Officer and 24 men. It was therefore arranged that each party should send parties across from front to front during the night. Another Platoon of D Coy had to be used to relieve 2 Lieut HARRISON's party on his left of "B" Subsector. The relief was somewhat tardily completed owing to the fact that the Officer who was sent to make the arrangements for the relief with the Company commander of the right Company Lieut Gordon Geils, was mortally wounded whilst making his arrangements and afterwards a heavy barrage delayed it. Relief complete was reported at 6.45 am. On the night 7th/8th the Battalion was relieved by the 20" Manchester Regt. The relief was again rather protracted the Manchesters arriving with 2 Companies instead of 4 and there was consequently slight delay in issuing new orders and obtaining guides. The relief was complete at 11.30 hrs but the report which was received from OC D Coy included the relief of both front line and support platoons. This was not noticed and the relief of the two front line platoons was carried until dawn when it was discovered that Coy Hqrs. already knew about.	

Army Form C. 2118.

WAR DIARY
INTELLIGENCE SUMMARY.
(Erase heading not required.)

Instructions regarding War Diaries and Intelligence Summaries are contained in F. S. Regs., Part II. and the Staff Manual respectively. Title pages will be prepared in manuscript.

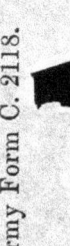

Place	Date	Hour	Summary of Events and Information	Remarks and references to Appendices
	8/10/17		After relief the Battn moved to dugouts on Western side of KILLEBEKE LAKE	
	9/10/17		The 2nd Queens Regt relieved the Battn which marched to camps near DICKEBUSCH	
	10/10/17		The Battn marched to CANORA Camp in the WESTOUTRE Area, arriving about 7.30pm.	
	11/10/17 to 22/10/17		The Battalion remained in CANORA camp, and carried out training. Battalion arrangements.	
	23/10/17		The Battn marched to camp near VIERSTRAAT arriving about 4.0pm	
	24/10/17		The Battn moved from camp at 3.0pm and proceeded via HEDGE ST and DUMBARTON LAKES to the front aid South of the MENIN ROAD, relieving the 16th and 17th Sherwood Foresters on a line running from J.21.c.30.12 on the MENIN ROAD, to J.21.c.9.7. opposite LEWIS HOUSE. C Coy occupied the front trench of this line with D Coy in close support. A and B Coys occupied a line about 250 yds in rear. Battn HQrs were established among some huts near the road. Intermittent shelling of front line took place during the night, with heavy shelling of B.H.Q's area from 1am to 3am.	
	25/10/17		At 6.15am and 6.20am small parties of enemy were seen attempting to enter LEWIS HOUSE. Lewis Gun and rifle fire inflicted some casualties and the parties dispersed. The enemy was fairly quiet throughout the day. The absence of machine gun and rifle fire on our front was especially noticeable. The enemy shelled intermittently	

WAR DIARY
or
INTELLIGENCE SUMMARY.
(Erase heading not required.)

Army Form C. 2118.

Place	Date	Hour	Summary of Events and Information	Remarks and references to Appendices
	26/9/17		all areas around Hillhouse including Bass Wood	
			The Batt. was ordered to attack and hold a line forming the point J.22.c.10.45	
			(in GHELUVELT VILLAGE) and J.22.c.10.05. Known as the RED LINE. The attack was	
			part of an operation to be carried out by the 20 INFANTRY BRIGADE. The P?	
			DEVON Regt and the 2nd QUEENS were attacking simultaneously on the left and	
			right respectively. After the objective had been captured the 2nd GORDON HDRS	
			were to leapfrog and establish a Blue Line parallel to the RED LINE and about 500	
			yards in advance of it.	
			The attack was carried out under a creeping barrage timed to start at 5.40am	
			and to reach the objective at 6.36am. The Batt. advanced in normal formation	
			"C" Coy on the right D Coy on the left. B Coy mothers and A Coy in Support	
			The Batts formed up on the tramline tehis at 60 yards distance the front taking	
			formed the point J.21.b.40.08 and J.21.C.55.71.	
			At 5.40am the Batts advanced over very marshy ground, through which the men were	
			only just able to move "C" Coy on the right advanced into the valley in J.21.a. where	
			they got stuck in the mud up to the waist and were almost entirely wiped out	
			Captain DEMPSTER was killed and 2nd Lieut STEPHEN was wounded. Machine Gun	
			fire was opened from LEWIS HOUSE on the right, the Robber Trees on the left at	
			J.21.d.7.9 as soon as our barrage opened.	
			D Coy on the left finding that the ground was impassable to their immediate front	

Army Form C 2118.

WAR DIARY
or
INTELLIGENCE SUMMARY.
(Erase heading not required.)

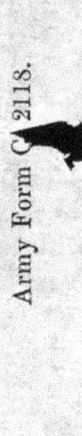

Place	Date	Hour	Summary of Events and Information	Remarks and references to Appendices
			moved over towards the MENIN ROAD. Practically the whole Brigade was wiped out by machine gun fire in an attempt to take the hidden wires at FM of 7.9. The survivors returned on a craters in the road before the hidden wires. The rear waves of B Company which had also moved to the left were the next to come up against the hidden wires with the same result as before. An attack was then made from the Crater but only no sight overcome Captain J. MOORE and 2nd Lieut INKPEN were killed in this attack and more of B & D Coys were casualties. A Company now came up and proceeded to attack the hidden wires. One of these was taken and a machine gun captured but the remaining three conceived of fire from LEWIS HOUSE defied all attacks to take them. Capt J.W. LITTLE collected the remains of B & D Coys and a few DEVONS, and advanced along the line of the road. Lieut LITTLE remained of A Company to attempt to take or keep down the hidden wires. Captain LITTLE took his party forward to within about 150 yards of CHEQUERS where he took up a line of shell holes. The DEVONS on the 6th returned to have pushed well forward. On the right the 2nd QUEENS had not been able to make head a number of men had sent away to the left of the road and a few had sent to the right amongst the QUEENS. LEWIS HOUSE The reason of the former was that it was impossible to make along the	

(10)

WAR DIARY
or
INTELLIGENCE SUMMARY.
(Erase heading not required.)

Army Form C. 2118.

Place	Date	Hour	Summary of Events and Information	Remarks and references to Appendices
			Original line of advance and consequently the men had to move to the left to the nearest belt of ground on the right of the road. This LofR was covered by Machine Guns in the hedge trees which were just on the right of the road, and was caught by Machine Gun fire from LEWIS HOUSE. The natural tendency therefore was to get on to the left of the road, and in fact, for the line to believe at all it was forced to do to the North of the road.	
			At 7am a handful of men went across to CHELUVELT village and were about the ruins of the CHURCH.	
			By 9am it was evident that the objective could not be reached with the small number of men left. On the right the 2nd QUEENS were establishing a line on the original line. On the left the situation of the DEVONS was not clear. The DEVONS appeared to have got forward and to be holding roughly the line of the Railway. A miscellaneous body of men were holding a salient South from the front where the railway joined the Road to about J.21.b.51 from that point to TOWER HAMLETS there was a gap. It was therefore decided to hut out to the along the original line as back to connect up between the different flank ending at J.21.b.51 so far to the right no hussies. By this time there were only about 40 men of the Batts left out of the attacking Companies. The remainder were either casualties or had been to our left and became mixed up with the DEVONS. The GORDON HIGHLANDERS were	

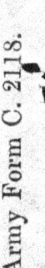

Army Form C. 2118.

WAR DIARY
or
INTELLIGENCE SUMMARY.
(Erase heading not required.)

Place	Date	Hour	Summary of Events and Information	Remarks and references to Appendices
			Apparently North of the road and South of LEWIS HOUSE. It was reported that a large number had gone North of the road and were amongst the DEVONS, they could not be found however and sub men sent out at first light with the DEVONS when the Brigade was relieved. The air run that had been collected to hold the line South of the road were holding from the road to a point at T.21.d.2.9. South of this there was a gap to TOWER HAMLETS and there Coy remained until the Battalion was relieved at 11.15 pm by 1st R. WELCH FUSILIERS and proceeded to tent shelter at the western end of ZILLEBEKE LANE	
	27/10/17		The Battalion was conveyed by motor transport to Camp at BLARINGHEM	
	28/10/17		The Battalion moved to billets between BLARINGHEM and RENESCURE	
	29/10/17		The Battalion remained in billets and resumed	
	30/10/17		Training was carried out under Bn arrangements	

Casualties for month

	Killed		Wounded		Missing	
	Officers	O.R.	Officers	O.R.	Officers	O.R.
1st–7th Oct	2	39	11	195	1	18
26th Oct	5	6	2	174	1	126
1st Oct		1		1		

33 Other ranks were evacuated sick during the month

The following reinforcements joined during the month.
Infants. 2/Lt Infwood, W.P Atkinson, M. Forbyson, L Bell on 23/10/17.
S.L Hawkins, Burton, R Davidson, F.L Savier, H.J Michaels on 26/10/17.
J.C Graham, S. Hogestan, W.E Rowe, C.C. Alley R.Fitt on 6/10/17.

4 O.R on 1½ 3 O.R on 10½ 4 O.R on 13½ 2 O.R on 14½ 3 O.R on 16½
3 O.R on 17½ 31 O.R on 18½ 3 O.R on 20½ 31 O.R on 21st 232 R on 22.0
158 O.R on 30/10/17 40 O.R on 31/10/17.

[signature] Major.
Comm'g 2nd Bn Border Regiment.

7th DIVISION.

20th INF BDE.

2nd BORDER REGIMENT.

NOVEMBER 1917.

2ND BN BORDER REGT.

WAR DIARY or INTELLIGENCE SUMMARY

Army Form

Ref. maps. Belgium and France.
Sheet 27 and 27A SE HAZEBROUCK
LENS II

NOVEMBER 1917

Place	Date	Hour	Summary of Events and Information	Remarks and references to Appendices
	1.11.17		The Battn. continued training in the BLARINGHEM area. No 33082 Pte HULBERT and No 10154 Pte PEACOCK returned to the Battn, having been found by a patrol of the 1st R.W. Fus inside the German lines on the MENIN ROAD. They only asked the latter where they were to be relieved. Heavy rain these two nights. Their clothing at their feet was abominable by the G.O.C. 7th Div.	
	2.11.17 5.11.17		The Battn continued training. 2nd Lieuts J. RENDELL and E.H. JOHNSON joined the Battn on 3.11.1917	
	6.11.17		The Brigadier inspected the 150 Draft at 10.30am. 10 O.R. joined Battn.	
	7.11.17		The Battalion continued training. A/Major W. KERR DSO MC wounded	
	8.11.17		A/Major W. KERR DSO MC took Command of the Battn. The Battalion took part in an inspection of the 7th Division by ALBERT King of the Belgians at EBBLINGHEM at 11.30am. Followed by a march past in close column of platoons A/Lt Col W. KERR DSO MC, Capt. Capt A/M F.W. MITCHELL and 76 other ranks of the original 7th Division that landed in BELGIUM in October 1914. were present at the Inspection. The Divisional General sent congratulations to the Regiment on its smart appearance.	
	9.11.17 11.11.17		The Battalion continued training	
	12.11.17		The Battn marched from BLARINGHEM to billets at WAVRANS S of LUMBRES arriving at 3.15pm. No 11106 Pte T. MASON was awarded Military Medal for Gallantry on Oct 24th – 26 17. Lieut G.H.E. PRYNNE rejoined the Battn from the R.F.C. and 2nd Lieut A. ELLISLIE joined from ENGLAND.	
	13.11.17		The Battn marched from WAVRANS to AVROULT arriving at 12.30pm	
	14.11.17		The Battn marched from AVROULT to COUPELLE VIELLE near FRUGES arriving there at 1.15pm	
	15.11.17		The Battn marched from COUPELLE VIELLE to HUMIERES near ST POL on the TANKS area	

WAR DIARY
or
INTELLIGENCE SUMMARY.

(Erase heading not required.)

Army Form

Instructions regarding War Diaries and Intelligence Summaries are contained in F. S. Regs., Part II. and the Staff Manual respectively. Title pages will be prepared in manuscript. SHEET 2

Place	Date	Hour	Summary of Events and Information	Remarks references to Appendices
	16.11.17		For the 4 days march only 2 men fell out. A Draft of 202 O.R. under Captain C.A. HILL joined the Battn.	
			The Battn. remained at HUMIERES.	
			The following were awarded the Military Medal for Gallantry on Oct 24th to 26th	
			15242 Serjt H. WOODBURN. 16660. Pte F. FARRINGTON. Pte W. BUCKLEY. 24133. Pte F. GREENWOOD	
			14784 Pte S. HARRISON. 203019 Pte R. McELROY. 3883. Pte F. HULBERT. 10154. Pte T. PEACOCK.	
	17.11.17		The Battalion entrained Embarkatory to a move to ITALY.	
	18.11.17		The Battalion marched to huts at DENCHY CAYEUX arriving there at 3 O.Am.	
			The following message was received from Lieut Gen. MORLAND. Commanding X'th Corps.	
			"To GOC and all ranks 7th Division - On your departure from the X'th Corps I wish	
			"to thank you for all your good and gallant work whilst under my command."	
			"In wishing you goodbye, which I do with regret, I wish you all success and good"	
			"fortune wherever you may find yourselves in the future."	
	19.11.17		The Battalion marched to WAVRANS Station to entrain for ITALY.	
			The 1st train started at 9.12 am Contained Lieut-Col W. KERR DSO OC 15 other officers	
			and 402 other ranks of "C" and "D" Coys.	
			The 2nd train started at 1.12 pm Contained Major G.C. KARISSOTICH DSO MC 14 other officers rest	
			359 other ranks of "A" and "B" Coys.	
			Both trains followed the same route, making halts for meals and exercise were	
			arranged. But as the trains always came late the duration of the halt was	
			shortened. As a rule the men were ready for hot water for making tea or using as water	
			for washing since the train left FRANCE the hot water usually being taken from the engine.	

WAR DIARY
or
INTELLIGENCE SUMMARY.
(Erase heading not required.)

Army Form C. 2118.

SHEET 3

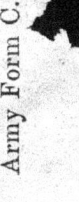

Place	Date	Hour	Summary of Events and Information	Remarks and references to Appendices
	20.11.17		The route was as follows:- WAVRANS ST POL COURCELLE ALBERT LONGUENEAU near AMIENS BOVES CREPY CHATEAU THIERRY EPERNAY CHALONS-SUR-MARNE. The train went through the UPPER MARNE and SAONE Valleys to/at LANGRES GRAY. LOUHANS.	
	21.11.17		In the early morning the train halted at CULOZ, among the Alps of SAVOIE. Hence along the edge of LAC BOURGET to AIX LE BAINS. There was a short halt at ST PIERRE D'ALBIGNY and a long one at MODANE, where the train caught sight of the Mont Cenis. The Battalion reached ITALY via the MONT CENIS Tunnel between 8pm and 12pm. The following Officers WO's and Staff Sgts of the Batn. entered ITALY:- Lt.Col. W. KERR DSO M.C. Major G.C. RAMSBOTTOM DSO. Capt. S.T.C. RUSSELL M.C. Lieut R.K. SHREWSBURY Lieut E.T.H. METHRIN 2nd Lieut E.J. PEACOCK. Capt + Qm. F.W. MITCHELL. No 9479 RSM. R.L. BOOTH and No 7824 CQMS. G.N. CLUFF. A Coy:- Capt. C. DAND Lieut GN.F. PRYNNE 2nd Lieut. J.H. GRAHAM. E.H. JOHNSON. J. RENDELL R.K. LONGMIRE W.I. ATKINSON No 7890 C.Sm. J. STREETER M.C. 6607 Cq.M.S. W LEE B.Coy:- Capt. F.W. LITTLE M.C. 2nd Lieut. H.T. HAYNES M. TOMLINSON. T. BALD. A. AINSLIE. H. DAVIDSON 6403 CSm. T. FLETCHER Ho2 PIGGINS J. SALES C Coy:- Capt. FARGUES Lieut C.A. HILL 2nd Lieut S.F. HAWKINS A.E. WILSON S.F. FORBES-ROBERTSON No 2096, CQM. F. LARKIN No 6445 Sgt H. LOUGHMAN D Coy:- Capt. J.G. CAMPBELL 2nd Lieut M.J. MELVILLE R. KIRK F.S. SAMUT RADEY No 7883 CSm. W MILLARD No 7744 CQMS W. FRASER Capt R.M. BURMANN (C/Bde Major) and Lieut W.E. KELLY Came with Brigade Headquarters.	

WAR DIARY or INTELLIGENCE SUMMARY.

Army Form C. 2118.

Ref. Maps.
VERONA PADOVA 1/100,000
PADOVA 1/10,000

SHEET 4.

Place	Date	Hour	Summary of Events and Information	Remarks and references to Appendices
	22/11/17		ITALY. TURIN was passed in the very early morning. Streets were empty and no one knew how long the half would be as they were due only at the line about 10.30am. The hot water was troubled and it was very difficult to obtain early tea on the snow of the Alps. The weather was sunny and the men were cheery. A first view was obtained of the snow on the Alps. The men singing and laughing on the trucks on the train passed along creating much amazement and a sort of impression amongst the Italians who gave them a very friendly welcome. The train went across the plains of LOMBARDY passing through PAVIA CODOGNO CREMONA and MANTOVA	
	23/11/17		The 1st train reached LEGNAGO about 9.15am. The half Battalion with transport had detrained by 10.30am and after breakfasting near the Station marched across the route ADIGE to MINERBE arriving there at 3.0pm. The 2nd train reached CEREA about 9.15am. This half Batn after detraining and breakfasting marched to LEGNAGO to MINERBE arriving at 11.45pm.	
	24/11/17		The Battalion remained at MINERBE clearing up before resuming its march forward. The Guard mounted evening on the Piazza at 4pm caused much interest among the inhabitants.	
	25/11/17		The Battn marched from MINERBE via MONTAGNANA and NOVENTA to LOZZO in one day's march. The march was from 22 to 24 miles. No men failed to arrive with the Battalion. Flowers were showered on the men as they passed.	
	26/11/17		The Battn marched from ALBETTONE to LUSIA at BARBARANO at the foot of	

Army Form C. 2118.

WAR DIARY
or
INTELLIGENCE SUMMARY.

(Erase heading not required.)

Instructions regarding War Diaries and Intelligence Summaries are contained in F.S. Regs., Part II. and the Staff Manual respectively. Title pages will be prepared in manuscript. SHEET 5

Place	Date	Hour	Summary of Events and Information	Remarks and references to Appendices
	27/11/17	1.45pm	The BERICI Mountains arrived at 1.45pm. The Band playing "Retreat" on the Piazza were enthusiastically applauded by the townsfolk, who crowded round shouting cries of welcome and throwing their hats in the air. The country was was found to be much hotter than the thin Bivy shelter or light winds. The Battn was engaged in Inspections and Lewis Gun practice. The roads of Guns was used for the first time in ITALY. A Boat of 12 of Joined.	
	28/11/17		The Battn marched to billets N of MONTEGALDA crossing the river BACCHIGLIONE and arriving about 10am. Local Italian townsfolk. 3 small horse waggons was sent for the first time for blankets etc. Officers were issued bullet wagons.	
	29/11/17		The Battn remained in billets. The weather continued sunny by day and frosty by night. The farm fact in whom the Battn was quartered were very friendly.	
	30/11/17		The Battn marched to billets in S.GIORGIO in BOSCO 4 miles S of CITTADELLA a distance of 26 Kilometres arriving at 5.15pm. The river BRENTA was crossed by a timber bridge, the other bridge having been blown up by the Germans at CAMPO S. MARTINO. A German aeroplane was seen about midday.	
			61 Other ranks were evacuated Sick during the month.	

M. Kent Lieut Colonel
Commanding 2nd Bn Border Regiment

www.ingramcontent.com/pod-product-compliance
Lightning Source LLC
Chambersburg PA
CBHW080807010526
44113CB00013B/2342